2nd Edition

WHY UNIVERSAL LIFE

THE NATIONAL UNDERWRITER COMPANY
CINCINNATI, OHIO

DEDICATED

To the industry we earnestly strive to serve

PUBLISHER'S PREFACE
TO SECOND EDITION

The rapid pace of events affecting the life insurance industry and particularly its hottest selling product, Universal Life, impels the publication of this second edition of *Why Universal Life*. While much of the first edition is sound and completely useable, far too much of what was said a year ago has been superceded by the events of the past 12 months.

This book contains four chapters of new material plus numerous other changes. These were generated by the public and private events surrounding Universal Life insurance since the issuance of a Private Letter ruling to Massachusetts Mutual in July of 1982. The passage of TEFRA superceded the ruling almost before the ink was dry.

This new legislation rapidly became the focus of an unprecedented number of speeches, seminars, and internal tax planning activities at the major life insurance companies. The frequent appearance of claims and counterclaims which permeated the trade press, and sometimes periodicals of general circulation, has given way to a steady stream of new product announcements.

The National Underwriter Company's current publications show a tripling of the number of companies selling Universal

Life in one of several forms. It appears that up to 300 insurers will be active in the market by the first anniversary of this second edition's publication.

This edition continues to reflect the balanced viewpoints of its three authors; an actuary, an agent, and an attorney. It is written with the life insurance agent in mind, but as the interest in its subject continues to broaden, we would not be surprised if others begin to benefit by reading it.

Universal Life will continue to generate action for years to come. The replacement issue, marketing, computer technology and the unresolved tax questions will affect you, your policyholders and the industry. We believe this second edition will help all those concerned better understand the scope of this revolutionary product.

Cincinnati, Ohio
May, 1982

CONTENTS

LIST OF FIGURES

Figure

LIST OF CASE STUDIES

CHAPTER 1

Origins of the Universal Life Policy

Trouble

Not long ago, a successful life insurance agent marched into his general agent's office with determination in each step. His brow was furrowed and his demeanor was pessimistic in stark contrast to the optimism of his good years in the marketing end of life insurance.

"I have made a decision," he said to the general agent. "You will have to get along without my new business. I'm going to Europe for a year. Please straighten out this product mess before I get back." With that, he turned and walked out the door.

What was this agent talking about? What would make a successful man turn his back on a career that had been good enough to him to enable him to go to Europe for one year?

The cause was a new product generically called "Universal Life." Let's do some exploring.

Questions

Traditional whole life insurance is in trouble. Urged on by headline attention to interest rates, the public is demanding a better life insurance product. Universal Life, or something like it, may be the last, best chance of the insurance industry to regain its percentage of the public's investment dollar. As inflation has steadily decreased the worth of the dollar, non-insurance institutions and other investment organizations have competed with increasing success for the money which previously flowed into permanent life insurance. The public, apparently, believes they can now get a better deal elsewhere.

If Universal Life does what it appears to be capable of doing, life insurance companies will be able to get off the defensive side of the competition and take the offensive. But important questions abound:

How does Universal Life work?

Can Universal Life actually replace whole life insurance?

How much does it pay for the life insurance agent to sell it?

What is the legal background on the tax issues?

How should these issues be resolved?

The most important question, as is often the case, is a marketing one:

Will the public have confidence in this new version of life insurance?

Term and More Term

For years, the public has been shifting its purchases of life insurance to individual term and other forms of low cost life insurance. From 1976 to 1981, purchases of individual term policies have risen dramatically to 143% of permanent sales.

Including group and credit insurance, 75% of all life insurance sold in the United States in 1981 was a form of low cost insurance.

Figure 1.1

1981 LIFE INSURANCE SALES

Form of Insurance	Amount (000,000 omitted)
Whole life and Endowment	$192,000
Term	275,000
Credit	85,000
Group (all types)	208,000

Two more observations clinch the point. The sale of permanent life insurance on a minimum deposit basis, a form of leveraged insurance, responds to the public's interest in low cost coverage. If we assume that half of the permanent individual sales are made with minimum deposit in mind, then the percentage of 1981 volume sold as low cost life insurance rises to over 87%. Add in, if you wish, the large number of pre-1981 permanent buyers who are borrowing their cash values to invest for higher yields, and the dismal outlook for traditional whole life insurance seems undeniable.

An Introduction

The Universal Life concept is *the* topic facing the insurance industry today. It has the potential to change the marketing strategies and structures of life insurance companies so much that traditional home office administration and investment practices may never be the same.

It is the intent of this book to help explain the implications of Universal Life so the reader will be able to form an understanding of its concepts and power. Along with the questions raised above, we will attempt to also explain:

3

How the product meets the insurance needs of the public.
How the policy contract reads.
Marketing procedures.
How computer technology serves the agent and client.

A Historical Perspective

This chapter traces the origins of Universal Life from its modest beginning, which we place in the year 1967. We give our version of the changes in the marketplace with emphasis on the organizational environment of life insurance over the past 15 or 20 years. We try to concentrate on those events which have contributed to the key features of the Universal Life contract.

We don't pretend to be historians; there isn't space in this book to chronicle the lengthy history related to the development of this product. Nor do we attempt to identify all the personalities, or begin to reprint even a significant part of the articles, policies, legal precedents and other events which have led up to 1982. In particular, many people who have contributed to the origins (or impeded earlier development) of Universal Life are not recognized in these few pages.

There are many insightful quotes and anecdotes available. In preparing this chapter, several thousand pages of file materials were reviewed. Certain items stood out for the style and word choice. These are included with our interpretation of their meaning. Often, we suspect, the message we discovered in 1982 is not what the origional author had in mind at the time he wrote or spoke the words.

Glimpses of the Future

In the last quarter of 1981, some 250 people attended seminars on Universal Life conducted by Tillinghast, Nelson & Warren, Inc., a well-known actuarial consulting firm based in Atlanta, Georgia. The attendees were a mix of technical, data processing, and marketing personnel from a cross section of the life insurance industry.

They completed a questionnaire which, in part, identified their employers' plans with respect to Universal Life. The usable questionnaires returned from the insurers totaled 168. The following summary, Figure 1.2, was provided by T, N & W, Inc. and is reprinted with their permission.

Figure 1.2
TILLINGHAST, NELSON & WARREN, INC.
QUESTIONNAIRE RESULTS

- One question requested the company's current and future direction on Universal Life.

  20 companies currently offered Universal Life.

  79 added companies planned to introduce Universal Life in the future.

  69 companies were undecided as to the introduction of Universal Life.

  0 companies had decided against the introduction of Universal Life.

- Dates of introduction, either completed or planned, were distributed as follows:

  8 companies introduced Universal Life in 1980.

  19 companies had introduced or were planning to introduce a Universal Life product in 1981.

  65 companies planned to introduce Universal Life in 1982.

  7 companies planned to introduce it in 1983.

- Reasons for being undecided were requested. The following six items were identified in the questionnaire; more than one response was allowed.

  46 companies listed administrative systems.

  40 companies listed company taxation.

  37 companies listed policyholder taxation.

  35 companies listed agent compensation.

  26 companies listed product profitability.

  25 companies listed internal replacement.

Prophecies from the Past

Of course, this was a biased group, since the participants paid a fee to learn of then current developments in nontraditional life insurance products. The plans of many of these insurers will never materialize. Many others will be making (and changing) plans in response to the marketplace.

Those who accuse the life insurance industry of failure to innovate have generally had myopia. Many different products have been tried in response to the perceived interests of the public. Some concepts have succeeded grandly. Consider the so-called enhanced protection policies which have lowered the cost of permanent insurance by roughly 25% to 40%.

On the other hand, some have failed totally. See the anecdote below about "no load" life insurance. Some have done passably well, but only for a few companies. And, we venture to say, other concepts have been well conceived but failed because the minds that conceived them were in companies that did not have the marketing ability or people to have the impact the product deserved.

The following are several quotations from the recent past to lend perspective to the origins and the future of Universal Life.

First, does anybody remember the excitement over mutual fund combination sales? A number of companies, seeking market share and a piece of the equity action, made major commitments.

"The life industry has underemployed three matchless assets: an unequaled sales force, investment brains with a century of performance, and a stupendous pool of money. Life insurance, which had been a major factor as a savings and protection vehicle, found itself in 1960 in the protection business only. Its share of the savings market has been taken over by savings banks, savings and loans, Wall Street and mutual funds. Life insurance had its competitive position due to the low interest rate and high commission structure inherent in its product.

"Once the move into mutual funds by life insurers is complete, these companies can then diversify into a broad range of other services. Many insurers have now formed real estate, data processing, mutual fund, and other service subsidiaries. Each of these new companies will be backed by decades of experience, millions of dollars, and the most effective sales force at work today."—John D. Brundage, President, Bankers National Life; speech to a 1968 conference sponsored by the Reinsurance Division of Continental Assurance in Chicago, Illinois; quoted in *The National Underwriter*, October 5, 1968.

There were problems. Mutual funds caused criticism of improper replacement practices, a complaint that is current in the marketplace today with respect to Universal Life.

"Combination purchase makes a lot of sense. But the raping of cash values by the mutual fund salesmen, and by many life agents who obtained National Association of Security Dealers (NASD) licenses and went on to the mutual fund trail of gold, ultimately ended up with dissatisfaction on the part of many disillusioned policyholders. In other words, a rapacious salesman, destroying a program of permanent insurance in order to make a mutual fund sale, buoyed up by a term insurance program, did not always offer a wholly satisfactory approach to estate planning or estate building."—Mr. Michael H. Levy, President, Standard Security of New York; "Prefers Term Over Cash Value Coverage, but Opposes Dual Sale"; quoted in *The National Underwriter*, February 1, 1969.

Combination funds rose in favor with parts of the industry. Although there are substantial residues, the impact on the insurance product was minimal. Marketing constraints, notably commission differentials, dampened the agent's enthusiasm.

Variable Life

Next, we have two views from the comparatively recent history of variable life insurance, the last ground swell of product innovation comparable to Universal Life. This product, which traces its early beginning to Canadian development beginning in 1961, was big news in the early 1970s. It was first introduced by New York Life Insurance Co. in 1969. At hearings held by the Securities and Exchange Commission (SEC), testimony given by life insurance executives indicated that an estimated 20% to 40% of new business would be on the variable life plan. The SEC asserted jurisdiction over variable life.

"I believe that we're on the threshold of an exciting and important new development in the life insurance industry. Variable life insurance will be beneficial for the public because it will offer them a unique combination of an equity investment element tied in with all of the plus factors (including important guarantees) that can be provided only by life insurance companies."—Letter from Gilbert W. Fitzhugh, Chairman of the Board of Metropolitan Life Insurance Co., dated February 18, 1972.

"It would be a tragic mistake if the introduction of variable life insurance were to encourage a replacement of, or retard future sales of, permanent life insurance. While there may be room for equity-oriented life insurance products on a moderated basis, these should be considered as supplementary to a sound permanent life insurance program and not as a substitute for it. One should not lose sight of the fact that the prime functions of life insurance are protection of the survivors and the guarantee that an estate goal can be realized."—Charles M. Sternhell, Executive Vice-president of New York Life; "Fixed Premium Variable Benefit Life Insurance", *Fall 1970 Gold Book*, New York Life Insurance Company, 1970, p. 145.

At one point, nearly twenty companies had filed policy forms and prospectuses. The contract is currently offered by only three companies, Equitable Life Assurance Society, Monarch, and John Hancock. Sales were virtually nonexistent until recently. John Hancock entered the market in September of 1980.

One year later, their production, measured by annualized premium, had risen to well over $1 million *per month*. In April 1982, monthly face amount sales were over $100 million. It certainly appears that variable life insurance is alive and well in Boston, though far short of the high expectations of many major companies.

No Load Life

Next, we present an odd and thought-provoking failure, turning first to *Forbes* magazine to make the story short.

Financial Assurance, Inc., a subsidiary of Gates Rubber Co. at the time, undertook to sell "a new kind of insurance without salesmen. The new policy is new in two ways. First, it is 'whole life' insurance sold through the mails. Second, the new policy guarantees a cash value that is never less than the total premiums paid. Holders of Financial Assurance's new policy can cancel even after the first month and get their premiums back in full."

The company's president at the time, James O. Richards, is quoted as boasting, "We've made the technological breakthrough of this generation in life insurance." *Forbes* closed the piece with this observation, "He [Richards] may find out, as have others before him, that pioneers are pioneers because they are ahead of their time. Whether or not America is really ready for self-service life insurance remains to be seen. And even if it is, the pioneer may not be the one to reap the harvest."—Quotes are from *Forbes*, "From No-Load Funds to No-Load Insurance", June 1, 1973.

Figure 1.3 is a summary of this small company's new business issued and overall premium income during this time period.

Figure 1.3

FINANCIAL ASSURANCE, INC.
YEARLY FIGURES 1972-1976

Year	Whole Life and Endowment	Term Insurance	Total Premium Income
1972	$ 2,808,000	$ 24,392,000	$ 1,391,000
1973	10,345,000	2,156,000	1,573,000
1974	5,289,000	1,178,000	1,794,000
1975	5,410,000	1,898,000	1,275,000
1976	6,190,000	6,883,000	2,933,000

In the fall of 1975, the company reactivated the portfolio of whole life and term plans through reestablishment of more customary sales operations. At the end of 1975 the company's total insurance in force was $44,000,000 less than the year before the "insurance without salesmen" was written up in *Forbes*. This was a decrease in business of 17%. During 1976, there was a change in ownership. The company survived the pioneering experiment. The product didn't.

Attempts such as this to change the nature of the life insurance product and the compensation of agents have generally not been successful. Apparently innovations of this kind have failed because they have not had sufficient positive effect on benefits to alter the motivation of the public. Or as a cliché of the trade puts it, "Insurance is not bought, it is sold."

Universal Life

To close this collection of quotes, the following was written by an innovative CPA who put together his own small company in the suburbs of Chicago in 1979, a company structure to sell only Universal Life insurance.

"It [Universal Life] is a product that is remarkably easy to sell as opposed to a conventional ordinary policy. It is because the consumer understands his own needs in terms of flexibility, simplicity, cost effectiveness, and tax efficiency. A Universal Life world is at least as good of a bet as any other scenario with which I am acquainted as a means of not only protecting but expanding the field force while making them much more productive. I don't think anyone knows exactly how best to market a Universal Life policy as the concept is still too new. Further, many companies that I am personally aware of have been frightened by the specter of the myriad of administrative problems of Universal Life and the cost and time involved in solving them. I am certainly not recommending that any company undertake the development of the Universal Life product unless they think that it is right for them. But I strongly urge you to watch the further development of those products, because as *Fortune* magazine recently pointed out about such products; 'The industry as a whole will likely be hauled kicking and screaming toward this kind of product. It will not win popularity contests with insurance agents nor will it bring in low cost savings on which the insurers can make large investment profits. But it is a product that seems grounded in rationality and just might take off.' "— Ron Butkiewicz, President, First Penn-Pacific Life Insurance Co., Oak Brook, Illinois; "Universal Life, A Product Whose Time Has Come", speech to A Conference for the Insurance Executive entitled "Marketing . . . The Skill of the Eighties", sponsored by the Life Reinsurance Division of CNA, Chicago, Illinois on September 4-5, 1980.

Mr. Butkiewicz subsequently sold his company to Lincoln National Corporation for several million dollars. In his case, Universal Life worked out well!

Marketing Change

This book presents many examples of the Universal Life policy to illustrate the evolution of the life insurance contract. While the form has been altered substantially, the marketing change has been even more dramatic. In this part of the chapter, we describe the evolution from the customer and agent perspective.

Small Policies in the Good Old Days

Over 100 years ago, life insurance, as a means of providing family security, began to be a desirable tool in the financial affairs of the public. Owning life insurance might even have been labeled "fashionable." The early history of assessment and benevolent societies has been well chronicled by other authors. By sharing the risk of premature death, thousands of men and women were able to pool their money through life insurance and protect their families.

For many years, policies were issued in relatively small amounts. Up until 15 or 20 years ago, face amounts typically ranged from $500 to $5,000. Premiums were relatively high for each $1,000 of insurance. The cash value of the policy was routinely considered a part of the death benefit. Equity or investment considerations were not of major importance. The rate of inflation was modest, 2% to 4% per year, and policyholders were content to accumulate a few hundred to a few thousand dollars in the contract to guarantee the small death benefit.

The amounts of money held by life insurance companies were small enough that noninsurance financial institutions were more or less content with the status quo. Real economic growth over many years averaged 3% or so. With modest inflation levels, a growth rate on cash values at the general level of 4% to 6% seemed reasonable to the typical life insurance buyer. The concept of leaving your cash values in the policy for an emergency or retirement was frequently a part of the agent's sales presentation. The policyholder accepted this as a good long-term plan for saving money.

Transition to Large Amounts and Lower Premiums

This quiet accommodation of product and need persisted until the 1950s. At that time, the economic environment of life insurance operations began to show signs of change. Interest rates, which had been relatively stable and predictable, started increasing. The well recognized relationship between interest and inflation received increasing attention by business and the public. The walls that divided existing financial institutions started to crumble, as each type of financial institution made its move to get a larger percentage of the consumer's investment dollars. One of the many contemporary developments was the competition for pension dollars between the self-insured bank trust funds and newly designed group annuity insurance contracts.

The comfortable concept of preserving cash values for emergency borrowing and retirement gave way to tax leverage approaches in the form of minimum deposit plans. Higher federal and state income taxes prompted many people to buy insurance with the partial objective of thwarting the revenue collectors.

In the 1960s, the sale of $25,000 and $50,000 life insurance policies became more common. The late 1970s marked the emergence of large face amount sales, frequently term sales, of $100,000 and up. Life insurers introduced policy fees and expanded various forms of "banding" to compete by using larger quantity discounts. Figure 1.4 shows the average premium current in 1970.

Figure 1.4

ANNUAL PREMIUM PER $1,000
MALE AGE 35 BASED ON REPRESENTATIVE
COMPANIES IN 1970

	Whole Life Insurance Policies		5-Year Term Life Insurance[a]	
	Participating	Guaranteed Cost	Participating	Guaranteed Cost
Lowest	$21.40	$17.03	$5.35	$5.23
Highest	24.86	19.18	7.58	6.67
Average	23.08	18.60	6.23	6.01

[a] Standard term, renewable and convertible at increasing rates to age 65.

By 1982 a premium on the order of $10.00 per thousand for permanent life insurance was available in several of the new competitive policies. Term insurance premiums cracked the $1.00 per thousand barrier at age 35 and were still dropping for the low-cost re-entry policies available to preferred (nonsmoker) risks.

One company, Northwestern Mutual Life, offered a participating term to 65 plan with paid-up additions (and no loan values) which provides essentially level insurance for the whole of life. The guaranteed level premium for this policy stops at age 65. At issue age 35, the premium is less than the 5-year term premium of $7.58 shown in Figure 1.4.

Cash values are no longer measured in hundreds of dollars. With the increase in face amounts and the decrease in the value of the dollars, cash values in the thousands are routinely involved.

The Shift to Low Cost Life Insurance

There were parallel developments in group life insurance.

Group term insurance amounts offered by employers grew from levels of $1,000 per employee to $5,000, $10,000, and then $25,000. Most state legislatures recognized this trend by raising or eliminating legal limits on the certificate amounts of group term. Today $250,000 per employee is not uncommon. In the same span of years, minimum group premium laws, originally passed to protect the companies against unwise competitive pricing, were repealed in New Jersey and New York.

Group term and other low-cost products accelerate a trend toward buying term and investing the difference. The rapid growth of mutual funds which allowed the client to invest in small dollar units enhanced the options available for regular investment. By the 1970s, the race for the savings dollar was on in earnest.

In 1980, inflation reached a level where the new money market funds were paying 10% and more. People started moving money from traditional savings vehicles of all sorts—cash values, banks, savings and loans, and low-yielding bonds—to the money markets. In the early 1980s, 18% low risk money markets all but crushed the traditional 5% interest haven of millions of dollars as these funds moved to the new high-yield instruments.

Everybody, it seemed, became an investment expert. The stockbroker took up a new role in the marketplace and placed billions of dollars in money market funds at zero commission, just to establish new clients. Life insurance companies paying commissions of 50% to 100% on new premium dollars were at a competitive disadvantage with the no load money market funds. Sales of term insurance soared as sales of cash value life insurance dropped.

If owning life insurance was once fashionable, in 1981 borrowing cash values to seek a better return became a cocktail party topic. Some companies turned to the "replacement market" to enhance sales, and dropping one's whole life insurance to buy term became common. The idea of buying a policy and keeping it for life was replaced by the combination of cheap term and noninsurance investments paying 10% and more.

In reaction to these developments, segments of the life insurance industry aggressively sold high-yield annuities. These single premium annuities, marketed with substantial emphasis on the tax-shelter they provided, paid 10% to 16% in 1981, competing with money market and other mutual funds as well as other life insurance company cash value products.

Some stockbrokers became part-time life insurance or annuity agents. The brokers were in an advantageous position to advocate buying term and investing the difference. A number of life insurance companies achieved marked success with combination sales.

As broad evidence of the impact these product shifts have had on life insurance companies, Figure 1.5 shows the dramatic changes in premium income and permanent/term new business for the years 1976 to 1981 (estimated).

Figure 1.5

PREMIUM INCOME AND PERMANENT/TERM NEW ISSUES (000,000 OMITTED)

Year	Life Premium	Annuity Premium	Annuity as % of Life	Issues of Permanent	Issues of Term	Term as % of Perm.
1976	$31,200	$5,807	18.6%	$113,665	$107,732	94.8%
1977	33,736	6,423	19.0	125,653	128,634	102.4
1978	36,594	15,391[a]	42.1	140,766	150,697	107.1
1979	39,040	17,856	45.7	154,105	184,260	119.6
1980	40,907	22,746	55.6	173,457	224,812	129.6
1981	43,000	29,500	68.6	192,000	275,000	143.2

[a]Premium figures from 1978 on include annuities and other fund deposits.

The Economic Recovery Tax Act of 1981 added another major development. Now, the working investor can deduct

$2,000 for himself and $250 for his spouse (if not working) or $2,000 for his spouse if working by establishing an Individual Retirement Account (IRA). The attractiveness of this tax deferral will undoubtedly have an impact on traditional life insurance. The concept of buying term and investing the difference has taken on a new dimension—buy term and tax deduct the difference. The small investor will be wary of equity investments and likely will be attracted to the low-risk, tax-deductible IRA account.

Organizational Change

Consider the following two quotes, from different sources and with different purposes in mind.

"Because of uncertainty about future rates of return and because of the lifetime commitments contained in traditional life insurance products, insurance companies have been unable to raise the promised rate of return on policies cash values to levels which can compete with other forms of saving. This has resulted in traditional life policies falling into disfavor with consumers."—Massachusetts Mutual request to the IRS for a private letter ruling, June, 1981.

"Question: Is Universal Life a good policy for me to own in a time of rapid inflation? Answer: Yes. Universal Life is a policy which provides the opportunity of keeping policy benefits current with, or ahead of, inflation. If the purchasing power of the dollar continues to decline, you can keep your insurance current by paying more of the 'cheaper' dollars in premium payments. Your insurance coverage can be decreased or increased, subject to insurability. The flexibility of Universal Life makes it sensitive to inflation, which makes it a unique insurance product."—Inter-State Assurance Company brochure about their Flexlife policy.

Why Universal Life? What are its origins? If it answers the challenge of inflation, why didn't the life insurance industry offer the product or something like it in the 1970s when inflation was recognized publicly as the worst domestic problem the country faced? In this part of the chapter, we trace major events which have impacted the business, with emphasis here on the home offices and the state regulators whose business relationship determines the product and services made available to agents and their clients.

The Law on Policy Contracts

As the readers of this book know, all insurance companies are subject to the laws and regulations of the states. No policy may be sold without the consent of the state. No agent may sell life insurance without the approval of the commissioner or director of insurance in the state of the application. Furthermore, every state has specific requirements under which a contract of life insurance must be formed.

The specific requirements which apply to policy form approvals include such weighty statutes as the Standard Nonforfeiture and Standard Valuation Laws. These complex combinations of legal and actuarial jargon leave all but the most persevering reader in a state of utter confusion. We do not recommend that anyone try to read and understand what these laws say. They assume a policy structure of the traditional variety, that a contract with fixed premiums and fixed benefits. It is often a challenge for actuaries and policy form analysts at the state insurance departments to interpret and apply them to specific policy contracts. As a result, the laws were applied in a very rigid way by the states for many years.

In the early 1970s, the first major crack in traditional fixed policies appeared when life insurance companies began to market the new Keogh annuities. Annuities were not a substantial part of company income before that time. The flexible premium annuity (FPA) made its appearance. The payment of unscheduled or flexible premiums gained ready acceptance in the marketplace. After processing hundreds of FPA form filings, the regulators became accustomed to flexible premiums. Incidentally, approvals were not hard to come by since there was no general minimum cash value standard applicable to the FPAs.

After some initial struggle, new data processing and accounting systems were developed to handle the unfamiliar billing and interest crediting practices required by the FPAs. Thus the companies and various computer firms gained experience with a nontraditional product.

There was another effect of FPAs which is part of the origins of Universal Life. FPAs are nothing more than money accumulation products with the interest rate virtually the sole factor to consider at purchase. And so it was that other financial institutions competed for Keogh money. They were often successful, in part because, with no commissioned sales person involved, the banks and others were able to sell their product on a no-load basis. IRAs and Tax Sheltered Annuities (TSA) followed. In order to compete in these new markets, the companies found it necessary to reduce commissions from those customarily offered on fixed premium deferred annuities. Over a short time span, first year commissions were squeezed down to the 5% and 10% level, with even lower renewal commissions. A few companies moved to introduce higher yield annuities. Among these were the Bankers of Iowa which offered a group funded product using "floating" cash values based on a bond fund. (In early 1982 Bankers went further, offering a "current yield annuity" for the first time.)

The acceptance of such low commissions came hard for many agents, but, in the end, it became a matter of accepting a small part of what were often fairly large annuity premiums or getting a larger part of nothing. Low load annuity products, the forerunner of early Universal Life policies, were born as a result of the tax-shelter made available by the federal government.

Federal Government Studies

This same time period saw the birth of broad federal legislation commonly referred to as "Truth in Lending." Hailed as a long overdue disclosure of important consumer facts, this legislation spawned a maze of complex regulations and mandatory paperwork which still helps to fill the mailboxes of the country. "Truth in Life Insurance" was not far behind.

In 1973 Ralph Nader and a number of other consumerists made headlines from Washington, D.C. when they testified before Senator Hart's Subcommittee on Antitrust and Monopoly of the Senate Committee on the Judiciary (93rd Congress, 2nd Session 8, 1974). The companies remained quiet, preferring to suffer the pain of adverse publicity rather than counter with their side of the story and increase the publicity.

In 1977 life insurance was again in the news from the Potomac. Congressman Moss held hearings of the Subcommittee on Oversight and Investigations of the House Committee on Interstate and Foreign Commerce, Report on Life Insurance Marketing and Cost Disclosure (95th Congress, 2nd Session 3, 1978). Again, the companies remained quiet.

In the meantime, various industry committees and insurance departments had been moving to improve the available consumer information on the cost of life insurance. The Buyer's Guide and a model regulation requiring the use of interest adjusted cost indices were the result of considerable cooperation between the companies and the National Association of Insurance Commissioners (NAIC). While this constructive development was taking place, the single most significant public relations event of this century affecting the life insurance business occurred, again in the nation's capitol.

At 10:00 A.M., EDT, Tuesday, July 10, 1979, the Staff Report to the Federal Trade Commission (FTC) was released. The headline of the press release read:

CONSUMERS LOSING BILLIONS YEARLY BY "ILL-INFORMED AND INAPPROIATE" LIFE INSURANCE CHOICES, FTC STAFF SAYS

Savings Element of Whole-Life Policies Yielding 1 to 2 Percent on Average: Holders of Older Policies May be Losing Money

This time the insurance industry had had enough. The first public response was from the Chairman and Chief Executive Officer of Massachusetts Mutual who immediately labeled the report "irresponsibly misleading and based throughout on faulty and incomplete analysis." The President of the American Council of Life Insurance (ACLI), Blake T. Newton, Jr., introduced his response in the *CLU Journal* by writing, "At a time when the President of the United States feels it necessary to appear on national television to discuss a 'crisis of confidence . . . the erosion of our confidence in the future,' and to urge us all to 'say something good about our country,' it is ironic that our government should itself be the source of a deceptive and misleading report, aimed at the heart of an institution which has served this nation well throughout its history; which accumulated a vast reservoir of consumer confidence; and which is one of the largest pools of capital in existence for the future growth and strength of the America economy. The publicity tactics surrounding the report of the Federal Trade Commission . . . represent an inexcusable and apparently deliberate attempt to destroy public confidence in the life insurance business, and to create headlines through accusations which are so misleading they can only be called deceptive."

The ACLI demanded and received a hearing before the Senate Commerce Committee, but the damage was done. Rice E. Brown, Chairman of the Committee on Federal Law and Legislation of the National Association of Life Underwriters (NALU) testified at the hearing.

"We believe that, as it now stands, this FTC Staff Report, and the more scandalous statements contained in or fairly to be derived from it, will be misused for years to come to cause dissatisfaction with existing life insurance, to cause its ill-advised replacement, and to prevent the sale of much of the kind of life insurance that has represented a high-quality purchase for millions of consumers for so long a time.'

Thomas J. Wolff, President of the NALU, also testified. He reacted strongly to another public relations blow that followed shortly after the release of the FTC Staff Report.

"On August 18, on WGN-TV in Chicago, and subsequently on approximately 150 other television stations throughout the United States, the *Phil Donahue Show* devoted its entire hour of television to life insurance, with particular reference to the FTC Staff Report and its allegation that life insurance companies pay 1.3% on life insurance 'savings.'"

Abandoning its customary low-key approach, the industry requested equal time. Tom Wolff and Robert A. Beck, Chief Executive Officer of Prudential Insurance Company of America subsequently appeared with Donahue to try to "set the record straight." But the damage was already done.

In January 1980, President Carter took his turn. He wrote the nation's governors that state and federal authorities needed to do more together to help consumers reduce life insurance costs. Again, Blake Newton responded, this time with a statement that "the proposed changes in disclosure regulations were never adopted by the FTC and were thoroughly discredited." And again, the damage was already done.

The negative impact of these federal activities are a part of the origins of Universal Life. By spotlighting the relatively low investment return of traditional products, the information and misinformation conveyed to the public has undoubtedly had a catalytic effect on the interest of the press and public in Universal Life. One wonders how many newspaper editors would have been unaware or unimpressed by stories about replacement of life insurance or Universal Life products had their interest not been piqued by the clamor which arose after July 10, 1979.

In a spirit of fairness and because these events were so extraordinary, we offer the following true/false summary of the FTC Staff Report. Each of the four points were keys to the Report.

1) *The life insurance industry is a major repository of consumer savings.*

TRUE if "savings" means the reserve funds needed to pay all the benefits of life insurance policies. FALSE when the words "savings" implies that life insurance surrender values are the same as a savings account with a bank. They are not. They are much more.

2) *In 1977 the industry paid its policyholders less than 2% on their savings.*

FALSE. The 1.3% (and similar low numbers given in the Report) are misleading and incorrect. The FTC treats the insurance industry like a bank which sells only cheap one-year term insurance. The calculations which result are full of holes. Proof of these serious errors, with accounting detail, was provided by the ACLI.

3) *Life insurance companies paying 2% after 20 years (using a theoretical rate of return calculation) compete successfully against companies paying 5%.*

As far as it goes, this is TRUE. Each company has a different market, underwriting, service and profit outlook. So, premiums and the theoretical rate of return also vary by company. Fixed premium whole life insurance, which does not pay dividends, competes poorly in a time of high inflation.

4) *Penalties for early withdrawal are remarkably severe but unannounced.*

It is TRUE that early lapses of permanent policies cause the consumer severe losses. The word "unannounced" is totally FALSE. Every contract issued and every policy summary used by the companies shows the premium and the early year cash values. The NAIC Buyer's Guide has a strong warning about this. The FTC summary statement on this matter is clearly biased.

The Impact of Consumerists

A variety of speakers, writers and educators have contributed in various ways to the origins of Universal Life. Some have merely added confusion. It is certainly the case that anyone with a view, pro or con, on traditional or nontraditional life insurance policies can find a quote ready-made for his purpose. Thus, it happens that thousands of reprints of super-critical publications have been distributed throughout the country. Chapter 13 of Venita Van Caspel's book, *The New Money Dynamics*, is typical. The title of Chapter 13, first edition, was "Life Insurance—The Great National Consumer Fraud?"

On the side of constructive criticism, a number of educators have contributed worthwhile ideas. We note especially Professor Joseph Belth of Indiana University on the subject of cost disclosure and Professor Harold Skipper, Jr., of Georgia State University for his most recent work on replacement regulations. Other consumerists are unshakeably wedded to the concept of buy term and invest the difference. As one example, a 1981 column by Jane Bryant Quinn summed up her view of Universal Life as, "Whole life buyers might want to wait for the next IRS ruling before buying (or switching to) Universal Life. For the most bang for the buck, it still makes sense to buy a low-cost term insurance policy and keep your savings somewhere else."

A discussion of origins would be incomplete without some discussion of policy disclosure matters and policy simplification. Agents and companies alike have come a long way from the days when the premiums paid less dividends and cash values were used to measure the cost of life insurance. It seems clear that the NAIC model regulation on cost disclosure is a considerable improvement over the old methods for traditional products.

On the other hand, the use of new money methods and nonguaranteed premiums has left the regulations woefully out of date. Other imponderables exist to further confuse both agent and client. The indices do not consider (1) the value of the service of an agent or company; (2) the relative strength and reputation of the company; or (3) other differences in the policy provision such as supplemental benefits and the options available at the time of claim. It may well be that no method can be found that is fully satisfactory to all parties. One actuary we know has commented that the best approach would be to require a detailed prospectus, such as that mandated on securities by the SEC. This document would be so long and ponderous that no one would read nor understand it.

All of the suggestions, national committees, and insurance department hearings have failed to keep up with the movement in the industry toward Universal Life. We can hope for something better, but it is unreasonable to expect this while the industry itself is experiencing considerable turmoil.

One other area under the broad heading of disclosure deserves a more positive report. This is the thrust of the states toward requiring more readable policy contracts. Begun in Massachusetts in the 1970s, the idea that insurance and other complex consumer legal documents should be readable has moved rapidly through many of the state legislatures. After some initial consternation, the companies have gone to work and responded well to this development. Naturally, some simplified policies are better than others. In this book, we have illustrated the degree of improvement by including a detailed look at one of the best simplified Universal Life policies. The consumer has benefited by improved clarity in the wording of his life insurance contract.

The effort to keep things simple—and understandable—has had an impact on Universal Life. A key feature of the contract's administration is the furnishing of an annual report to the policyholder which attempts to explain just how the premium and benefits work and what are the costs. Movement toward simplification has even shown up in advertising copy. One company, The Acacia Group, offered a simple respite from the blare of advertising claims and counterclaims. In a copyrighted advertisement in late 1981, they featured the headline, "The last life insurance ad you'll ever have to read."

The Role of State Regulators

Historically, the insurance departments have been primarily concerned with the solvency of insurance companies. There are no state statutes which mandate price control or rate approval processes for life insurance premiums. The only area of substance which affects the final price of the product and falls under state supervision is that of surplus distribution, that is payment of policyholder dividends. This is a highly technical and judgmental area, loosely regulated.

The states have frequently become involved in certain kinds of product related matters. There have been a number of life insurance products and marketing approaches in this century which have caused concern. Going back to the early 1900s, the history of endowment policies and excessive company expense was at the heart of the historic Armstrong investigations in New York. More recently, annual endowment or coupon policies led to restrictive regulations in at least 12 states by 1964. Founder's policies and so-called profit sharing plans were sometimes sold by stock company promoters in such a way as to confuse the insurance policy with an investment in the company itself. State action followed to correct the recognized abuses.

Variable life created special problems because of the involvement of the SEC. The compromise, which grew from the state-federal compromise over this product, required a great deal of energy by those departments able to contribute qualified people to the NAIC activities. Deposit term was the controversial product just before the full-blown emergence of Universal Life.

The states have often exercised their authority in ways which shape the design and marketing practices of new and unusual product designs. This is happening in the case of Universal Life. More than two dozen states have developed some form of regulation, formal or informal, dealing with the Universal Life contract. One of the more detailed examples thus far is South Carolina.

Besides the usual policy form material, South Carolina requires submission of sales material for approval prior to use. A statement must appear that illustrative values may materially change. The policy summary must indicate when the cash value would be exhausted based upon the stipulated premium/amount relationship. A 60-day grace period must be provided before lapse without value, with notice of impending lapse being given at least 30 days before lapse. An annual report must be given to the policyholder summarizing policy activity and results during the past year.

Many of these requirements are specified in Universal Life contracts now being sold. In fact, it appears that a number of states developed their regulatory approach by simply reviewing early company practices and regulations then developing requirements believed to be of benefit to their citizens. A half-dozen states have special requirements dealing with details of the annual report. California has expressed a concern with the level of actuarial reserves, but has not prevented companies from marketing the product. A task force of the NAIC has undertaken development of a model regulation scheduled for a vote in late 1983 or early 1984.

New York approved legislation for Universal Life in July, 1982. An insurance department circular letter giving initial policy approval guidelines was developed in the Spring of 1983 thus making New York the last state to allow the sale of Universal Life. This letter contained rather stringent requirements in several areas; new and controversial limits on field compensation were included.

In general, the states have accepted the product as one that suits the times. The regulators had to accept the new approach to cash values and they have. To understand how this is involved with the origins of Universal Life, a discussion of product development and changes in the Standard Nonforfeiture and Standard Valuation Laws will be helpful.

Actuarial Developments

Actuaries have played an important role in the origins of Universal Life. The so-called retrospective approach to the policy has been mentioned numerous times in actuarial literature. A Canadian actuary, George R. Dinney of the Great-West Life Assurance Co., did some very early work on flexible products in that country. He is credited with coining the phrase "Universal Life Plan" in a speech called, "A Descent into the Maelstrom of the Insurance Future" delivered at Niagara Falls, Ontario, in 1971.

In the past twenty years or so in the United States, Maurice H. LaVita, a consulting actuary in Washington, D.C. produced several papers dealing with variable products. One such paper, "A Flexible or 'Stop and Go' Life Plan," was presented in 1965 about the time the earliest Universal Life policy was being developed in the United States.

Walter Chapin at Minnesota Mutual (1970) and the actuaries at Bankers Life of Iowa (1977) also made original contributions to flexible policies in the form of their companies' Adjustable Life plans. James C. H. Anderson of Tillinghast, Nelson & Warren wrote the most quoted paper at the Pacific Insurance Conference, September 1975 entitled, "A Universal Life Insurance Policy." Alan Richards, who was President of Life of California before it became E. F. Hutton Life and catapulted Universal Life into public consciousness (1979), is also an actuary.

An unusual group of actuaries figures in the origins, and very probably the future of Universal Life. This was the Special Committee of the Society of Actuaries, chaired by Henry Unruh, Chairman of the Provident Life & Accident Company. The Unruh Committee (1972-1974) developed a comprehensive report on the changes needed to update the Standard Nonforfeiture Law. Nontraditional policies were one of dozens of topics dealt with in the Committee's report. The Committee had among its working papers the North Central policy discussed elsewhere in this chapter. One of the Committee members who studied this early Universal Life policy and developed a positive view of its potential was Alan Richards.

In a report to the American Bar Association in January 1982, Alan Lazarescu and Harold Leff of Metropolitan Life gave the following summary of the new model law:

"The new Standard Nonforfeiture Law, approved by the NAIC in December 1980 and already enacted in about 17 states, does not specifically address nonforfeiture requirements on Universal Life. It does not even define or mention Universal Life. There is a catch-all section, Section 6, which allows the insurance commissioner to promulgate regulations governing the approval of any plan of such a nature that minimum values cannot be determined by the other sections of the Nonforfeiture Law. In others words, Universal Life burst on the scene so quickly that even a very up-to-date Nonforfeiture Law does not directly address it. The prior Nonforfeiture Law dates principally to the 1940s, and even the catch-all section is not contained therein."

The catch-all section appears to have played an important

role in the approval process of Universal Life contracts. A number of the key state regulators, men like John Montgomery from California and Ted Becker from Texas, met frequently with the members of the Unruh Committee. After due attention to the matter, they agreed that a catch-all section was desirable to encourage innovation and not force future policy designs into the rigid mold of the prior law.

Quoting Lazarescu and Leff again: "The basic problem with the Nonforfeiture Law is that cash values are defined in terms of present values (prospectively), while Universal Life cash values are calculated in terms of an accumulation since issue (retrospectively)."

A regulator could argue that the model law before 1980 does not allow Universal Life since it is impossible to define the present value of future premiums when the amount of such premiums is unknown. Nevertheless, enlightened by the actuarial exchange of views, the regulators accepted the new actuarial reasoning of the Hutton product design from which all of the Universal Life product variations subsequently developed take their cue.

Acceptable actuarial methods for determining cash values and reserves have been developed. NAIC model regulations will continue to be updated as new product designs are developed.

New York's 1982 law has a unique requirement for policy loans on Universal Life contracts. The difference between the policy loan interest rate and interest credited on loaned cash values may not exceed 2% (unless the insurer can justify a larger spread). Thus, a loan of say, 8%, dictates a minimum rate of 6% to be credited on loaned cash values.

The other major development which has contributed to the origins of the policy is the new technology. Without the computers of the 1980s, the calculations required to illustrate the Universal Life policy in the field and administer it in the home offices would be quite cumbersome.

The First Universal Life Policy

The folks who became E. F. Hutton Life Insurance have frequently been given credit for originating Universal Life in the United States. Our research uncovered a policy developed and sold by the North Central Life Insurance Company of St. Paul, Minnesota. We would like to nominate this small company as the first to have made a commercial success of Universal Life.

According to John T. Beck, Executive Vice-president of the company, their policy was developed in the early 1960s. The policy form we have was approved by a midwestern insurance department on April 24, 1967. The original release paid commissions based upon the face amount. Loadings were level with the first year cash values as high as 65% of the premium. After indifferent sales results, the company shifted to a traditional percentage commission basis and sales from their small sales force mushroomed. During 1972 through 1975 some 15,000 Flexible Life policies were sold. At its peak, the reserves on this contract had accumulated to $8,000,000, in round figures.

Why did North Central stop selling the plan? As related above, the attitudes of insurance departments have changed markedly in recent years. It took several years of arduous work at the company to obtain approval of Flexible Life. When the company determined that it needed to update the contract, they decided it would not be worth repeating the huge effort needed to refile with the departments. At about the same time, they had developed a new approach using an annuity policy with a term rider. They stopped selling this early version of Universal Life.

What happened to the business in force? North Central felt it should not raise the interest credited on Flexible Life. Some of the company's ex-agents started to twist out the business in force. In order to conserve the policies, North Central allowed conversion of Flexible Life to their new no load annuity. Ironically, over half of the policies sold were replaced by the annuity. Reserves for this early Universal Life policy are roughly $3.5 million today. It presently credits interest at $7\frac{3}{4}\%$.

Summary

The important product features of Universal Life are rooted in the material discussed above. Inflation in the 1970s spurred demand for a higher current interest return from life insurance products. Noninsurance institutions and money market funds competed successfully. Annuity products began to offer current new money returns, and Universal Life followed naturally.

Inflation encouraged a new cost consciousness among the public. Low cost life insurance for greater death benefits caught on. Universal Life mirrored this public demand in its initial low-load product designs. After the E. F. Hutton policy brought national attention to the product, policies began to appear with nonsmoker mortality costs, following the low cost term products developed in the late 1970s.

The idea that death benefits need not be fixed emerged with variable life insurance. Flexible premiums, a key product feature of Universal Life, became familiar to companies, regulators and computer firms as the industry developed flexible premium annuities to help consumers benefit from the government's new tax shelters.

With its studies, notably the Truth in Lending legislation and the ill-famed FTC Staff Report, the Federal government encouraged state activities to simplify policy wording and improve cost disclosure methods. Consumerists and eventually actuaries played their roles in responding to the increasingly pressurized atmosphere in which the life insurance companies had been operating since inflation reached the double-digit level.

Old products were rewritten and repriced. New products, of which Universal Life is the most striking variation, came swiftly on the scene in the 1980s. One who simply sits and compares this product with the standard whole life policy of ten years ago might well wonder what happened to bring about so profound a change. To those who trace the origins, Universal Life seems to evolve quite naturally from the past.

CHAPTER 2

One Policy for Life

Life Style

Everyone is unique—the leader of a different life pattern. And no one life insurance policy could meet all the demands and differences of a man or woman—except Universal Life. For example, let's assume a man and woman decide on the following pattern:

a. He secures a job.

b. They marry.

c. The wife secures a job and wants to help save money for a home.

d. They purchase a home.

e. They have two children.

f. The wife returns to work when the children are in school.

g. Their children go to college.

h. Their children graduate from college, and husband and wife have more disposable income.

i. He retires, and they need additional income to support their leisure years.

j. He dies, and his widow needs income to support herself.

Given this train of events, we present one way in which a single Universal Life contract can be tailored to meet the needs of this man and his family. Each of the events above is described and then keyed by letter to the illustrative sales proposal, Fig. 2.1.

a) A male, age 22, graduates from college and secures a job with an annual salary of $20,000. He allocates 6% ($1,200 per year) to purchase a $100,000 Universal Life policy.

b) At age 27, he marries and increases his premium each year by $400 and his protection by $10,000 each year. After 5 years the totals are $3,200 premium and $150,000 protection respectively.

c) The wife secures a job and wants to help save for a home. They increase their premium by an additional $3,200 per year for 3 years.

d) A home is purchased for $100,000 and a withdrawal is made from the Universal Life policy for $25,000 to make a down payment. Insurance is increased to $175,000 to cover the mortgage.

e) Two children are born and for 5 years the premiums on the Universal Life policy are reduced to $3,000 per year. The policy is increased to $275,000 to protect the children.

f) At this time the children are in school and the wife goes back to work. The premiums are increased to $5,000 per year.

g) The children go to college and the premiums are discontinued. $10,000 per year is withdrawn for 8 years to help cover college expenses.

h) When the children graduate the family decides to start making premium payments of $10,000 per year to build a retirement fund.
i) Upon retirement at age 70, the husband and wife decide to withdraw $100,000 per year to life expectancy, estimated at 15 years, to help fund retirement.
j) At the husband's death the wife receives a lump sum settlement in the amount specified by the contract (obviously a very large sum if high interest rates should continue until late in the life of the family).

The bottom line is that one Universal Life policy, with flexible premiums, cash withdrawals, and death benefits, solves a family's lifelong financial security needs.

Note that the premiums, withdrawals, and death benefits can be adjusted according to the interest rate earned. As Figure 2.1 shows, the program will work well with a 12.36% interest rate, but at 4% and 8%, the benefits as well as the premium will have to be rearranged. It is reasonable to adjust benefits because no one can know in advance the salary he will earn or the benefits he will desire during his lifetime.

The Universal Life contract has the flexibility necessary to allow these adjustments and deliver the benefits. One policy will do the job—for life.

Figure 2.1
ONE POLICY ILLUSTRATION[1]

AGE	YEAR	ANNUAL PREMIUM	4.0% BASIS (guaranteed)		8.0% BASIS (illustrative)		12.36% BASIS (current)	
			CASH VALUE	DEATH BENEFIT	CASH VALUE	DEATH BENEFIT	CASH VALUE	DEATH BENEFIT
22[a]	1	1,200	224	100,000	253	100,000	265	100,000
23	2	1,200	1,179	100,000	1,240	100,000	1,265	100,000
24	3	1,200	2,172	100,000	2,307	100,000	2,390	100,000
25	4	1,200	3,204	100,000	3,462	100,000	3,657	100,000
26	5	1,200	4,277	100,000	4,711	100,000	5,083	100,000
27[b]	6	1,600	5,740	110,000	6,428	110,000	7,069	110,000
28	7	2,000	7,620	120,000	8,662	120,000	9,695	120,000
29	8	2,400	9,931	130,000	11,454	130,000	13,043	130,000
30	9	2,800	12,692	140,000	14,849	140,000	17,200	140,000
31[b]	10	3,200	15,918	150,000	18,898	150,000	22,269	140,000
32[c]	11	6,400	22,319	150,000	26,438	150,000	31,263	150,000
33	12	6,400	28,982	150,000	34,593	150,000	41,385	150,000
34	13	6,400	35,918	150,000	43,413	150,000	52,774	150,000
d→YEAR 14:		25,000	PARTIAL	CASH	WITHDRAWAL			
35	14	0	10,883	175,000	19,478	175,000	30,769	175,000
36	15	6,400	16,950	175,000	26,973	175,000	40,739	175,000
37[e]	16	3,000	19,635	275,000	31,386	275,000	48,124	275,000
38	17	3,000	22,486	275,000	36,235	275,000	56,519	275,000
39	18	3,000	25,398	275,000	41,446	275,000	65,937	275,000
40	19	3,000	28,366	275,000	47,046	275,000	76,508	275,000
41	20	3,000	31,387	275,000	53,073	275,000	88,384	275,000
42[f]	21	5,000	36,361	275,000	61,533	275,000	103,784	275,000
43	22	5,000	41,469	275,000	70,655	275,000	121,105	275,000
44	23	5,000	46,714	275,000	80,491	275,000	140,594	275,000

[1] This illustration has not been changed from the first edition. The death benefits at 8% and 12% do not meet the TEFRA corridor requirements at all ages. The case studies in Chapter 11 are also unchanged from the first edition. However, this in no way diminishes the illustration of the policy's flexibility

The TEFRA corridor requirements are fully discussed in Chapter 8, "TEFRA 1982—Tax Issues and Guidelines." The sales proposals in Chapter 5, "Creating the Proposal", are in compliance with these 1982 changes to the Federal law.

45	24	5,000	52,099	275,000	91,096	275,000	162,530	275,000
46	25	5,000	57,621	275,000	102,526	275,000	187,231	275,000
47	26	5,000	63,284	275,000	114,853	275,000	215,065	275,000
48	27	5,000	69,086	275,000	128,156	275,000	246,457	275,000
49	28	5,000	75,029	275,000	142,525	275,000	281,793	309,972
50	29	5,000	81,113	275,000	158,061	275,000	321,457	353,603
51	30	5,000	87,342	275,000	174,882	275,000	365,977	402,575
52	31	5,000	93,721	275,000	193,114	275,000	415,944	457,538
53	32	5,000	100,254	275,000	212,898	275,000	472,017	519,219
54	33	5,000	106,947	275,000	234,390	275,000	534,935	588,429
g → YEARS 34 thru 41: 10,000 PARTIAL CASH WITHDRAWAL YEARLY								
55	34	0	98,613	265,000	242,006	267,006	589,187	648,105
56	35	0	89,759	255,000	250,273	275,300	650,033	715,037
57	36	0	80,339	245,000	259,179	285,097	718,268	790,095
58	37	0	70,302	235,000	268,761	295,637	794,772	874,250
59	38	0	59,590	225,000	279,067	306,974	880,529	968,582
60	39	0	48,131	215,000	290,146	319,161	976,628	1,074,290
61	40	0	35,850	205,000	302,050	332,255	1,084,280	1,192,710
62	41	0	22,655	195,000	314,834	346,317	1,204,840	1,325,330
63 h	42	10,000	28,563	195,000	349,148	384,063	1,361,240	1,497,360
64	43	10,000	34,467	195,000	386,063	424,669	1,536,310	1,689,940
65	44	10,000	40,359	195,000	425,760	468,336	1,732,230	1,905,450
66	45	10,000	46,228	195,000	468,414	515,256	1,951,320	2,146,450
67	46	10,000	52,065	195,000	514,220	565,642	2,196,200	2,415,820
68	47	10,000	57,857	195,000	563,384	619,722	2,469,790	2,716,770
69	48	10,000	63,606	195,000	616,128	677,741	2,775,320	3,052,850
i → YEARS 49 thru 63: 100,000 PARTIAL CASH WITHDRAWAL YEARLY								
70	49	0			555,302	610,832	2,994,290	3,293,720
71	50	0			489,724	538,696	3,238,480	3,562,330
72	51	0			419,076	460,984	3,510,790	3,861,860
73	52	0			343,005	377,306	3,814,300	4,195,730
74	53	0			261,133	287,246	4,152,260	4,567,490
75	54	0			172,621	197,621	4,528,020	4,980,830
76	55	0			76,888	101,888	4,944,980	5,439,480
77	56	0					5,406,930	5,947,630
78	57	0					5,917,940	6,509,740
79	58	0					6,482,400	7,130,640
80	59	0					7,105,010	7,815,510
81 j	60	0					7,790,550	8,569,610

The Advantages of Universal Life

Let's look in some detail at the following characteristics of Universal Life:

1) Simplicity
2) Flexibility
3) Cost Effectiveness
4) Tax Effectiveness
5) Complete Cost Disclosure
6) Commissions
7) Sales Applicability

1) SIMPLICITY

The simplicity of Universal Life is made possible by the unbundling of the traditional Whole Life policy. "Unbundling" means that the insurance contract is broken down into three components—interest, administrative costs and pure death benefit. In this form, the consumer can understand each element of his contract and its related cost. Also, he can clearly see the effect of the interest rate on the cash value of his policy.

This is accomplished by a computerized proposal at the time of purchase and an annual statement of account, sometimes called an "Annual Report." The proposal shows the cash values based on the minimum guaranteed interest as well as the cash values based on the current high interest rates (such as 12% in many of this book's illustrations). The proposal shows the amount of total death benefit, calculated at both the guaranteed and current interest rates. Each client, therefore, receives a "road map" of exactly which direction his program can take. The understanding of his contract is reinforced annually as he receives his annual report. A typical annual report is shown in Figure 2.2.

Figure 2.2

A N N U A L   R E P O R T

INSURED   **JOHN Q. DOE**   REPORT DATE 08/01/2005   REPRESENTATIVE
ADDRESS   100 MYRTLE LANE   ISSUE AGE 35 MALE   JAMES M AGENT
           HOMETOWN OH   23200   POLICY CI12345678   HOMETOWN OH

-----------------------STATUS AS OF REPORT DATE-----------------------

SPECIFIED AMOUNT   250,000.00   MATURITY DATE   08/01/2040
NET DEATH BENEFIT   250,000.00   SCHEDULE PREMIUM   1,799.00
COVERAGE TYPE   PAYABLE ANNUALLY
    FLEXIBLE PREMIUM ADJUSTABLE LIFE   NET CASH VALUE   58,867.96
    SPECIFIED AMOUNT   NET SURRENDER VALUE   56,205.83

--------SUMMARY OF TRANSACTIONS FOR YEAR ENDING ON REPORT DATE---------

MONTH ENDING	PREMIUMS RECEIVED	EXPENSE CHARGES	INTEREST CREDITED GUAR'E	EXCESS	%	INSURANCE DEDUCTIONS	PARTIAL WITHDL	END OF MO CASH VAL.
08/2004	1,799.00	161.90	184.55	217.81	9.00	221.40	0.00	56,774.69
09/2004	0.00	0.00	185.14	218.53	9.00	221.19	0.00	56,957.16
10/2004	0.00	0.00	185.74	219.25	9.00	220.98	0.00	57,141.16
11/2004	0.00	0.00	186.34	219.97	9.00	220.77	0.00	57,326.69
12/2004	0.00	0.00	186.95	220.70	9.00	220.56	0.00	57,513.78
01/2005	0.00	0.00	187.56	221.44	9.00	220.34	0.00	57,702.44
02/2005	0.00	0.00	188.18	222.18	9.00	220.13	0.00	57,892.67
03/2005	0.00	0.00	188.80	222.93	9.00	219.91	0.00	58,084.49
04/2005	0.00	0.00	189.43	223.68	9.00	219.69	0.00	58,277.91
05/2005	0.00	0.00	190.07	224.45	9.00	219.47	0.00	58,472.97
06/2005	0.00	0.00	190.71	225.21	9.00	219.24	0.00	58,669.64
07/2005	0.00	0.00	191.35	225.99	9.00	219.02	0.00	58,867.96

INTEREST HAS BEEN CREDITED MONTHLY IN THE DETERMINATION OF CASH VALUE.
GUARANTEED INTEREST IS BASED ON AN EFFECTIVE ANNUAL RATE OF 4%. EXCESS
INTEREST FOR EACH MONTH IS BASED ON THE EXCESS OF THE EFFECTIVE ANNUAL
CURRENT INTEREST RATES (SHOWN ABOVE) OVER THE GUARANTEED RATE. EXCESS
INTEREST IS NOT CREDITED ON THE FIRST $1,000 OR ON THE PORTION OF CASH
VALUE BORROWED UNDER LOAN PROVISIONS.

The client has the opportunity to review his monthly transactions, both premiums paid and benefits provided. The exact expense charges, guaranteed interest, excess interest, insurance deductions, partial withdrawals, and the end of month cash values are shown. The unbundling of the policy enables many clients, for the first time, to understand how their policy is structured.

By keeping the annual reports each year, a client has a complete record of all his transactions. He no longer has to wonder what happened during the year with respect to his contract. He simply reviews the annual report and knows exactly how the policy performed.

2) FLEXIBILITY

Flexibility is three-fold in the Universal Life contract. There is flexibility in (a) premium payments, (b) current interest credits, and (c) adjustable low cost protection. This is shown in Figure 2.3, a typical sales illustration.

Figure 2.3

UNIVERSAL LIFE SALES ILLUSTRATION

- FLEXIBLE PREMIUM PAYMENTS—Subject only to certain administrative requirements (ranging from 7.5% to 10.5%), premiums may be paid at any time and in any amount. Payments made, less specified percentage expense charges, are credited to an individual cash value account.

  PREMIUM
  PAYMENTS → \<CASH VALUE\>

- CURRENT INTEREST CREDITS—Interest is credited each month in the determination of the cash value account, based on attractive current yield rates. And, this interest is accumulated tax-free.

  PREMIUM   INTEREST
  PAYMENTS → \<CASH VALUE\> ← CREDITS

- ADJUSTABLE, LOW-COST PROTECTION—The amount of life insurance coverage is adjustable; it may be increased or decreased to meet changing protection needs. The cost of protection is based on low, monthly rates, and each month the cost of pure protection and certain specified expense charges are deducted in the determination of the cash value account.

  PREMIUM   INTEREST
  PAYMENTS → \<CASH VALUE\> ← CREDITS
  ↓
  COST OF PURE PROTECTION
  (AND EXPENSE CHARGES)

The flexible premium payment allows the policyholder to determine when, and in what amounts, payments are to be made. No longer is a loan required if a periodic premium is not paid. No longer is the Automatic Premium Loan provision activated when a premium is not paid. No longer is a minimum deposit required to get the flexibility in premium deposits. The average client can appreciate that earning a high current interest will help pay for future pure death benefit costs and that premium payments are not mandatory.

In traditional whole life policies there is an incentive to make a policy loan if he is a high taxpayer. He borrows at 8% gross interest, a net of about 4% after tax. Under the Universal Life contract the policyholder can earn current rates tax sheltered. For example, 10% tax sheltered current interest gives the same net return as 20% taxable interest to the 50% taxpayer. This solves the insurance industry's problem of large policy loans.

Under the flexible, low cost protection there are two types of pure death benefit coverage options available under a standard Universal Life insurance contract:

Option A— The death benefit is equal to a "specified amount" as selected by the buyer, which includes the cash value.

Option B— The death benefit is equal to a "specified amount" as selected by the buyer, plus the cash value accumulation.

The type of option may also be changed. If one goes to Option A from Option B, or increases the amount of pure death benefit coverage, new evidence of insurability may be necessary. Going from Option A to Option B will be a reduction in protection as long as the "specified amount" is not increased. Such a reduction requires no evidence of insurability.

Benefit changes may usually be scheduled and underwritten at the time the policy is issued. Subsequent increases and decreases may be made within wide limits. Evidence of good health is typically required for such an increase. A policy provision which grants cost-of-living increases without evidence is available in many Universal Life contracts. In some other cases, ad hoc options to increase the specified amount are offered, say, annually.

In the typical Universal Life contract, the amount of pure death benefit is equal to a minimum amount, such as the greater of $10,000 or 10% of the cash value of the contract. Under Option B, the minimum pure death benefit amount creates what is called a "corridor" of life insurance. This corridor causes the total death benefit, which consists of the pure death benefit plus cash value, to increase as the cash value increases once the minimum amount of pure death benefit is provided by the policy. See Figure 2.4.

Figure 2.4
PURE DEATH BENEFIT

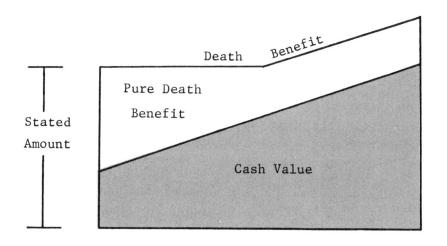

3) COST EFFECTIVENESS

Cost effectiveness is achieved by the fact that Universal Life enables an insurance company to match other companies' portfolios of insurance products with only one product. The "one" product allows cost savings in administration and these savings can be passed on to the policyholder.

The loads and fees taken from Universal Life premium deposits are generally lower than under traditional life products. These savings make the product cost efficient and the savings can be passed on in the form of additional values. The reduced load also allows a substantial first year cash value, in comparison to traditional whole life policies.

The contract guarantees a minimum interest that will be credited each month. However, the current interest paid is a reflection of current interest being paid on other cash investments. Therefore, the client currently receives a rate of interest competitive in the market place. It is important to note that the Universal Life policy must pay current rates that are competitive, since the client can withdraw his funds and invest elsewhere at any time.

There are two types of approaches being used in determining the current interest that will be credited. The first approach is for the insurance company to determine the interest it will pay and declare a specific current rate in advance. The second approach is to index current interest with a prevailing rate on another investment, such as the prevailing rates on long-term U.S. Government Bonds. The rate is then automatically adjusted on a predetermined time frame. Such an index is typically guaranteed for a definite period in advance. The advantage of the index method to the client is that he currently has an up-to-date rate that is not determined by the insurance company. Many traditional life companies have declared higher dividends on new policies being issued but not raised dividends commensurately for old policyholders.

4) TAX EFFECTIVENESS

Tax effectiveness is obtained by the fact that, as is true with any life insurance contract, interest credited to the policy's cash value is sheltered from current income tax. For example, if a person has a cash value of $10,000 in his Universal Life contract that earns 12% interest this year, he earns $1,200. This $1,200 is credited to his contract free of current income tax. Since money accumulates much faster on a tax-sheltered basis, this is a good reason for clients to utilize their Universal Life contracts to accumulate long term savings.

A policyholder may also take either a partial cash withdrawal or a policy loan from his contract. If a partial withdrawal is made, there is no interest charged. However, if the withdrawal is larger than the total premiums deposited, the amount withdrawn over the tax basis will be taxed as current income. Therefore, under certain circumstances, a client may prefer a policy loan. Policy loans are usually made at interest rates of 6% to 8% and the total cash value may be withdrawn with no current income tax on amounts borrowed over the tax basis. The interest charged normally should be tax deductible to the client and the policy pays the minimum interest guaranteed on borrowed funds. If a $10,000 loan is taken at 6% interest, and the contract pays minimum interest of 4%, the following happens:

$600.00	gross interest is
300.00	net interest after-tax in 50% bracket
− 400.00	guaranteed interest credited to contract
$100.00	gain to policyholder

If the interest paid is 8% gross, 4% net in the 50% tax bracket, then the $400.00 in net interest is offset by the guaranteed interest of 4% on the amount borrowed.

5) COMPLETE COST DISCLOSURE

Complete cost disclosure is an important part of the Universal Life contract. It appears that the federal government and state insurance regulatory agencies have intensified their interest in getting complete and full disclosure for the consumer, both at the time of the sale and throughout the life of the contract. With this effort on the part of the regulatory agencies, it is completely appropriate that a Universal Life product provides full disclosure.

All charges for expenses and costs of pure protection are described in the plan documents as is the crediting of interest. The annual report shows, for each month, the actual amounts of premium received and credited; expense charges and costs of pure protection deducted; interest credited and the accumulated cash value; any cash withdrawals. The major objections of many critics have been answered.

6) COMMISSIONS

The agent's commission may be significantly lower than is available under a typical whole life product.

Therefore, it will be necessary for the life insurance agent to sell an increased amount of Universal Life insurance in order to maintain his standard of living. The commission payments on a Universal Life contract generally consist of the following sums:

a) The agent is paid a fee to sell the policy which normally runs from $100.00 to $300.00.

b) The agent receives an initial commission which can be anywhere from 50% to 100% of the cost for the pure death benefit provided.

c) The agent receives a percentage of the total premium paid which is generally 2% to 5%.

For example, suppose a male client, age 40, purchases a $100,000 Universal Life contract that has a yearly premium of $2,000. The first year's commission to the agent could be a policy fee of $225.00 plus $5.00 per thousand of life insurance purchased, $500.00, plus 4% of the total premium, $80.00 which totals $805.00. In subsequent years, the agent would receive a commission equal to 4% of the premiums paid. In addition, the policy may provide a commission on the pure death benefit maintained under the contract, such as $.20 per $1000. As with any typical insurance commission, administrative expenses and costs of the secretarial staff would, of course, have to be paid from the commissions received.

Nevertheless, if the Universal Life contract does what it purports that it will do—that is to put the policyholder in a secure position where the policyholder will not be threatening to turn over the policy year after year—the agent will find that he has much less of a responsibility regarding existing policyholders, and can count on his existing policyholders to keep up with the annual premium payments without constant prodding and hand-holding. Witness, for example, the tremendous amount of money which is constantly pumped into the money market funds without the prodding of any marketing experts. Thus, in time, the successful Universal Life agent may find the product frees tremendous amounts of time to pursue new clients and new opportunities while at the same time paying reasonable renewals.

When Universal Life first came out, many agents were concerned that the commissions were so low that they could not possibly sell enough Universal Life insurance to maintain their standard of living. However, a number of Universal Life contracts have been developed which pay full or nearly full regular life commissions. Also, some companies are paying commissions on the replacement of their existing contracts as long as the pure death benefit is increased by a specified amount and the premium is increased. Thus, there are tremendous opportunities for the life insurance agent to make substantial commissions from the sale of Universal Life insurance.

The range of commissions paid in practice is illustrated by Figures 2.5, A-D. (We are indebted to the actuarial consulting firm of Tillinghast, Nelson & Warren, Inc. for permission to use these figures which they developed in October 1981.)

Figure 2.5A

Comparison of Compensation[a] - Universal Life Policies
Age 35 - Rates per $1,000

Policy Size (000)	Company A		Company B		Company C	Company D
	Smoker	Nonsmoker	Smoker	Nonsmoker	Aggregate	Aggregate
			Premium[b]			
$ 50	$7.73	$6.18	$7.51	$5.08	Not Sold	$11.37/5.81
$100	7.17	5.66	7.38	4.98	$9.83/6.10	7.31/5.43
$500	6.62	5.15	7.38	4.98	5.46	4.94
			Commission Amount			
$ 50	7.61/.31	7.19/.25	3.08/.38	2.13/.25	Not Sold	8.25/.33
$100	6.09/.29	5.28/.23	3.07/.37	2.09/.25	7.75/.38	4.81/.30
$500	4.87/.27	3.85/.21	3.07/.37	2.09/.26	3.53/.36	2.10/.28
			Commission Rate[c]			
$ 50	.98/.04	1.16/.04	.41/.05	.42/.05	Not Sold	.73/.06
$100	.85/.04	.93/.04	.42/.05	.42/.05	.79/.06	.66/.06
$500	.74/.04	.75/.04	.42/.05	.42/.05	.65/.07	.42/.06

[a]Commissions include General Agent overwrite. "/" shows 1st year/renewal.
[b]Premium is the minimum annual amount per $1,000 for a "whole life" target policy. The Universal Life policy is illustrated at a specified death benefit to age 95. It endows for the policy size.
[c]For example, .98/.04 is 1st year of 98% then 4% for at least 9 years.

Figure 2.5B

Comparison of Compensation[a] - Universal Life Policies
Age 55 - Rates per $1,000

Policy Size (000)	Company A		Company B		Company C	Company D
	Smoker	Nonsmoker	Smoker	Nonsmoker	Aggregate	Aggregate
			Premium[b]			
$ 50	$27.36	$23.15	$28.44	$20.94	Not sold	$24.08
$100	26.45	22.27	27.74	20.34	23.97	22.78
$500	22.66	21.50	27.73	20.34	22.75	21.48
			Commission Amount			
$ 50	18.89/1.09	18.73/.93	13.19/1.42	8.28/1.05	Not Sold	14.84/1.35
$100	15.86/1.06	15.69/.89	13.16/1.39	8.25/1.02	17.52/.92	11.26/1.28
$500	13.43/1.03	12.98/.86	13.16/1.39	8.25/1.02	13.46/.88	8.37/1.20
			Commission Rate[c]			
$ 50	.69/.04	.81/.04	.46/.05	.40/.05	Not Sold	.62/.06
$100	.60/.04	.71/.04	.47/.05	.41/.05	.73/.04	.49/.06
$500	.52/.04	.60/.04	.47/.05	.41/.05	.59/.04	.39/.06

---

[a]Commissions include General Agent overwrite. "/" shows 1st year/renewal.
[b]Premium is the minimum annual amount per $1,000 for a "whole life" target policy. The Universal Life policy is illustrated at a specified death benefit to age 95. It endows for the policy size.
[c]For example, .69/.04 is 1st year of 69% then 4% for at least 9 years.

Figure 2.5C

Comparison of Compensation[a] - Universal Life Policies
Age 35 - Rates per $1,000

Policy Size	Company E		Company F	Company G		
(000)	Plan 1	Plan 2	Aggregate Premium[b]	Smoker	Nonsmoker	Aerobic
$ 50	8.65/6.52	9.04/6.61	9.35/6.78	9.96/7.23	9.72/6.66	9.48/6.03
$100	5.98	9.04/6.08	6.23	9.96/6.98	9.72/6.41	9.48/5.80
$500	5.28	9.04/5.53	5.48	9.96/6.80	9.72/6.24	9.48/5.64
Commission Amount						
$ 50	5.93/.20	6.78/.20	6.11/.37	9.76/.36	9.53/.33	9.29/.30
$100	3.90/.18	6.78/.18	3.90/.35	9.76/.35	9.53/.32	9.29/.29
$500	2.32/.16	6.78/.17	2.19/.33	9.76/.34	9.53/.31	9.29/.28
Commission Rate[c]						
$ 50	.69/.03	.75/.03	.65/.05	.98/.05	.98/.05	.98/.05
$100	.65/.03	.75/.03	.63/.06	.98/.05	.98/.05	.98/.05
$500	.44/.03	.75/.03	.40/.06	.98/.05	.98/.05	.98/.05

---

[a]Commissions include General Agent overwrite. "/" shows 1st year/renewal.
[b]Premium is the minimum annual amount per $1,000 for a "whole life" target policy. The Universal Life policy is illustrated at a specified death benefit to age 95. It endows for the policy size.
[c]For example, .69/.03 is 1st year of 69% then 3% for at least 9 years.

Figure 2.5D

Comparison of Compensation[a] - Universal Life Policies
Age 55 - Rates per $1,000

Policy Size	Company E		Company F	Company G		
(000)	Plan 1	Plan 2	Aggregate	Smoker	Nonsmoker	Aerobic

Premium[b]

Policy Size (000)	Plan 1	Plan 2	Aggregate	Smoker	Nonsmoker	Aerobic
$ 50	22.30	27.86/21.58	24.75	27.96/27.64	26.76/25.69	25.56/23.68
$100	21.31	27.86/20.84	23.69	27.96/27.10	26.76/25.17	25.56/23.16
$500	20.48	27.86/20.19	22.80	27.96/26.72	26.76/24.79	25.56/22.80

Commission Amount

Policy Size (000)	Plan 1	Plan 2	Aggregate	Smoker	Nonsmoker	Aerobic
$ 50	10.82/.67	20.90/.65	11.49/1.42	27.40/1.38	26.22/1.28	25.05/1.18
$100	8.84/.64	20.90/.63	9.35/1.38	27.40/1.36	26.22/1.26	25.05/1.16
$500	7.25/.61	20.90/.61	7.63/1.36	27.40/1.34	26.22/1.24	25.05/1.14

Commission Rate[c]

Policy Size (000)	Plan 1	Plan 2	Aggregate	Smoker	Nonsmoker	Aerobic
$ 50	.49/.03	.75/.03	.46/.06	.98/.05	.98/.05	.98/.05
$100	.41/.03	.75/.03	.39/.06	.98/.05	.98/.05	.98/.05
$500	.35/.03	.75/.03	.33/.06	.98/.05	.98/.05	.98/.05

[a]Commissions include General Agent overwrite. "/" shows 1st year/renewal.
[b]Premium is the minimum annual amount per $1,000 for a "whole life" target policy. The Universal Life policy is illustrated at a specified death benefit to age 95. It endows for the policy size.
[c]For example, .49/.03 is 1st year of 49% then 3% for at least 9 years.

7) SALES APPLICABILITY

As we develop in detail in Chapter 11, "Marketing Ideas and Case Studies," the Universal Life contract can be used in almost any sales situation where a typical whole life contract would be used. In fact, the flexibility alone is enough to give it the nod in most situations. The disclosure of the way the policy works, and the availability of high current interest rates, enables the agent to deal with the most competitive sales situations.

1) Is it possible to satisfy both present and future insurance needs with just one policy?

Yes. You may increase your protection as needs occur, such as marriage, children, the purchase of a home, going into business, etc. You may also increase premiums to provide increased protection and to build larger cash values for retirement. You may decrease your protection as your business and family needs diminish and thereby build larger cash values for retirement.

2) Is it more economical and convenient to own one life insurance policy instead of owning several?

Yes. Most life insurance companies charge a policy fee for issuing and maintaining each life insurance policy. Most Universal Life contracts only charge one policy fee. Subsequent increases and decreases in the contract's death benefits and premium deposits do not require an added policy fee. The Universal Life contract is more convenient than owning several policies, since there is only one premium to pay, one address to change, one beneficiary arrangement, and one cash value "account." All of this makes it a simple matter to prepare statements of personal or business net worth, and to make and update financial plans.

3) Could there be a time when I might need two Universal Life contracts?

Yes. You may well have different personal and business insurance needs. This might require the issuance of two separate Universal Life contracts.

4) *Would I ever want more than one policy issued within my family?*

Yes. You might want a policy issued on your wife and each child in addition to your own Universal Life contract.

5) *Is it possible for my family to collect the cash value and specified amount of death benefit at my death?*

Yes. Universal Life offers two options. Option A offers a death benefit equal to the specified amount of insurance. Option B offers a death benefit equal to the cash value of the policy plus the specified amount of insurance.

6) *What changes am I allowed to make within my Universal Life contract?*

You can make the following changes:

- Increase or decrease the premium amount you pay.
- Make premium payments any time you wish and in any amount you desire, as long as you have sufficient cash value to cover expenses and mortality costs.
- Make as few or as many premium payments as you like during your life.
- Increase or decrease your specified death benefit. (Evidence of insurability will generally be necessary to increase the benefit.)
- Change between Option A (death benefit equal to specified amount) and Option B (death benefit equal to cash value plus the specified death benefit). Again evidence of insurability will be necessary. There are no requirements to switch from Option B to Option A if the insurance coverage is not increased.
- If the policy permits, you may add additional insureds to your one Universal Life policy.

7) *Is it possible to stop paying premiums on my Universal Life policy?*

Yes. As long as your contract has sufficient cash values to cover the costs of mortality and company expense charges, you may discontinue premium payments.

8) *What range of Universal Life contracts are available?*

The range of plans in the one policy is unlimited. The computer technology, discussed in Chapter 4 of this book, allows you to select any combination of premium, protection, and cash values. You can create a single premium policy, arrange a term to 65 benefit, or build a 10-year endowment. The computer handles the mathematics which makes a ratebook unnecessary for Universal Life.

9) *How does the cash value of my Universal Life contract accumulate?*

After the first year, roughly 90% to 93% of each premium dollar goes into the cash value. The current interest rate offered by the insurance company is credited to your cash value but would never be less than the 3%-5% guaranteed interest, again depending upon your policy provisions. Costs of pure insurance protection are deducted each month from the cash value. In the first policy year, there may be an added deduction for policy fees or monthly expense charges. First year policy fees run from $0 to $600, and monthly expense charges are typically zero to fifty cents per month per thousand of insurance.

10) *Can I borrow the cash value of my Universal Life contract?*

Yes. Depending upon the policy provisions, you can generally borrow up to the entire cash value, less the interest due at the end of one year.

11) *Can I withdraw money from my policy and not pay interest?*

Yes. You can surrender all or part of your cash value. No interest is charged, but the amount of the withdrawal reduces your death benefit by a like amount. Some companies charge a fee for each withdrawal.

12) Will I receive any communication during the year about the status of my policy?

Yes. At the end of each policy year, you will receive an annual report or accounting statement showing your amount of insurance, cash values, premium payments, expense charges, guaranteed interest, excess interest, mortality charges, loans, partial withdrawals, and other pertinent information.

13) Is there a minimum guaranteed rate of interest that will be credited to my Universal Life policy?

Yes. Depending upon policy provisions, the minimum rate of guaranteed interest will be between 3% and 5% per year.

14) Can the interest credited to my Universal Life policy be higher than the minimum guarantee?

Yes. You will never receive less than the minimum guarantee. However, you will be credited with the insurance company's current rate of interest each year if higher than the guarantee. The current rate can be credited by one of the following methods, depending upon your policy's provisions:

   i) A current rate is declared once a year by the insurance company's board of directors.

   ii) An index, such as the rate of current 90-day T-Bills, is used to determine the current rate. Adjustments may be made for company expenses and profit.

   iii) Some companies use a dual index. An example: A policy may provide you with the higher of the 90-day T-Bill rate or the 20-year U.S. Government Bond Funds rate, adjusted for company expenses and profit.

An index may be changed quarterly, semi-annually, or annually, depending upon your policy provisions. Typically, the applicable rate or index is guaranteed for a specified period.

15) What interest rate will I be charged if I take a policy loan?

Normally, a fixed annual rate of 5% to 8% will be charged. As traditional policies begin to use the variable loan interest rate which is now legal in about 20 states, it is likely that some Universal Life policies will start to use variable rates.

16) Does Universal Life offer me any tax advantages?

Yes. Universal Life policies should be subject to tax in the same manner as any other life insurance policy. As long as the cash value is received as a death benefit, you should not be required to pay income tax on that cash value including the portion that represents interest income. If you surrender the policy, or make partial withdrawals, only the amount received less the sum of premiums paid should be taxed as current income.

A policy loan in any amount may be taken at any time free of current income tax.

17) How does the interest credited to my Universal Life cash value compare to other currently taxable investments?

Figure 2.6 indicates the amount of currently taxable interest you would have to earn to match 10%, if that is the rate that is credited to your Universal Life policy. (Rates of 12% are common at the present time.)

Figure 2.6

TAXABLE INTERSET TABLE

Income Tax Bracket	Tax-Deferred Universal Life	Current Taxable Investment
14%	10%	11.60%
30%	10%	14.28%
50%	10%	20.00%

18) Can other persons, such as my wife and children, be insured under my Universal Life policy?

Yes. Most Universal Life companies have riders which allows benefits on family members. Also, some companies offer special riders to meet a business person's need to cover more than one person.

19) Will my Universal Life policy be affected by inflation?

Yes. Your current rate of interest should keep increasing as inflation goes up and should come down as inflation comes down. Benefits can be automatically increased with a cost of living rider offered in many contracts. Your policy is very flexible in this important area.

20) Can I add waiver of premium, guaranteed insurability rider, and accidental death benefits to my Universal Life policy?

Yes, if your policy provisions permit.

21) Can I add term and annuity riders to my Universal Life policy?

No. There is no need to do this. You can increase your death benefit at any time (with evidence of insurability) and increase your premium when you desire to build your cash value. However, the premium payment under a Universal Life contract does not qualify as a tax deduction to an IRA, so if you desire to utilize this new government benefit, a separate IRA should be established.

CHAPTER 3

What the Policy Looks Like

Few people ever read a life insurance policy. For that matter, few people ever read any insurance policy, except perhaps when they have a casualty loss or they themselves are a casualty and are anticipating the medical bills.

In the case of Universal Life, this truism may be false. At least it will be for the reader of this book who takes the time to read this chapter.

Universal Life has been called a transparent product, one comment which is understandable. This transparency contrasts with traditional policies, especially with the standard contract written 10 or less years ago. Now, because of new state standards requiring minimum levels of readability, most life insurance companies have vastly improved their policy contracts.

We first present a general analysis of the product features which seem to be of most importance in today's environment.

This is followed by a complete analysis of one of the most readable of the new style of contract. It is a Universal Life policy currently marketed by Inter-State Assurance Company, a small mutual insurer in Des Moines, Iowa.

This policy came to the attention of the authors during the summer of 1981. It is, as a matter of interest, patterned very closely after a traditional whole life form developed by Security Mutual Life Insurance Company of Lincoln, Nebraska.

Important Product Features

A. Current Investment Return. Without question this is the key feature of permanent insurance contracts in the life insurance marketplace today. The public has been besieged by advertising of all sorts, from institutions of all sorts, and bombarded by the constant stream of news regarding housing and mortgage rates, IRAs in dozens of guises, "low-cost auto financing at 13.8%," and so on. As a result, potential buyers of life insurance are more sensitive to the earning power (and cost) of money than ever before.

Life insurance competition prominently features the current return available. Rates, nearly all at double-digit levels, are quoted in connection with wrap-around annuities, IRA programs, and all of the most popular Universal Life insurance plans being offered. The rate-of-return cost disclosure advocates have had their influence as well. And the replacement market plays off the accusatory low returns of traditional life insurance quoted from various sources and given nation-wide attention in the 1979 Staff Report of the Federal Trade Commission. (For the authors' view of this phenomenon, see Chapter 1.)

So pervasive is the public's fascination with interest rates, and so ballyhooed are the best of the returns being paid, that other factors listed below pale in comparison. In addition to this fascination, the mechanics of insurance pricing also stress the importance of interest. From an actuarial perspective, interest earnings are by far the most powerful factor in developing life insurance products which may double as attractive savings products.

The current interest rate under Universal Life policies varies from 9% to 12.5%. As we fully discuss in Chapter 7, the interest rate may not always be so attractive when compared to typical whole life insurance contracts.

B. Low Load on Savings Element of Premium. Another key feature of at least the first generation of Universal Life products is the low load or expense feature of policy design. Low load implies low sales compensation. Since the competing financial institutions offer their accumulation or savings mechanisms with little or no direct sales expense, this development should come as no surprise. Neither is it surprising that the consumer-oriented press and academic communities have seized on low load products as innovative, desirable and overdue.

Also to be considered is the major financial penalty to the policyowner who terminates his traditional permanent policy in its early years. A low load Universal Life policy reduces this loss to more acceptable levels, reducing one impediment to a sale.

Just as Universal Life policies can differ in the interest they credit, they also can differ significantly in the loads charged up front.

C. Reasonable Mortality Cost. The cost of insurance under traditional whole life policies is, at best, difficult to determine. Consumerists justly claim that sales presentations obscure the real cost of the insurance. Interest adjusted indices are poorly understood by agents and clients alike. No simple approach to unravel traditional policies has been found, and none is likely to be available any time soon.

Universal Life moves in the right direction. When the cost per dollar of insurance is clearly set out in the policy or made available in an annual report to the policyowner, the confusion is reduced. (Also see, "F. Clarity of Wording.") Again, the cost of mortality varies significantly from Universal Life policy to Universal Life policy. The guaranteed rates are generally those based on the 1958 Commissioners Standard Ordinary table.

D. Flexibility of Premiums. Many nontraditional products provide for flexible or stop-and-go premiums. Agents and their clients became familiar with this concept during the 1960s when flexible annuities were introduced to take advantage of Keogh plans and IRA tax shelters. Flexible premium annuities and their relationship to the origins of Universal Life are discussed in Chapter 1, "Origins of the Universal Life Policy."

Although there has always been considerable flexibility in traditional whole life, through use of loans, dividend options, and premium deposit funds, the typical client usually does not bother to take advantage of this flexibility. He may buy because of it; he seldom implements the steps each year required to make his out-of-pocket cost fit the various proposals suggested at the time he buys the policy.

Contributing to this failure to use flexible policy features has been the normal situation wherein the client is a policyholder in several different companies or has multiple policies with a single company and no common premium billing system.

With the Universal Life contracts, nearly total flexibility is the rule. The only limitations may occur when the yearly value of the policy is too large in comparison to the pure death benefit.

E. Flexibility of Benefits. For many years, the ability of companies to provide flexible benefits or life cycle changes in insurance policies was impeded by the state regulators. Dozens of trade articles have been written about the perceived benefits of such flexibility. With increasing inflation, the need for greater benefits has accelerated and flexibility of benefits has become more important.

In the 1960s and much of the 1970s, hide-bound interpretations of the Standard Nonforfeiture and Valuation Laws discouraged innovation and left weary those few companies who tried to develop new products. Many of the attempts to innovate failed, apparently because the fear of inflation was not so high as to develop an effective selling argument. Sometimes, too, the actuaries, in an attempt to recoup development expenses, priced flexible benefits at a level which decreased the product's marketability, or they made the fatal mistake of reducing commissions in order to preserve profit margins. Even such obvious devices as allowing a special dividend option to buy increasing term insurance failed in their purpose. More of this history is referred to in Chapter 1, "Origins of the Universal Life Policy."

Inflation has tipped the balance of thought. Flexibility in the amount and underwriting of benefits is a sought after quality in a life insurance policy. As was demonstrated in Chapter 2, "One Policy for Life," a Universal Life contract may be the only policy an individual will ever need. Thus, it offers the ultimate in flexibility.

F. Clarity of Wording. "Clarity" combines the twin virtues of simplicity and understandability. Home offices have gradually adapted their thinking and methods to produce policies with clear policy wording. Legalese is on the decline. The requirements of several states which mandate minimum Flesch readability test scores on policy forms evolved in the mid-1970s, at precisely the time the first nontraditional products were being readied for market.

Clarity, as a general term, also includes information about how the policy works. A better knowledge of the product leads to confidence that the hoped for combinations of benefits, including a reasonable investment return, will be realized.

Few would doubt that clarity is a virtue. It is not enough to have the flexibility and design features listed above. The customer must understand them to appreciate their continuing value to him. We think the illustrated policy enables the customer to understand what the Universal Life policy can do for him.

The simplicity of Universal Life insurance, as measured by mechanical tests, is satisfactory. Although most Universal Life insurance forms have been drafted to comply with state simplified language requirements, the Flesch readability test scores generally are near the minimum of 50.

In Chapter 9, "How Others Expect to Compete," the key features of other types of policies are briefly discussed and we have attempted to compare the attractiveness of these features. On the following pages are the Inter-State Assurance Company's form called "Flexlife." Our analysis and comments are printed on the left hand page of the book. The actual policy language, as filed with the state insurance departments, is printed on the right hand page. (Incidentally, for the reader who has an interest in the simplified language requirements, the policy has a Flesch readability test score of over 80!)[1]

You may prefer to read through the policy before looking at our comments. The policy is a refreshing change from the standard of years past. Even regulators seem to appreciate the style and simplicity.

---

[1] The NAIC Model Regulation Service provides four pages of guidelines on how to establish policy language and the establishment of a minimum score of 40 on the Flesch reading ease test or "an equivalent score on any other comparable test ..." The Act reads in part:

"The NAIC Life and Health Insurance Policy Language Simplification Model Act was meant "to establish minimum standards for language used in policies, contracts and certificates of life insurance, health insurance, credit life insurance and credit health insurance delivered or issued for delivery in this state to facilitate ease or reading by insureds.

"This Act is not intended to increase the risk assumed by insurance companies or other entities subject to this Act or to supercede their obligation to comply with the substance of other insurance legislation applicable to life, health, credit life or credit health insurance policies. This Act is not intended to impede flexibility and innovation in the development of policy forms or content or to lead to the standardization of policy forms or content."

Specific instructions on how to determine the minimum score for the Flesch reading ease test and other information regarding this Act can be found under Life Insurance, Volume II, 575-2 of the Official NAIC Model Insurance Laws, Regulations and Guidelines.

In any event, the policy and our comments should enhance your understanding of the concepts and marketing appeal of Universal Life.

1 → Clarity of layout. The policy contains much white space. It uses an outline form which greatly improves readability. This type of layout leads to the high score on mechanical tests of readability.

2 → Customer information. The suggestion to read the policy is meaningful here because the policy can be understood.

3 → Clarity of wording. This is as close to the ideal promise as a company is likely to get. The clear message is, "We pay when you die."

4 → Flexibility of insured persons. "An insured" can refer to one of several people. Refer to the sample list of benefits in the POLICY SCHEDULE.

5 → Customer information. A simple warning is given without complex wording. Misrepresentation is not mentioned, but the message is clear.

6 → Note on clarity. You have already noticed the use of personal pronouns in referring to the company. There are different views on whether this approach suits a formal document on a matter as intensely personal as death. The reader can judge for himself.

7 → Clarity of wording. This policy is simply called "Adjustable Life" or Flexlife in the company's sales literature. The term "Universal Life" is not defined in most laws, regulations, textbooks, or elsewhere. Even the simple name "Adjustable" can be confusing within the industry. (See Chapter 9, "How Others Expect to Compete," on the general product with this accepted name.) The client should not be confused.

8 → Customer information. Some Universal Life companies now provide free telephone service. They may even list an 800 area code on the policy and on various other mailings to the owner.

1 ➜   LIFE INSURANCE POLICY

POLICY NUMBER   012345
EFFECTIVE DATE   December 24, 1982
PRIMARY INSURED   Good Buyer Jones

2 ➜ THIS IS A LEGAL CONTRACT—READ IT CAREFULLY

3 ➜ WE PROMISE to pay the death benefits to the beneficiary on death of 4 ➜ an insured, subject to the terms of this policy.

LOOK AT THE APPLICATION FORMS

This policy is based on answers in the application forms (see copies in back). 5 ➜ If all answers are not true and complete, the policy may be affected.

10 DAY RIGHT TO RETURN THE POLICY

This policy may be sent back to 6 ➜ us or 6 ➜ our agent within 10 days after it was received. We will send back all premiums within 10 days after we get the policy.

7 ➜   Adjustable Life—Participating
Premiums Payable During Life
of Primary Insured

(Signature)   (Signature)
Secretary   President

I N T E R - S T A T E
ASSURANCE COMPANY
8 ➜ 420 Keosauqua Way
Des Moines, Iowa 50308

Form 605

1 ➜ Clarity of wording. The word "Guide" is more descriptive than "Table of Contents" or "Index."

2 ➜ Customer information. This is the first mention of the Annual Report, one of the key features which makes Universal Life stand out from traditional.

3 ➜ Note on clarity. This reference introduces a remarkable simplification of the usual long and confusing settlement option provisions. See further discussion on this page of the policy.

4 ➜ Note on clarity. "Incontestability" is a confusing legal concept. The word itself is confusing. Universal Life policies share this communication problem with traditional policies.

5 ➜ Clarity of wording. Notice the dropping of the term of art the actuaries love. The policy substitutes "Options When Policy Terminates" for "Nonforfeiture Options."

1 ➙ GUIDE TO YOUR POLICY

1 → Flexibility of insured persons. Universal Life lends itself to insuring several persons under one policy. Using "Primary Insured" and "Spouse Insured" is just the beginning of the possibilities for business and family situations. Options which allow a new insured person to replace someone already insured are easily handled. Death benefits payable on the death of the last survivor of two (or more) persons will be available from an increasing number of companies.

2 → Flexibility of death benefits in the basic policy. The policy draws attention to the option of increasing the death benefit by including the cash value as an addition to the specified level amount.

3 → Flexibility of premium. Different terms are used for the premium which is needed to accomplish the client's plan. Most often this will be the level premium which would be paid for life, or to a specified age, such as 65 or 70, to provide whole life—if the current assumptions are realized.

4 → Flexibility of benefits. A cost of living rider is a popular example of flexibility. Note the others including coverage on children and a total disability rider priced as a percentage of premiums paid for the other benefits.

5 → Flexibility of benefits. This "Scheduled Increase Option" is simply an option to purchase specified additional amounts of insurance on scheduled dates without evidence of good health. It illustrates one way in which Universal Life companies can offer benefits which have been popular in the sale of traditional policies.

POLICY SCHEDULE

POLICY NUMBER   012345

EFFECTIVE DATE   December 24, 1982

1 →PRIMARY INSURED   Good Buyer Jones

AGE AND SEX	35-Male
RATE CLASS	Standard
INITIAL SPECIFIED AMOUNT	$25,000

2 → DOES ~~NOT~~ INCLUDE CASH VALUE

INITIAL PREMIUM	$500.00

3 →PLANNED PERIODIC PREMIUM $500.00 Per Year

SPOUSE INSURED   Mary Jane Jones

AGE AND SEX	35-Female
RATE CLASS	Standard
INITIAL SPECIFIED AMOUNT	$10,000

OTHER BENEFITS

FORM NUMBER	EFFECTIVE DATE°	BENEFIT TITLE	BENEFIT AMOUNT	MONTHLY COST OF BENEFIT
430		Children's Insurance	$ 1,000	$0.50
431		Total Disability	N/A	2.5%°°
432		Accidental Death-Primary Ins.	$25,000	$2.00
433		4 → Cost of Living	N/A	N/C
434		Accidental Death-Spouse Ins.	$10,000	$0.80
435		5 → Scheduled Increase Option	$10,000	$1.50

°If Other Than the Policy Effective Date
°°Percentage of any premium paid

1 ➙ Cost of insurance. This table gives the factors used as the maximum or guaranteed cost of insurance. The monthly factors which are shown here for all attained ages are derived from the current minimum valuation table, the 1958 Commissioners Standard Ordinary table. The figures used by other companies may vary. See Chapter 7, "Company vs. Company vs. IRS," for a general discussion of the impact on overall cost of these numbers.

2 ➙ Cost of substandard. If the insured is substandard, the table may show higher guaranteed rates. More often, the policy will specify that the rates are an appropriate multiple of the table based on the rate class on the first page of the POLICY SCHEDULE. Many of the Universal Life policies offer distinctly lower substandard rates than traditional policies. The reasons for this include: (a) different treatment of commissions, (b) pricing which reflects more recent mortality assumptions than many of the largest companies, and (c) the industry practice of paying dividends for mortality savings primarily on the standard risk. It is common to charge 100% additional premium for term insurance Rate Table 4, but pay the same dividend on both a standard and substandard issue.

3 ➙ Note on costs. The table continues with the rates for all ages at which death benefits are available. Most Universal Life forms stop at age 95 yet there are variations and more than one table may be used. Rates for women, substandard rate classes, and supplemental benefits such as accidental death and premium waiver may be included.

1 →   POLICY SCHEDULE Page Two

Table of Monthly Guaranteed Cost of Insurance Rate Per
1,000
2 → For Standard Rate Class

Attained Age	Rate
0	.36927
1	.13669
2	.12420
3	.11918
4	.11459
5	.11043
6	.10669
7	.10376
8	.10167
9	.10084

3 →

10	.10168
. . .	
15	.12502
. . .	
25	.16211
. . .	
35	.21463
. . .	
45	.46600
. . .	
55	1.16471
. . .	
65	2.77608
. . .	
75	6.38757
. . .	
85	14.06748
. . .	

1 → Clarity of wording. This part defines the personal pronouns used to make the policy more readable. Note the
careful distinction in the policy between the definitions of
"owner" and "insured."

2 → Flexibility of benefits. A "Supplemental Policy Schedule"
may be provided at any time according to the company's
rules. This policy provides for requested changes monthly
while other companies limit the change to an annual basis.
Exceptions to these sorts of rules will often be granted
and, therefore, no new policy will be needed. Since the
policy is not returned to the home office for endorsement,
paperwork and costs are reduced for all parties.

3 → Clarity of wording. "Notice" and "Proof" are given clear,
common sense definitions. This is surely better than words
like, "Proof of continued satisfactory insurability must be
provided on the company's approved forms and will not
be accepted until such forms are signed and received at
the Home Office of the Company during the continued
lifetime of the above named Insured."

4 → Clarity of layout. This is the first part of the policy which
uses an outline format. With careful punctuation, this
style lends itself to understanding and easy reference.

5 → Flexibility of benefits. The right to this flexibility is given
here. Details are shown throughout the contract.

6 → Flexibility of premium. The right to this flexibility is given
here. Details are shown primarily in the part called
PREMIUMS.

IN THIS POLICY

1 ➡ YOU or YOUR means the owner of the policy, as shown on the initial application, unless changed.

WE, OUR or US means the Inter-State Assurance Company.

INSURED means either the primary insured or the spouse insured name on the schedule. An insured person may or may not be the owner.

SCHEDULE means the Policy Schedule or the 2 ➡ Supplemental Policy Schedule most recently sent to you by us.

ANNUAL DATE means the same date each year as the policy effective date.

MONTHLY DATE means the same day of each month as the annual date.

3 ➡ NOTICE TO US means information we have received at our home office which is written, signed by you, and is acceptable to us.

PROOF means evidence satisfactory to us for insurability or for other matters which require proof.

This is an adjustable life insurance policy. We will pay the death benefit if an insured dies while the policy is in force, subject to the terms of this policy.

Premiums are payable during the lifetime of the primary insured.

4 ➡ Your rights available while the primary insured is living:

5 ➡ • Right to change the specified amount;
6 ➡ • Right to change the premium payment pattern;
    • Right to assign this policy;

1 ➡ Note on dividends. This policy is issued by a mutual company. It provides for the possible payment of dividends. No dividends were illustrated by the company at the time this book was written, a practice which has become common on low premium term policies issued in recent years.

2 ➡ Note on cost. By itself the 3½% interest rate appears to be quite low, and it is. The client may actually read the policy. If he does, the agent will want to make sure he knows that the current interest being credited is actually higher. Some day, when policies are printed by computer, the current rate can be included within the policy.

3 ➡ Clarity of layout. The outline form adds understanding to what would otherwise be complicated wording. The policyowner can quickly calculate the death benefit by going step by step through the outline.

4 ➡ Note on benefit minimum. These words introduce the "corridor benefit" which many companies use to be sure that there is always a true death benefit in the policy. See Chapter 7, "Company vs. Company vs. IRS," for further discussion on the need for this. The policy shown here uses a minimum "level amount" which differs by issue age. See the discussion in Chapter 6, "Policyholders and Taxes—the Legal Background."

5 ➡ Flexibility of death benefits. This part activates a major option in the policy. See note 2 in the POLICY SCHEDULE above.

- Right to change the owner or beneficiary, except if beneficiary is named as being irrevocable;
1 ➔ - Right to receive any dividends;
- Right to terminate this policy;
- Right to make loans;
- Right to make withdrawals.

DEATH BENEFIT

We will pay as soon as we get proof that an insured has died while this policy is in force.

When the benefit is paid in one lump sum, we will include interest from the date of death to the payment date. The rate of interest will not be less than 2 ➔ $3\frac{1}{2}\%$ per year.

3 ➔ The payment will include:
- the specified amount in force at the date of death;
- the cash value if not included in the specified amount. (Refer to the schedule.)

We will subtract:

- any loan;
- any premium needed as set forth in the Grace Period section.

Death of the primary insured:

- If the cash value is included in the specified amount, the benefit will be the 4 ➔ larger, at the time of death, of the specified amount or the sum of the cash value and the level amount. The level amount is $10,000 if the policy was issued prior to age 60, or $5,000 if issued at age 60 or older.
5 ➔ - If the cash value is not included in the specified amount, the benefit will be the specified amount plus the cash value at the time of death.

1 → Clarity of wording. This is a "built-in" rider. It avoids the need for a separate rider or supplemental benefit using added pieces of paper and extra words to bind a spouse benefit to the basic contract. When computers print policies, all added benefits will be built in.

2 → Flexibility of benefits. This key provision of Universal Life sets up the policy as a lifetime contract. The words in this policy insist on a one year wait before a change is made. Administrative practices and the language of policies offered by other companies offer more leeway.

3 → Cost of mortality. This part defines a last-in first-out basis for death benefit decreases. This is needed in order to charge a fair price when death benefit changes go along with a change in rate class. If an insured has added benefits before, which were rated substandard, a later decrease should be made from the higher priced benefits.

4 → Clarity of wording. Recall that "proof" is defined above as "evidence satisfactory to us of insurability."

5 → Flexibility of benefits. This decrease is a simple matter. A signed letter request should be enough.

6 → Note on underwriting. No proof is required for this change. The policyholder should read this part carefully. The true death benefit, called the net amount at risk by actuaries, does not change. A simple formula is used to determine the new specified amount.

7 → Flexibility of benefits. Minimum benefit amounts such as are shown here may be imposed for different reasons:
   a. Technical requirements of the Standard Nonforfeiture Law, or
   b. Company standards set by expense considerations. Some Universal Life policies are available only for larger amounts such as $100,000. These have different minimum amount rules in operation.

1 ➜ Death of the spouse insured:
- The benefit will be the specified amount of the spouse insured at the time of death.

DEATH BENEFIT CHANGES

2 ➜ You may change any death benefit, after it has been in effect for one year, by notice to us. Any change is subject to the following conditions:

- A decrease will be effective on the monthly date following our receipt of the request. Any reduction will be 3 ➜ in the following order:
  1. against the most recent increase in insurance;
  2. against the next most recent increases;
  3. against the initial specified amount.
- Any increase will required 4 ➜ proof. An approved increase will have an effective date as shown on the Supplemental Policy Schedule.
5 ➜ • The specified amount may be changed to include the cash value, by notice to us. The effective date of change will be the monthly date following our receipt of the notice.
- The specified amount may be changed to exclude the cash value, by notice to us. 6 ➜ In such case, the specified amount will be reduced so that the death benefit is not increased as of the date of change. The effective date of change will be the monthly date following our receipt of the notice.
- The specified amount after any requested change must be at least:
  7 ➜ 1. For the primary insured:
       $25,000 for issue ages 0 through 54;
       $20,000 for issue ages 55 through 59;
       $15,000 for issue ages 60 through 64; and
       $10,000 for issue ages 65 and older.

1 → Flexibility of benefits. This minimum is a company standard. The insurance works like a traditional term rider for a spouse.

2 → Clarity of wording. These seven words replace over one thousand words and numbers in a traditional policy. Note that this same simple approach can be used by any policy, subject only to the occasional whim of a policy form reviewer in a state insurance department.

3 → Customer information. The owner is told about his right to control the payment of funds.

4 → Clarity of wording. "Effective annual rate" cannot be easily understood without some background in financial mathematics. Nevertheless, this phrase is better than trying to give all the rules for daily or monthly interest.

5 → Note on cost. Here again, the $3\frac{1}{2}\%$ interest rate appears to be quite low, and it is. The current rate will be higher. It should be disclosed to enhance the sale unless printed in the policy.

6 → Flexibility of benefits. This part completes the benefits for the spouse by adding the usual right of conversion.

7 → Clarity of wording. Note the use of the simple one syllable word "stop." This is used frequently in the rest of the policy.

8 → Note on wording. Presumably "permanent plan" refers to a traditional policy. Another of Inter-State's Universal Life forms refer to a "level premium permanent plan." It is not clear whether spouse insurance may be converted to another Universal Life policy.

1 → 2. For the spouse insured: $10,000.

HOW THE FUNDS ARE PAID

The funds can be paid:
- in one lump sum; or
2 → • in any way you and we agree.

3 → Before an insured dies, you can choose how the funds are to be paid. If you have not made a choice before an insured dies, the beneficiary can choose how funds are to be paid.

Funds left on deposit with us will earn interest at an 4 → effective annual rate not less than 5 → $3\frac{1}{2}\%$.

SPOUSE INSURED

You may apply for coverage on the spouse if not covered by your policy. Our application form should be sent to us. Approval by us will be subject to proof. Any approved spouse insurance will have an effective date as shown on the schedule.

6 → CONVERSION OF SPOUSE INSURANCE

You may convert the insurance on the spouse insured if:

- the insurance has been in force at least one year;
- the spouse is not over 65 years old;
- the insurance 7 → stops for a cause other than lack of premium payment; and
- the request is received within 31 days of the date insurance stops.

Conversion will be at the attained age, sex and rate class for the spouse, with no need to give us proof. Benefits added to this policy by rider cannot be converted without our consent. Conversion can only be to any 8 → permanent plan available from us.

1 → Note on dividends. If dividends were to be declared, two options are available. The other possible options, such as dividend accumulations and paid-up insurance additions, are not needed. The flexible benefits and cash value accumulations give the same result.

2 → Flexibility of premium. Added money may be put into the contract at any time. The limit to once a month will normally be waived. It is included simply to avoid the expense of many small premiums if an individual client should want to put in a small amount, say $5.00 weekly. The $25.00 limit has the same purpose.

3 → Customer information. Billing is optional. Automatic monthly check payment plans are always available. Of course, since premiums are not required unless the cash value is very small, this is merely a customer convenience.

4 → Flexibility of premium. The traditional one month grace period is often extended for Universal Life. This benefits the client. It also gives the company added time after its monthly accounting has been completed to determine that the available cash value will be insufficient to continue benefits.

5 → Note on benefits. No extended insurance is needed. The only time a grace period comes about is if the cash value has been used up. See also OPTIONS WHEN THE POLICY TERMINATES.

DIVIDENDS

As long as the policy is in force, you will receive any dividends we declare.

1 → You have these options:
  - Use the dividends to increase the cash value; or
  - Take the dividends in cash.

You may choose either option or change options by notice to us. If neither is chosen, the first option will be used.

PREMIUMS

The initial premium is the amount paid on or before delivery of this policy. You may make other premium payments:

2 → • at any time, but not more often than once each month.
  - for any amount $25.00 or more and less then any maximum amount we may set.

3 → We will send premium notices if you request. They can be sent each 3, 6, or 12 months. Premium payments may be made to our home office or to one of our agents in exchange for a receipt signed by our President, Vice-President or Secretary and countersigned by the agent.

GRACE PERIOD

Starting on the monthly date when the cash value less any loan is less than the monthly deduction for the policy month to follow, a grace period of 4 → 61 days will be given for the payment of enough premium to cover the monthly deduction.

The cash value and monthly deductions are described in the Policy Values section.

If the premium is not paid within the grace period, 5 → all insurance stops. If an insured dies during the grace period, the death benefit will be paid but reduced by the premium needed to cover the monthly deductions through the month of death.

1 → Clarity of layout. This page is a fine example of the outline format. The conditions for stopping and reinstating benefits, and the procedure for making loans are clearly spelled out.

2 → Clarity of wording. Here is simple wording at its best. Short sentences and one syllable words are the key.

3 → Note on clarity. Here the policy wording could be better. Interest in arrears is more familiar and understandable. Interest "in advance" reflects the common insurance practice of the early 1900s. Inter-State may simply want to be consistent with their other policies.

4 → Customer information. Clear direction of what the owner should do to make a loan are given. The right to defer making the loan is required by law, and has not been exercised by any insurance company for many, many years.

1 → TERMINATION

The policy will terminate and all insurance will stop:

- on the first monthly date after you request it by notice to us; or
- when the primary insured dies; or
- when a needed premium is not received before the end of its grace period.

REINSTATEMENT

You may put this policy back in force by notice to us if:

- each insured gives us proof; and
- payment is made of enough premium to cover past monthly deductions not made, plus 6% annual interest on each from the date it would have been made; and
- interest on any loan is paid at the rate of 6% annual interest from the date insurance stopped; and
- the notice is received within 5 years of the date coverage stopped.

LOANS

2 → This policy may have a cash value. You may want to use the cash value. This may be done by a loan. The most we can loan is:

- the cash value; less

3 →
- loan interest in advance to the next annual date; less
- old loans and the interest on them.

4 → You may ask for a loan at any time. Nothing else is required for the loan. We have the right to wait to make a loan up to 6 months after we receive notice.

1 → Cost of interest. The policy provides for variable loan interest. With the passage of the new model law in many states, many Universal Life companies are likely to provide for this flexibility and replace the maximum 8% annual rate with the indexed rate permitted.

2 → Clarity of wording. This part shows the company's calculation of policy values one step at a time. The formula used by other companies is different.

3 → Cost of expense. The 9% charge is made every year. It is the basis for payment of renewal agency compensation and home office expense. Note there are additional charges in the first policy year as set out in the MONTHLY DEDUCTION.

4 → Note on wording. The "monthly deduction" is defined in the following paragraphs.

5 → Cost of expense. Here is the first calculation. It gives the value of (a) at issue. Note the same 9% deduction as for later premiums.

6 → Note on wording. The "cost of insurance" is defined in the following paragraphs.

LOAN INTEREST

Loan interest is payable in advance. The rate of interest is 1 →
flexible but will not exceed an effective annual rate of 8%. We
will add interest to the loan on each annual date.

LOAN REPAYMENT

A loan may be paid back in full or in part at any time. Each
payment must be at least $25.00.

POLICY VALUES

- CASH VALUE
- The cash value will be calculated on each monthly date as
  follows:
  2 → (a) plus (b) plus (c) less (d) less (e):
  (a) the cash value on the prior monthly date;
  (b) one month's interest on (a);
  (c) 91% of the premium received for the policy in the prior
      month 3 → (the 9% deduction is an expense charge);
  4 → (d) monthly deduction for the prior month;
  (e) one month's interest on (d).
    - On any day between monthly dates the cash
      value will reflect any premiums paid and time
      elapsed since the prior monthly date.
  5 → • The cash value on the effective date of this policy
      is 91% of the initial premium for the policy.

- MONTHLY DEDUCTION
    - The monthly deduction for each policy month is (a)
      plus (b):
      6 → (a) the cost of insurance and the cost for any pol-
              icy riders except for disability premium pay-
              ment riders;

1 → Cost of expense. The company reduces the cash value fund by this formula during the first 12 policy months. The amount the company keeps; $30.00 times 12 or $360.00 plus $0.12 per $1,000 of insurance is used to pay the agent and help cover home office issue and other administrative expenses. This cost varies widely among Universal Life companies. See the discussion of commissions and other expense subjects in this book.

2 → Credit of interest. This is a key part. The excess interest or current interest rate which leads to low premiums compared to traditional products is set out here. In this policy, which does not use an index, the excess interest is available "at our option."

3 → Credit of interest. Money loaned does not receive the excess interest; neither does money taken out as a partial withdrawal.

4 → Note on clarity. This part is needed to be clear on the cost when the death benefits are increased at different times using different rate classes. It uses a last-in first-out method like that used in DEATH BENEFIT CHANGES above.

5 → Clarity of wording. These four lines define the true death benefit, i.e. the amount at risk, without using this technical phrase. This calculation accounts for the fact that the cost of insurance goes down each month during any policy year (unless there is a withdrawal).

1 ➔ (b) $0.12 per $1,000 initial specified amount on the primary insured and the spouse insured, plus $30.00. This applies only to the first 12 policy months.

- INTEREST RATE
  - The guaranteed rate to be applied to the cash value is 0.32737% per month, compounded monthly (same as 4% compounded yearly). 2 ➔ An interest rate exceeding the guaranteed rate can be used at our option. 3 ➔ We will not use an excess rate on that part of any cash value which equals any loan.

- COST OF INSURANCE
  - The cost of insurance is determined each month for each specified amount by using the insured's age on the prior annual date.
4 ➔ • If the specified amount includes the cash value and the specified amount has been increased, the cash value will first be considered part of the initial specified amount. If the cash value is greater than the initial specified amount, it will be part of any additional specified amounts in the order of the increases.
  - The schedule shows whether the cash value is included in the specified amount.

- PRIMARY INSURED
  1. If the specified amount is the death benefit and it includes the cash value, the cost is (a) times the result of (c) less (b):
  5 ➔ (a) the cost of insurance rate;
  (b) the cash value at the beginning of the policy month; and
  (c) the specified amount divided by 1.0032737.

91

1 ➜ Note on wording. Part 2 and part 3 on this policy page carefully define the cost of insurance calculation for the other flexible death benefit methods.

2 ➜ Cost of mortality. This is a key part. The lower cost of insurance rates contribute to the low premiums compared to traditional products. As with excess interest, the lower rates are used "at our option."

3 ➜ Customer information. The client can see the results of the policy at least once each year. The reader will want to study the Annual Report descriptive material in this book.

1 ➜ 2. If the specified amount included the cash value, and the death benefit is the cash value plus the level amount, the cost is (a) times the result of (c) less (b):

(a) the cost of insurance rate;
(b) the cash value at the beginning of the policy month; and
(c) the result of dividing the sum of (b) and the level amount by 1.0032737.

3. If the specified amount does not include the cash value, the cost is (a) times the result of (c) less (b):

(a) the cost of insurance rate;
(b) the cash value at the beginning of the policy month; and
(c) the result of dividing the sum of (b) and the specified amount by 1.0032737.

- SPOUSE INSURED

The cost of insurance is the spouse's specified amount times the cost of the insurance rate.

- COST OF INSURANCE RATE

The cost of insurance rate is determined for each spcified amount by the sex, attained age and rate class of each insured person. 2 ➜ We can use lower rates than shown in the Table of Monthly Guaranteed Cost of Insurance Rates at our option.

ANNUAL REPORT

3 ➜ We will send you a report at least once each year showing your current cash value, premiums paid, loans and charges since our prior report.

1 → Clarity of wording. This part describes the nonforfeiture options, again without using this very confusing phrase. The "Paid-Up Term Insurance" option replaces the two traditional options of paid-up whole life and extended term. The automatic higher mortality cost usually charged for extended term is not charged.

2 → Note on wording. This right to defer payment is required by law.

3 → Flexibility of benefits. This right, often called a partial withdrawal privilege, enables the client to plan an accumulation of funds for a specified time. Chapter 1, "Origins of the Universal Life Policy," illustrates this use of Universal Life, as do several of the case studies in Chapter 11, "Marketing Ideas and Case Studies."

4 → Note on underwriting. The reduction of the death benefit is needed to prevent withdrawal of funds in anticipation of death. Of course, the death benefit may be kept the same with proof.

5 → Cost of expense. The fee covers the company's expenses. It is important, also, in considering the tax effect of Universal Life to policyholders. See Chapter 6, "Policyholders and Taxes—the Legal Background."

6 → Note on wording. Again, this right to defer payment is required by law.

7 → Note on wording. The COMPUTATIONS part is required by law. The state regulators have allowed some simplification in the words used.

8 → Note on wording. The policy is required to state the current legal mortality table and rate of interest used to determine the minimum cash values. The interest rate cannot exceed a low percentage, generally $4\frac{1}{2}\%$ or $5\frac{1}{2}\%$. As is the case in traditional life insurance policies, this table and interest rate have no direct effect on the cost of the insurance although they may effect the level of premiums charged by the company. For a more detailed discussion of this involved subject, the reader is referred to the actuarial literature.

9 → Clarity of wording. This simple statement avoids defining "adjusted premium" or "nonforfeiture factor", terms required in many traditional policies in the past.

1 → OPTIONS WHEN THE POLICY TERMINATES

If the policy terminates and there is cash value in excess of any loan, you may choose one of these options. The choice must be made within 61 days after the policy terminates.

- Cash Surrender—The cash value less any loan will be paid to you. 2 → We have the right to wait up to 6 months to pay.
- Paid-Up Term Insurance—We will use the cash value less any loan to continue the insurance on all insured persons until the end of the grace period.

Paid-up term insurance will be used if no election is made.

3 → PARTIAL CASH SURRENDER

You may surrender part of your policy for cash by notice to us, subject to any loan and the minimum specified amount of your policy. The amount surrendered will be deducted from the cash value. 4 → The amount surrendered will also reduce the death benefit of the primary insured. 5 → A $25.00 fee will be charged for each partial surrender. 6 → We have the right to wait to pay up to 6 months after we receive notice.

7 → COMPUTATIONS

Minimum cash values, options when the policy terminates, and reserves for this policy are based on the Commissioners 1958 Standard Ordinary Mortality Table Age Last Birthday with interest at 8 → 4% compounded annually.

All of the values are the same or more than the minimums set by the laws of the state where the application was signed. If required, we have filed a detailed statement about this with your State Insurance Department. 9 → It shows the figures and methods used.

1 → Note on wording. Much of the GENERAL PROVISIONS on this and the following policy page are required by law. The meaning in practice of many of these provisions is well settled and is identical for Universal Life and traditional policies. A few of the simplifications of this particular policy are discussed below.

2 → Customer information. The policyowner is put on notice that he should tell the truth when he provides information to the company.

3 → Flexibility of benefits. The policyowner is reminded that a new two year period begins with the date of application for an increase in benefits. Thus, part of the policy may frequently be contestable during the lifetime of the insured, depending upon the number of times the death benefit is increased. "Increase" in this context means a requested increase in the pure death benefit, not an increase in the total death benefit that is attributable to an increase in the cash value or the operation of a cost-of-living rider which does not require evidence of good health.

1 → GENERAL PROVISIONS

● POLICY

These pages are the whole policy. This policy is a legal contract and is issued in consideration of the application and the initial premium. Nothing else which has been said or put in writing is part of this policy unless it is attached. No one can change any part of it except the owner and one of our officers. Both must agree to a change and it must be in writing.

● RELIANCE

We have formed this policy according to the answers in the application or supplemental application. We have assumed all of them to be true and complete. 2 → If any are not, we may have the right to void the policy and send back all premiums. Read the copy of the application attached to this policy. If anything is not true or complete, please write to us so we can tell if it will affect the policy.

● INCONTESTABILITY

Except for accidental death and disability premium payment benefits, we cannot contest this policy after it has been in force for two years while each insured is alive, 3 → nor can we contest any increased benefits later than two years after the application for such increased benefits.

We cannot contest the policy or any benefits increased after the policy effective date unless:

1. an answer in the application for the policy or increased benefits was not true or complete; and
2. if we had known the truth, we would not have issued the policy or increased the benefits.

1 ➔ Note on wording. Much of this page is also required by law. The meaning in practice of many of these provisions is well settled and is identical for Universal Life and traditional policies. A few of the simplifications of this policy are discussed below.

2 ➔ Flexibility of benefits. The policyowner is told that each increase in benefits is subject to the same termination provision if there is a suicide. The last comment on INCONTESTABILITY applies here as well.

3 ➔ Note on wording. By making the payments to an assignee in a lump sum only, the insurer deprives the assignee of the advantages of different settlement options. (We do not agree with this approach.)

4 ➔ Clarity of wording. Remember that "you" refers to the owner of the policy.

1 → • SUICIDE

For the first two full years from the original application date, we will not pay if the primary insured commits suicide (while sane or insane). We will terminate the policy and give back the premiums paid to us less any loan and any partial surrender amount. In such a situation for death of another insured, the costs of insurance for that person will be refunded to the policy cash value. 2 → A like limitation applies to any increases in benefits and the date of the application for such increases.

• CONFORMITY WITH LAWS

This policy is subject to the laws of the state where the application was signed. If part of it does not follow that law, it will be treated as if it does.

• AGE AND SEX

Age in this policy means age last birthday. If any insured's age or sex has been misstated, we will adjust the policy values to those based on correct monthly deductions since the policy effective date.

• ASSIGNMENT

You can assign this policy. We will not be responsible for the validity of an assignment. We will not be liable for any payments we make or actions we take before notice to us of an assignment. 3 → Payments to an assignee will only be made in a lump sum.

• OWNERSHIP

While the primary insured lives, 4 → you have all rights in this policy. If you die before the primary insured, the "contingent owner" named in the application is the primary insured and becomes the new owner unless you tell us otherwise in writing.

1 → Customer information. This part sets up a typical family arrangement for beneficiaries which saves time for the agent. It also keeps these important provisions right in the policy instead of in the application copy or a separate piece of paper which may become lost, leading to confusion. This is one of the most desirable improvements made by this policy.

2 → Customer information. This wording is designed to clear up another common point of confusion.
3 → Clarity of wording. The final payee is defined as the estate of the owner.

A change of owner may be made at any time by notice to us. It will take effect on the date notice is received by us. We will record the change. A change of owner does not change the beneficiary.

BENEFICIARY

The beneficiary will get the funds when an insured dies. 1 ➔ Unless otherwise provided by notice to us, the beneficiary is as follows:

Person Insured	Beneficiary Designation
Primary Insured:	Primary: The spouse, if living.
	Contingent: The surviving children of the primary insured.
	Last Contingent: The owner.
Spouse Insured:	Primary: The primary insured, if living.
	Contingent: The surviving children of the primary insured.
	Last Contingent: The owner.

2 ➔ The spouse is the spouse of the primary insured at the time the original application is signed, unless we are told otherwise in writing. 3 ➔ If no beneficiary is living when an insured dies, we will pay to your estate.

1 ➔ Clarity of wording. This part has still more of the important details to expedite settlement of a death claim. The words needed to avoid estate tax problems which may arise from simultaneous death situations are given. Also, a precise definition of "child" and "children" is provided along with a common sense means to quickly ascertain the correct beneficiaries.

2 ➔ Customer information. The owner's right to change the beneficiary at any time is described. Note that this change, as is true with all insurance contracts, must be made prior to death. An individual cannot provide for a change of beneficiary of his policy in his last will and testament. This is the difference between a contractual right and a testimonial right and is the reason insurance proceeds, in most cases, avoid probate at death.

Unless we are told otherwise in writing, 1 ➜ we will follow these rules:

- We will pay equal shares when more than one beneficiary is to share the funds.
- No revocable beneficiary has rights in the policy until the insured dies.
- An irrevocable beneficiary cannot be changed without consent.
- If any beneficiary dies at the same time as the insured, or within 30 days after and before we make any payments, we will pay as if that beneficiary did not live as long as the insured, unless we are told otherwise in writing. However, we will not be required to delay payment until 30 days after an insured's death.
- When beneficiaries are not shown by name (such as "children"), we may find who they are from sworn statements and not wait for court records.
- The word "child" means only a child born to or adopted by the insured; it does not mean grandchild.

2 ➜ You may change the beneficiary at any time before the insured dies by notice to us. Any change must be approved by us. If approved, it will take effect on the date the notice was signed by you. We will not be liable for any payments we make or actions we take before the change is approved.

CHAPTER 4

New Technology and the Sales Process

An Overview

Without computer technology there would be no Universal Life. The computer is the key to flexible deposits and flexible death benefits. Before the computer and Universal Life, rates were calculated by an actuary and the rates were published in a rate book. Each age was accompanied by a rate per thousand for life insurance and matching cash values, dividends and paid-up insurance. Since Universal Life allows flexible deposits, death benefits, withdrawals, etc., the options are unlimited. No rate book could be large enough to contain all of the necessary information about all options. A computer is an indispensable piece of hardware for the Universal Life illustrations. All rates, cash values, premiums and death benefits are linked mathematically, and, as long as the computer has sufficient capacity, unlimited variations can be calculated for each client's situation.

It has been assumed for many years in the life insurance business that an annual premium would be paid each and every year by a client. This premium would generate guaranteed cash values, paid-up options, and other benefits. However, as the insurance business has developed in this century, it has become evident that the client is much more willing to utilize his life insurance contract as an investment vehicle than was originally anticipated. As a result, sizable policy loans have developed. With the recurring changes since 1946 in interest rates and investment opportunities, the use of a fixed premium, fixed interest rate product with guaranteed cash values and anticipated dividends has become less attractive. The consumer is looking for an investment product that has guaranteed death benefits and is very sensitive to interest rates.

During the same period of years, the public's awareness of investment opportunities has increased and, at the same time, there has been a leap forward in the availability of computer technology. The computer can react immediately to changes on the part of the policyholder, with respect to his insurance objectives. The client's desire to change his premium deposits, expected returns, and cash values can occur frequently. The computer is an ideal way to handle the administration required by these desired changes.

Insurance companies can increase their service capabilities and improve on the time required for illustrating policy proposals through the use of computers. The only limiting factors on computer use have been the cost of the equipment and the ability of the company to program required information into these computers. However, it appears that, in the foreseeable future, illustrations and servicing of issued policies will be handled almost exclusively by computers.

Computers can quickly do mathematical sales calculations. This was illustrated in Chapter 2, "One Policy for Life." As long as an agent has a policy number, he should be able to access contract information from the insurance company's data base and obtain a printout of current values.

With further technological advances, it is possible that small computers in the home will be able to access insurance companies' data banks and receive policy information. Since many checking accounts in the future will be serviced through home computers, it is possible that a person will be able to access his own insurance policy data using the same machine. Total policyholder service through a personal computer is technologically possible. However, this may enable the policyholder to bypass the skilled agent, and we know what kinds of problems this creates.

Further, technology is currently being developed whereby an entire insurance office can be run by way of small computers. As long as the home office data is available to the insurance office, the following activity can be visualized: An agency's corporate books, accounts receivable, accounts payable, check writing, billing, both estate planning and financial planning illustrations, commission checks, all policyholder service, and even policy issue could be run off the agency computer. Communications between the agent and the home office on agency administration, underwriting, or policyholder service could be handled via the computer without the need for personal communication by telephones.

The Sales Process

The sale of a Universal Life policy is not much different than any other policy. Let's take a look at how a typical, yet simplified, Universal Life sale might go.

STEP 1

The agent meets his client and secures a fact finder, containing information such as the client's family situation, income, assets, objectives he would like to satisfy through financial planning and so on. The agent will explain the types of planning that he can provide through his computer programs, such as personal planning, business planning, and estate planning. It is then decided which plan or combination of plans will be run on the computer.

If the agent and client have sufficient time, and a computer terminal is available, the illustrations can be printed at this meeting. Usually, the agent prefers to take the data gathered during the meeting back to his office to make a more thorough study and analysis. If no portable computer terminal is available, or the client can not come to the agent's office, a second meeting will be needed.

STEP 2

Once the data has been entered into the computer and a definite plan of action has been established, it becomes necessary to decide upon the type of policy illustration to be printed. Prior to Universal Life, the first thing to decide was how much premium the client could afford to spend and then to decide on a type of policy. This could be term, life, a combination of life with a term rider, or some form of minimum deposit. Using Universal Life, the agent's job is simplified. He has only one policy, which is life, term, and minimum deposit all under one wrapper. This is one of the advantageous features of Universal Life.

The agent enters the variables and the computer decides how the policy will be structured. For example, if the client has limited funds and wants a term product, the agent sets up a zero cash value at age 55, 65, 75, or any other selected expiration age. The agent enters the amount of insurance and the computer determines the premium. If the agent knows how much the client can spend and how much insurance he wants, the computer will calculate the cash values or tell the agent when the insurance will run out. If the client only wants to pay so many years, say 10, the agent enters 10 years premium and the computer will figure the cash values, etc. One policy does the job of all the policies that companies had in the past. Finally, the agent and the client can talk the same language. Universal Life is term, life, or any combination of plans the client might want or need.

STEP 3

Once the Financial Plan (Step 1) and the Proposal (Step 2) are completed, the agent is ready for the next meeting with the client to discuss the entire plan. It is common, when using Universal Life as the solution, for the client to want to make changes in the assumptions that the agent used in the preparation of the proposal. This is where the versatility of the product starts to show. For example, the client might have originally felt that he wanted $100,000 of life insurance with an annual premium of $2,000 and now decides that he would rather have $150,000 of life insurance with an annual premium of $2,000. The agent can easily solve this problem by entering new data in the computer. The computer solves the problem by establishing new cash values. The assumptions can be changed as many times as the client requests until the very best solution is found.

The client is further pleased with the fact that the next year he can change his policy to provide more life insurance or increase or decrease the premium, depending upon what type of cash value build-up he would like. The client is usually the first person to comment on the tremendous flexibility of the product. He likes the fact that in the future he can go from term to ordinary life, or from a high cash value policy to a low cash value policy. Most clients like the idea of not being locked into one policy for the rest of their lives.

STEP 4

The application is now completed and the first premium collected. The agent mentions that if in the future more insurance is needed, the policy can be increased in size.

The agent should also mention to the client that, in the future, he can skip premium payments if he so desires or can send in extra deposits any time he wishes. The only limitation is that there must be enough cash in the contract to pay the expense charge and the cost of the protection. If he fails to send in sufficient premiums to take care of the costs, then the insurance company will send a notice giving the client 60 days to forward the premium sufficient to keep the contract in force.

The above sales situation is generalized in order to illustrate the basic sales situation. Many interesting comments can be made to gain the attention of the client such as, "Wouldn't you like a policy in your pension plan that can be increased in size each year so you don't keep getting an additional new policy?" Or, "Wouldn't it be nice if you could insure you and your partner for the buy-sell agreement under the same policy? Since you and your partner are different in age by 10 years, wouldn't this solve the problem of the large difference in premiums that each of you pay?" Or, "Many clients are concerned that at death they only get the policy death benefit and lose their cash value. By using Universal Life, we can give you the death benefit and the cash value."

Most clients are fascinated by these new and exciting comments and are willing to continue the discussion to find out more about the product. The best way to gain the attention of the prospect is to actually let him place the data into the computer and run his own program. If you have the computer terminal with you, it is easy. If not, an invitation can be made for the client to come to your office to actually run the illustration. Once the client gets involved in the running of the program, you will definitely have his attention. This technique will allow the power of the computer to actually help make the sale.

Computer Systems

As we mentioned at the beginning of this chapter, there would be no Universal Life product without computer technology. And with the every day advances being made in this area, no purpose would be served by discussing all types of hardware and software available. There are, however, three types of computer hardware that are currently being used within the insurance business that we feel we should comment on. Also, we will discuss practical ways that this equipment can be used in the sale and service of the Universal Life product.

The three types of hardware that we will discuss are: (1) the small business computer sold or leased by Radio Shack, commonly referred to as the TRS-80 Model II computer; (2) the Apple II Plus computer; and (3) the Keypact portable computer terminal made available by Computone Systems, Inc. Our discussion is limited primarily to the field applications of these computers rather than attempting to give a detailed study of the actual programming and home office functions of the equipment.

1) THE TRS-80 MODEL II COMPUTER

In studying the TRS-80 Model II computer, we must first understand that this piece of equipment is designed as an in-house computer with four components. First, it has a keyboard similar to a typewriter which allows a person to feed information into the computer. Second, it has a screen to review the information as it is developed. Third, it contains a floppy disc on which information—programmed instructions or raw data—

can either be recorded at the home office or in-house. Fourth, it includes a printer which will print sales illustrations once they have been developed and approved on the screen.

The most typical application of the TRS-80 begins with the home office of the life insurance company providing a series of floppy discs. The discs contain the programs rates, cash values, and so forth that the agent will use in developing his actual sales illustration. Once a floppy disc is inserted in the machine, the program is called up by use of the keyboard and a series of questions are presented on the screen. After all of the questions are answered (via the keyboard), the computer calculates the values for the illustration and displays them on the screen. When the operator has approved the values on the viewing screen, he presses a key and the computer prints a formal illustration for use with the client. The "One Policy for Life" illustration in Chapter 2 was calculated on the TRS-80. Also, the TRS-80 has the additional capacity of being utilized as a word processor.

Since the TRS-80 stores all information on the floppy disc, it is important to understand the storage capacity of this equipment. The double-density disc drive provides 416,000 characters of storage for programs and data on interchangeable floppy disc diskettes. If that's not enough, you can add the Model II disc extension unit with one, two, or three more drives. Each added drive stores another 486,000 characters, bringing the total capacity of the four disc drive system to about 2,000,000 characters.

For the fastest possible access to a large amount of data, the Model II can be outfitted with up to four hard disc drive systems. The system can be expanded at any time to handle almost any agency situation and it will not become obsolete within a few years. One standard parallel port and two RS-232C serial ports allows you to add printers, plotters, digitizers, and communications with data bases and other computers. Internal plug-in card slots are also provided for other options, such as the hard disc drive interface. The TRS-80 has the capacity of not only running information that is recorded on floppy discs, but also act as a terminal for the insurance home office. The TRS-80 has the capability of handling the following types of programs (and more):

a) Universal Life sales. These illustrations are printed with the premiums, cash values and death benefits illustrated. Guaranteed values and those available using current interest and other assumptions can be shown. Some programs also provide for numbers to be illustrated which are in between the guarantees and the current basis.

b) Financial and estate planning. The home office can develop, on floppy discs, estate and financial planning programs that can be run by the agent as a part of developing the sale.

c) Accounting and agency management programs. The home office can provide floppy discs with programs for an agency to run its entire accounting system including accounts receivable, accounts payable, ledgers, journals, financial reports, etc.

d) Management and agent training programs. The home office can provide actual training programs pertaining to home office oriented training or training for CLU work, state insurance exams or special training programs.

e) Word processing. Radio Shack produces a complete word processing program that has advanced capabilities. A secretary can type her letters onto a screen before having them actually printed. Letters can be stored on floppy discs for future reference and recalled. If, for example, a mass mailing program is being developed, the standard letter can be merged with the names and addresses of all the recipients. One hundred letters and matching envelopes can quickly be printed.

For fancy effects, the graphic printer, called the TRS-80 Multi-Pen Plotter, offers color graphics at an affordable price. It comes with six standard color ball-point pens and draws lined charts, pie charts, and bar charts.

f) Individual programs developed by the agent. The system has the additional benefit of allowing those agents who acquire (or hire) programming skills to develop their own programs in-house. There is no limit to the combination of programs that an agent can assemble.

g) Communication with the home office. With the right expertise and cooperation, the microcomputer can be tied in by phone with a home office computer. The machine then works like a terminal. It will send and receive messages from the insurance company computer. In fact, this use is similar to the way the Keypact terminal operates. This piece of equipment will be discussed shortly.

These seven activities, plus many others, outline the capabilities that are available through microcomputers. A primary advantage of these machines is that they are inexpensive to operate compared to the use of the telephone. This advantage of inexpensive operation of microcomputers vs. microwave networks may change with increased competition through current advances in microwave networks. Using microcomputers allows an agent to spend an unlimited amount of time working on illustrations at virtually no cost. This certainly can be a major factor for the agency budget. With a TRS-80 Model II computer, a separate floppy disc is required for each insurance company's programs. Without access to the company's floppy discs, an agent is limited to the output he can generate with his microcomputer.

2) THE APPLE II PLUS COMPUTER

This is one of the most popular computers on the market today. The Apple II Plus is physically similar to the TRS-80

Model II computer in that there is a basic computer unit with a built-in keyboard, viewing screen one or multiple disc drives and a printer. The two pieces of equipment are somewhat physically different, however, in that the Apple II Plus has the basic computer and keyboard built as one unit, whereas the TRS-80 has the viewing screen and computer as one unit with a detachable keyboard. The Apple II Plus has a viewing screen which is detachable while the TRS-80 has the viewing screen attached as part of the computer unit. The disc drives on the Apple II Plus are separate units while the TRS-80 has one disc drive built into the basic computer along with the screen; the other multiple disc drives would be separate. The printers for both pieces of equipment are detachable and similar in nature.

Both the Apple II Plus and the TRS-80 operate in a similar fashion; the floppy discs, although different in size, are inserted into the machine; information is placed into the computer via a keyboard and viewed on a screen; the information is then checked for accuracy and printed. Once an operator learns the basic principles of operating the one piece of equipment, the techniques are readily transferable to operating the second piece of equipment.

The Apple II Plus has some advantages, though, over the TRS-80. Due to the modular nature of the Apple hardware and some of the add-on items developed by other manufacturers, it is a system which can grow with the user. The compatability of this equipment with the Apple II computer broadens the scope of the work that can be done.

The Apple II has proven to be one of the most reliable microcomputers in the marketplace due to its wide acceptance, and service is usually available wherever you are located. Also, with the rapid sales of the Radio Shack products in the past two years, and the number of Radio Shack outlets, the service available for their equipment is paralleling that of the Apple II Plus.

The number of languages available to the Apple II is also of significance. Using both Apple-developed peripherals and peripherals developed by others, the following systems and languages are available:

Machine Language	FORTH
Applesoft Basic	CP/M
Microsoft Basic	COBOL
Integer Basic	FORTRAN
UCSD Pascal	

The scope of languages and systems available make the Apple II capable of doing things no other single microcomputer is able to do at this time. Another advantage of the Apple II is its time-sharing program. By using the D.C. Hayes Micromodem II, the system can access MUFU, ISSS, Financial Data Planning Corporation and home office time-sharing services to provide those illustrations not yet available using Apple software.

In essence, then, the Apple II, when combined with other software, becomes a self-contained, extremely useful tool for the bulk of your computer needs. At the same time, it can serve as a terminal when the demands of the user exceed the capacity of existing software.

Pertaining to cost, we would like to make the general statement that the basic Apple II Plus computer would have a price of approximately $1,530. Disk drives available would run about $645 for the first drive, $525 for the second drive, and $220 for a good viewing screen. The total cost for these items would run a little under $3,000. The prices of the printers vary, going from $625 to $2,000 with the quality of the printing determined by the quality of the printer purchased. It would be safe to say that for under $5,000 a high quality computer system could be put together using the Apple components.

It should be sufficient to say that all of the basic programs available and the delivery systems as discussed under the TRS-80 Model II computer can be done using the Apple II Plus. It is felt by many Apple owners that the HI-RES Graphics that are available under the Apple II provides a dimension that is not offered by all microcomputer systems. There is more flexibility available in the graphics that can be displayed on the screen.

Another feature of the Apple II is that it has many more personal uses than some of the other computers, which are designed strictly for business purposes. There is always the possibility that the life insurance agents using the Apple II for business reasons might decide to play some computer games; this flexibility might not be available on any other business computer systems.

One other interesting dimension to the Apple II is that at least one company in the United States, L.P.A. Tech Corporation, has developed an entire software package for use with the Apple II Plus computer. Their current selection of software includes PFS/PFS: REPORT/ADMS. They have taken the best available user defineable data base system and designed three computer forms to go along with the PFS and PFS:report. With this system you can store a wide range of client information, such as a broker mailing list, or institute a computer base business tracking system. Wide flexibility of printouts are available along with single or multiple field searches.

We are sure that L.P.A. Tech Corporation is one of many companies that will be coming out with total software packages for use by life insurance agents. We are particularly pleased that L.P.A. Tech Corporation could make this information available to us for inclusion in this book.

3) KEYPACT

The third piece of equipment to be discussed is the Keypact portable terminal unit available through Computone Systems. In essence, it is a briefcase size, self-contained computer terminal. A special input system is used and the programmer is guided by templates marked with insurance terms. This allows the programmer, or agent, to use the system without the need for special computer or typing skills.

The key to the use of this piece of equipment is the availability of many companies' premium rates and policy values, which are stored on Computone's main computer located in Atlanta, Ga. To gain access to their figures and programs, the agent must attach a telephone to the Keypact unit, dial a toll-free number, interconnect with the computer, and receive information from the computer over the telephone. The illustration selected is received on the printer which is built-in to the Keypact terminal.

The advantage of Keypact over the TRS-80 Model II computer is that with the Keypact terminal, an agent can access many different insurance company's rates, as long as they are available on the master computer. Hundreds of companies have their rates available. Therefore, as long as the agent has the access number to that particular set of rates, he can run an illustration for that company. Some companies using the service offered by Computone allow anyone to run their policy illustrations, while other companies require the agent to have an access code, thus limiting who can gain access to their illustrations.

Keypact has the capability of producing illustrations for personal financial planning, business insurance, detailed policy illustrations, and estate planning. The partial list of programs shown in Figure 4.1 shows the capacity of Keypact to provide illustrations in each of these categories. Computone has under development 10 or more Universal Life programs. Several of these deal with sales ideas illustrated in Chapter 11, "Marketing Ideas and Case Studies."

The Keypact can provide a complete and total computer illustration system for an agent at a reasonable cost. With over 8,000 Keypact terminals currently in use throughout the United States, this should attest to its wide acceptance by the agents in the field. It can be a significant "secondary" computer system for those companies not wishing to develop their own field programs.

An additional benefit is the portability of the equipment. The agent can do planning and produce policy illustrations anywhere. He can work in his office, or he can take the Keypact in the field and run the illustrations while the prospect is involved in the interview. The impact of seeing the computer in action significantly enhances the sales potential and, as a result, use in the field may well be the preferred approach.

Figure 4.1
PARTIAL LIST OF PROGRAMS AVAILABLE ON THE COMPUTONE SYSTEM

FUNCTION

- Accumulating Annual Level Installments for Retirement
- Accumulation of Wealth Feasibility Study
- Adjustment of Tentative Federal Estate Tax for Gifts—Year of Death
- Asset Accumulations
- Business Financial Ratios
- Calculate Annual Outlay to Achieve a Given Income at Retirement
- Calculating Before Tax Earnings and Gross Sales Required to Fund a Business Purchase Agreement
- Defined Benefit Plans (up to 9,999 lives)
- Eligible Joint Interest in Farm or Business Property
- Estate Model — Hypothetical Illustration
- Executive Bonus
- Financial Planning Analysis
- Human Life Value
- Illustration of Flexible Outlay Policy, Annuity and Mutual Fund
- Income Tax Calculations
- Investment Projection and Analysis
- Investment Property Analysis
- Mutual Funds Hypothetical Past Performance Calculator/Interest Calculator
- Policy Comparison — Net Death Benefit
- Policy with Rider Illustration

FUNCTION

- Present Value Analysis of Lump Sum Distribution vs. Monthly Annuity After Death
- Present Value of a Series of Installments
- Profit Sharing and Defined Contribution Plans (up to 9,999 lives)
- Projection of Profit Sharing, Money Purchase or Thrift Plans
- Renewable and Convertible Term vs. Permanent Insurance
- Renting vs. Home Ownership
- Retired Lives Reserve
- Retirement Program Funded by a Single Sums(s) and/or Level Annual Installments
- Split-Dollar Program — Policy Illustration
- Split Funded Money Allocation Program
- State Inheritance Tax
- Tax Exempt Income from a Municipal Bond Fund to Purchase Life Insurance
- Tax Sheltered Dollars of an Annuity to Purchase Life Insurance
- Term Conversion or Exchange
- Using Life Insurance Equity to Prepay Mortgage
- Valuation of a Business — Valuation of a Keyman
- Working Capital Analysis (Bardahl Formula)
- Working Capital Analysis (Mead Formula)

The Keypact also has the definite advantage of implementing a total financial planning process from the data sheet all the way through to the printed illustration using one piece of equipment. The agent does not have to develop any of his own programs, nor does he have to rely on his home office to provide him with these programs. Updated numbers are available as soon as they enter Computone's computer. Computone and the Keypact terminal handle the numbers, while the agent handles the sale.

In early 1982 Computone announced limited compute capability for its terminal. The terminal can now be modified to incorporate a Z80 microprocessor similar to that of the TRS-80 Model II computer. There is no disc storage. The first announced program for their new system is "Financial Planning Analysis."

The disadvantage of Keypact is that it operates on a time-share basis. Multiple illustrations are often needed, particularly when the product and the Keypact terminal and programs are not familiar to the agent.

The authors have been informed by Computone that the average usage cost per Keypact terminal in early 1982 was between $70 and $80 per month. This cost covered the broad spectrum of programs utilized by the agents of many companies. For 250 agents specializing in Universal Life, the average in one month was $91.57. According to the company, the average cost per Universal Life illustration was $3.06. This is a reasonable cost if the agent is not required to make multiple illustrations to close the sale.

Cost and the Sales Process

As far as costs are concerned, a moderately powerful TRS-80 Model II computer can be purchased for $5,000 to $6,000. We have previously mentioned the costs for the Apple II Plus computer and related components. The Keypact unit used by most agents can be purchased for about $2,995. For more advanced network systems, the costs can range to whatever the agent and company are willing to spend. Of course, the capacity of the equipment and the range of operations will continue to increase.

Summary

Many agents may decide to purchase one or more of these computer systems. The Keypact, as noted previously, has the portable capability. The various insurance companies may decide to go with the Apple II Plus and a TRS-80 Model II computer to be able to produce the illustrations. If all illustrations will be run with one company in the office, the TRS-80 may be better. If the illustration is going to be run in the field in front of the client, and numerous companies are going to be used, the capability offered by Computone would probably be the obvious choice. The situation will determine which piece of equipment should be used.

We have talked with one major insurance company that is using an innovative system to get around the problem of various styles of equipment in their field offices. For those offices not using the company's standard computer system a clearinghouse will be established that will enable the agent to use the telephone lines. Using a telephone connecting device the agent will plug the phone into his microcomputer, type in the required codes, and receive the illustrations on his printer, regardless of what style of computer he has. We are sure that, as more and more companies provide the Universal Life programs and need computer delivery systems for illustration purposes, this variation will become more pronounced.

In our opinion, the ideal hardware, which is not yet available commercially, would be a portable version of a microcomputer which would have access to Computone and other information networks, both company based computers and "public" networks. This would be the best of both worlds.

We point out these situations because many people will be confused as to what type of computer system to purchase, fearing a mistake will be made. We believe it more important, however, to establish a basic system now that will solve most of your needs. Then, as more technology becomes available, adapt that system to the various software packages that will be developed.

In any event, the computer is a must for Universal Life illustrations and, as was discussed above, it can actually be viewed as your partner in the sales process.

CHAPTER 5

Creating The Proposal

As we mentioned at the beginning of the prior chapter, Universal Life products would not exist without computer technology. We discussed three types of computer processes that are being used by agents. In this edition of *Why Universal Life*, we have omitted a section from the first edition which dealt with home office computers. Instead, having gained additional experience with the new technology of microcomputers during the past year, we will discuss practical ways that computers can be used to understand and sell Universal Life.

Agents who consider the question, "Why Universal Life?" can expect significant rewards for their study as they develop their answers through use of the computer. We will discuss three dimensions of such computer oriented study:

1) Client Questions;
2) Computer Program Capabilities and Options; and

3) Universal Life Product Comparisons.

There is an important learning curve associated with the use of computers in the sales office. Companies have consistently found that an experienced agent often needs six to eight weeks of work with the computer before a solid understanding of the Universal Life policy is achieved. The agent then develops confidence in the product and the learning curve leads to a positive sales curve.

The next few pages should pull the reader well-up the learning curve. Our short course has only two prerequisites:

- A good grasp of the Universal Life policy as described in this book, and
- A state of the art computer program to perform illustrative calculations.

The policy used in this chapter is similar to the first Universal Life policy developed by the Union Central Life Insurance Company of Cincinnati, Ohio. The company's policy form is based on the policy illustrated in Chapter 3. The microcomputer program, believed to be among the most versatile currently available, was developed for the company by FIPSCO, Inc. of Park Ridge, Illinois.

The examples are geared to the family market. An agent can easily prepare comparable examples using other policies and computer programs offered by an increasing number of companies. Some of the advanced calculation features are not yet available in all such programs.

1) Client Questions

In discussing the four steps in the sales process, we stressed the importance of the computer proposal. We said,

"Usually the agent prefers to take the data gathered during the meeting (with the client) back to his office to make a more thorough study and analysis. . . . It becomes necessary to decide upon the type of policy illustration to be printed."

In order to make this important decision, the agent needs to respond to several questions which can arise at the point of sale. Sometimes the key question or questions will be apparent during the initial interview. If the interview was inconclusive, sales experience will point the way to the proper type of illustration. At all times the questions can be answered best with knowledge of how to use the computer to its fullest. The questions are:

- What will my insurance cost?
- What is the most insurance I can buy for a given premium?
- What premium should I pay for a given amount of insurance?
- How does Universal Life compare with traditional fixed premium life insurance?
- How can I keep my policy current with inflation?

Each question is first discussed in general terms. The next part of this short course is to study the computer input. After that, you can proceed to the sample proposals which show the way Universal Life works. This material concentrates on the specific information and numbers you need to make the sale.

We will answer most of these questions in terms of a policy which provides coverage to age 85, a close equivalent of traditional whole life. Universal Life policies which expire at an earlier age, or which seek to limit the age or number of years for which premiums are planned, may be similarly studied. Now, let us take a look at the general answers to the client questions.

What will my insurance cost?

Interest is the key feature in all forms of life insurance coverage designed to provide protection for the whole of life. This includes Universal Life. Cost, defined here to mean out-of-pocket cost or planned premium, depends heavily upon the interest credited by the company. To answer this question, study the interest rates projected by the computer. Compare the current (high) rate with the rate you expect the company to credit in future years. Differences between mortality costs and loading charges cannot be ignored, even though they are much less important overall. (These are discussed further in the product comparison part of this chapter and in Chapter 7 under the heading, "Mortality Charges—the Hidden Interest Cost.") The all-important relationship between interest and cost is given a great deal of attention in the sample proposals.

What is the most insurance I can buy for a given premium?
Pick an interest rate and the computer answers this question. If the agent and client are willing to assume continued high interest rates, the maximum benefit for a given premium can be determined. If interest credited in the future is lower, cash values will be reduced. When this happens, the cash value will often be depleted within the period of coverage initially illustrated. Increased premiums will then be required if the planned death benefit is to be continued.

What premium should I pay for a given amount of insurance?
Again, this question is answered best by studying the relationship between cost and interest. A proposal can be created which guarantees a minimum death benefit and cash value. It will be based upon the guaranteed interest and cost of insurance rates in the policy. In many respects, this proposal is like a traditional participating policy. The planned premium for each thousand of specified death benefit is high, and the policy values increase greatly with time as excess interest credits and mortality savings accumulate.

At the other extreme, if the agent and client are willing to assume a continuation of high interest rates, the planned premium is much smaller. We suggest that, for most people, *the desirable planned premium for a Universal Life policy be between these two extremes.* In the next part of this chapter, we will explain one way of settling on a premium which we believe is suitable. Other ways may be chosen by the agent. The computer is used to evaluate how each will work in a variety of possible future circumstances.

How does Universal Life compare with traditional fixed premium life insurance?

Expense and mortality costs on nontraditional and traditional policies can, if the actuaries so calculate, be made much the same. That is, in fact, the case with the Union Central policy used in our illustrations. If the amount of interest credited to traditional fixed premium policies begins to approach that credited to Universal Life, the cost of traditional whole life compares favorably. The answer to this question, once again, depends heavily upon the outlook for interest rates. The reader should refer also to Chapter 7 in which we discuss the question, "How Long Can the High Interest Continue?"

How can I keep my policy current with inflation?

This can be done rather easily by using the newest policy riders and computer techniques. Given a program option which allows increasing premium patterns and a cost-of-living increase in benefits, great creativity is possible in a minimum amount of time. To demonstrate the advanced use of the technology, one of many possible proposals is included in a later part of this chapter.

2) Computer Program Capabilities and Options

Now that you have a general idea of key client questions and answers, let us continue up the learning curve. As part of becoming familiar with the new technology, an agent will often wish to run a large number of proposals. What better way to see how Universal Life functions than to create proposals which are similar to traditional ledger sheets. If the agent has a computer readily available, and understands the program capabilities and policy options, it is quite common for him to run half a dozen proposals on a single client. Experience will reduce the number of proposals needed to make a presentation with confidence.

A warning may be in order for some of our readers. Creating the proposal can become so fascinating that excessive time is invested in studying options. You should, as quickly as you can, discover those types of proposals with which you are most comfortable. But don't forget to review other options from time to time. It is easy to forget a program feature that, although it does not help with most sales, will be the key variation on special cases.

Here is a true story, experienced by one of the authors. After nearly two years of selling Universal Life, our friendly author found himself in competition with another Universal Life company. Knowing the company he was representing had a strong product, he confidently presented a single Universal Life proposal using Option A and a level premium. The competition had figured out that a return of cash value at death was important to the prospect. Before the author thought to counter with an Option B proposal, the case had been closed by the competition.

Figure 5.2 shows part of a proposal from the FIPSCO computer program. (The format varies a bit from the "One Policy Illustration", Figure 2.1, found in Chapter 2.) We will explain how the program works and then show selected numbers from a wide range of proposals. Take a minute and study Figure 5.1.

Figure 5.1
SAMPLE OF FIPSCO COMPUTER INPUT

PROMPT	TYPED INPUT	FIELD NUMBER AND DESCRIPTION
0) RUN TYPE	1	0)- 3) Run and client information.
RUN ID	WHY ULI	
1) INSURED FIRST NAME	STANDARD PROPOSAL	
INSURED LAST NAME	- ENDOWMENT AT 85	
2) AGE	35	
3) SEX	M	
5) AGENT	I M GOODFELLOW	
6) PLAN CODE	UCL00	
PREFERRED RISK	Y	
7) # OF YRS	A85	7). . . Attained age or No. of Years.
SHOW ALL YEARS	Y	All? Input "No" or "N" requests print
8) LEVEL OUTLAY	Y	of only the first 20 years and every
		fifth year thereafter.
11) SPEC DEATH BENEFIT	100000	11)-15) Plan details for a level
12) DB OPTION-B ADDS CV	A	outlay, i.e. planned level premiums.
13) MODAL OUTLAY	0	13). . . Dollar amount. When zero is
14) PAYMENT MODE	A	typed, the computer calculates the
15) ASSUMED % INTEREST	7.5	needed planned premium.
		14). . . For loans and partial cash
		withdrawals, type "L" or "P".
201) NEW POLICY	Y	
202) ADDED INIT'L OUTLAY	0	202) . . Lump sum premium amounts.
203) ANN OUTLAY CHANGE	N	203) . . For annual increase or
		decrease in planned premium.
204) RATED	N	
205) SEARCH TYPE	2	205) . . Key field. The sub-field
CASH VALUE TARGET	100000	"RATE TO CALCULATE" has options:
END OF YR	A85	C =Current (12% in the example)
YRS TO PAY	A85	G =Guaranteed (4.5% in the Union
RATE TO CALCULATE	A	Central policy)
		A =Assumed (e.g. 7.5% input in
		field 15).
207) CHECK PREM LIMIT	N	207) . . Optional. See TEFRA chapter.
209) NUMBER OF COPIES	1	
211) TOTAL DISABILITY	N	211)- 217) No riders selected.
212) ACCIDENTAL DEATH	N	
213) GUAR. INSURABILITY	N	
214) OTHER INS - SPOUSE	N	
216) CHILDREN'S RIDER	N	
217) AUTOMATIC INCREASE	N	

The left column in Figure 5.1 shows the actual computer screen display used to produce the illustration. Each of the lines is called a "PROMPT." After the computer is turned on and the diskette inserted, the agent types the word "INPUT" followed by the "ENTER" or "CARRIAGE RETURN" key. A series of PROMPTs then flash on the screen in sequence. The proposal is created by simple answering each PROMPT with typed input. If a misteak (sic) is made, a new PROMPT appears to tell the agent what input is needed.

The PROMPTs change, depending upon what is typed. For example, typing "Yes" or "Y" in response to "204) RATED" will bring other PROMPTs which ask for the special class rating, flat extra rating, and the number of years the extra rating is to apply. The process is simple, very much like a programmed learning course.

The middle column in Figure 5.1 shows the typed input to create a standard whole life proposal. The agent (agency secretary or client) can create this proposal with no more than 70 key strokes plus the name of the client and agent. The right column gives a brief description of some of the PROMPTs. This information is taken directly from an operator's manual which is designed to explain all of the program's many capabilities, and includes samples of the most important types of proposals.

In order to study the relationship between cost and interest, simple changes are made to the input. For example, PROMPT "205) RATE TO CALCULATE" can be changed from "A", assumed rate or rates of interest, to "C", current rate of interest. Then another proposal can be run which gives the minimum premium required to answer the second client question in our list.

With changes such as this, it is easy to run two proposals in a batch at the same time (or any larger number of proposals for that matter). As suggested by the example of the interest rate change, it is not necessary to retype any information which is constant. Batching of several proposals at one time is also easy.

But we are getting ahead in our short course. Let us look again at each of the client questions, but this time in more depth.

What will my insurance cost?

Compare the cash values in Figure 5.2. Note that this calculation was based on a level interest assumption less than the current projected rate of 12%.[1] We used $7\frac{1}{2}\%$ as an estimate of long-term average interest on Universal Life policies being issued today. This rate approximates the net earnings of a life insurance company on its 8% policy loans, allowing $\frac{1}{2}\%$ for expenses.

As you would expect, the cash values after 10 or 20 years are much higher if the 12% interest continues. At the maturity age of 85, the cash value using 7.5% interest is the $100,000 requested of the computer with a death benefit of 5% more. This is to comply with the new IRC corridor requirement of Section 101(f) of TEFRA 1982 (see the tax discussion in Chapter 8 for a full explanation of the corridor). This compares with the 12% maturity value of $921,392. On the low side, the guaranteed cash value runs out in the 24th policy year and all benefits stop.

The illustration program has many other useful capabilities. One of these is to specify that interest rates change from time to time. If rates come down in the next few years, which seems likely, additional computer calculations will reveal the impact to the policyholder. Figure 5.3 is a proposal which assumes

----

[1]In the Union Central policy design illustrated, the first $1,000 of cash value is credited with $1\frac{1}{2}\%$ less interest than the balance of the cash value. Note also that the proposals in this chapter include the TEFRA corridor death benefits. The proposals in other chapters do not.

Figure 5.2
STANDARD PROPOSAL-ENDOWMENT AT 85

STANDARD PROPOSAL - ENDOWMENT AT 85   INITIAL SPECIFIED AMOUNT   100000
MALE, AGE 35

POLICY YEAR	AGE YR END	PLANNED OUTLAY*	CURRENT RATE 12.00%		ASSUMED RATE ***		GUART'D RATE 4.5%	
			CASH VALUE	**DEATH BENEFIT	CASH VALUE	**DEATH BENEFIT	CASH VALUE	**DEATH BENEFIT
1	36	631	51	100000	44	100000	42	100000
2	37	631	590	100000	558	100000	376	100000
3	38	631	1180	100000	1094	100000	714	100000
4	39	631	1829	100000	1661	100000	1044	100000
5	40	631 3156	2544	100000	2257	100000	1365	100000
6	41	631	3331	100000	2885	100000	1678	100000
7	42	631	4199	100000	3546	100000	1970	100000
8	43	631	5154	100000	4240	100000	2253	100000
9	44	631	6208	100000	4969	100000	2513	100000
10	45	631 6312	7371	100000	5735	100000	2739	100000
11	46	631	8656	100000	6541	100000	2940	100000
12	47	631	10080	100000	7390	100000	3104	100000
13	48	631	11660	100000	8285	100000	3218	100000
14	49	631	13415	100000	9231	100000	3277	100000
15	50	631 9467	15363	100000	10227	100000	3281	100000
16	51	631	17527	100000	11275	100000	3214	100000
17	52	631	19933	100000	12377	100000	3059	100000
18	53	631	22609	100000	13536	100000	2813	100000
19	54	631	25588	100000	14752	100000	2458	100000
20	55	631 12623	28906	100000	16028	100000	1986	100000
25	60	631 15779	52208	100000	23245	100000	0	0
30	65	631 18935	93416	108362	32082	100000	0	0
35	70	631 22090	163517	181503	43012	100000	0	0
40	75	631 25246	285792	302939	56679	100000	0	0
45	80	631 28402	498053	522955	73838	100000	0	0

PRESENTED BY I M GOODFELLOW   01/01/83

Creating The Proposal

| | AGE | | CURRENT RATE 12.00% | | ASSUMED RATE *** | | GUART'D RATE 4.5% | |
POLICY YEAR	YR END	PLANNED OUTLAY*	CASH VALUE	**DEATH BENEFIT	CASH VALUE	**DEATH BENEFIT	CASH VALUE	**DEATH BENEFIT
50	85	631 31558	856009	898810	100000	105000	0	0

* INCLUDES THE FOLLOWING RIDERS:

   *** NONE ***

OUTLAY PAYABLE ANNUALLY
NEGATIVE FIGURES INDICATE PARTIAL CASH SURRENDERS
# INDICATES FEDERAL PREMIUM GUIDELINE LIMITATIONS ARE EXCEEDED

UNION CENTRAL'S CURRENT INTEREST RATE OF 12.00% MAY INCREASE OR DECREASE BUT NEVER BELOW 4.5%. THE RATE ON THE FIRST $1000 OF CASH VALUE IS 1.5% BELOW THE RATES SHOWN, BUT NEVER BELOW 4.5%. THE OWNER MAY ADJUST THE FACE AMOUNT, PREMIUM AND DEATH BENEFIT OPTION TO INCREASE OR DECREASE THE ILLUSTRATED BENEFITS.

| **DEATH BENEFIT | OPTION | ***INTEREST RATE | THRU AGE |
| SPECIFIED AMOUNT | A | 7.50% | 85 |

5% INTEREST ADJUSTED SURRENDER COST INDEX	10 YEARS	20 YEARS
CURRENT	0.73	- 2.01
ASSUMED	1.97	1.70
GUARANTEED	4.24	5.74

AT LEAST ONCE EACH YEAR, UNION CENTRAL WILL SEND THE OWNER A REPORT SHOWING THE CURRENT CASH VALUE, AMOUNT OF INTEREST CREDITED, PREMIUMS PAID, CASH SURRENDERS, MONTHLY EXPENSE CHARGES, AND COST OF INSURANCE DEDUCTED SINCE THE PRIOR REPORT.

THIS ILLUSTRATION IS NOT A CONTRACT.   THE COST OF THIS POLICY CANNOT BE COMPLETELY DETERMINED WITHOUT TAKING INTO ACCOUNT THE INTEREST THAT WOULD BE EARNED ON THE PREMIUMS IF THEY HAD BEEN INVESTED RATHER THAN PAID TO THE INSURANCE COMPANY.

Figure 5.3
DECREASING INTEREST RATE PROPOSAL

DECREASING INTEREST PROPOSAL   INITIAL SPECIFIED AMOUNT   100000
MALE, AGE 35

POLICY YEAR	AGE YR END	PLANNED OUTLAY*	CURRENT RATE 12.00% CASH VALUE	**DEATH BENEFIT	ASSUMED RATE *** CASH VALUE	**DEATH BENEFIT	GUART'D RATE 4.5% CASH VALUE	**DEATH BENEFIT
1	36	581	28	100000	28	100000	21	100000
2	37	581	514	100000	514	100000	306	100000
3	38	581	1043	100000	1043	100000	592	100000
4	39	581	1625	100000	1616	100000	868	100000
5	40	581 2903	2264	100000	2231	100000	1133	100000
6	41	581	2965	100000	2886	100000	1386	100000
7	42	581	3737	100000	3576	100000	1616	100000
8	43	581	4584	100000	4297	100000	1833	100000
9	44	581	5517	100000	5043	100000	2024	100000
10	45	581 5807	6543	100000	5809	100000	2177	100000
11	46	581	7676	100000	6614	100000	2302	100000
12	47	581	8927	100000	7462	100000	2385	100000
13	48	581	10314	100000	8357	100000	2413	100000
14	49	581	11851	100000	9302	100000	2382	100000
15	50	581 8710	13555	100000	10297	100000	2290	100000
16	51	581	15443	100000	11345	100000	2121	100000
17	52	581	17538	100000	12446	100000	1859	100000
18	53	581	19865	100000	13604	100000	1498	100000
19	54	581	22449	100000	14820	100000	1019	100000
20	55	581 11614	25320	100000	16095	100000	417	100000
25	60	581 14517	45332	100000	23307	100000	0	0
30	65	581 17420	80688	100000	32139	100000	0	0
35	70	581 20324	141642	157222	43060	100000	0	0
40	75	581 23227	247499	262348	56716	100000	0	0
45	80	581 26131	431259	452821	73856	100000	0	0

PRESENTED BY I M CAUTIOUS   01/01/83

Creating The Proposal

POLICY YEAR	AGE YR END	PLANNED OUTLAY*	CURRENT RATE 12.00%		ASSUMED RATE ***		GUART'D RATE 4.5%	
			CASH VALUE	**DEATH BENEFIT	CASH VALUE	**DEATH BENEFIT	CASH VALUE	**DEATH BENEFIT
50	85	581	741150	778207	99998	104997	0	0
		29034						

* INCLUDES THE FOLLOWING RIDERS:

*** NONE ***

OUTLAY PAYABLE ANNUALLY
NEGATIVE FIGURES INDICATE PARTIAL CASH SURRENDERS
# INDICATES FEDERAL PREMIUM GUIDELINE LIMITATIONS ARE EXCEEDED

UNION CENTRAL'S CURRENT INTEREST RATE OF 12.00% MAY INCREASE OR DECREASE BUT
NEVER BELOW 4.5%. THE RATE ON THE FIRST $1000 OF CASH VALUE IS 1.5% BELOW
THE RATES SHOWN, BUT NEVER BELOW 4.5%. THE OWNER MAY ADJUST THE FACE AMOUNT,
PREMIUM AND DEATH BENEFIT OPTION TO INCREASE OR DECREASE THE ILLUSTRATED
BENEFITS.

**DEATH BENEFIT	OPTION	***INTEREST RATE	THRU AGE
SPECIFIED AMOUNT	A	12.00%	36
SPECIFIED AMOUNT	A	11.50%	37
SPECIFIED AMOUNT	A	11.00%	38
SPECIFIED AMOUNT	A	10.50%	39
SPECIFIED AMOUNT	A	10.00%	40
SPECIFIED AMOUNT	A	9.50%	41
SPECIFIED AMOUNT	A	9.00%	42
SPECIFIED AMOUNT	A	8.50%	43
SPECIFIED AMOUNT	A	8.00%	44
SPECIFIED AMOUNT	A	7.50%	85

5% INTEREST ADJUSTED SURRENDER COST INDEX	10 YEARS	20 YEARS
CURRENT	0.85	- 1.49
ASSUMED	1.41	1.17
GUARANTEED	4.16	5.69

AT LEAST ONCE EACH YEAR, UNION CENTRAL WILL SEND THE OWNER A REPORT SHOWING
THE CURRENT CASH VALUE, AMOUNT OF INTEREST CREDITED, PREMIUMS PAID, CASH
SURRENDERS, MONTHLY EXPENSE CHARGES, AND COST OF INSURANCE DEDUCTED SINCE
THE PRIOR REPORT.

THIS ILLUSTRATION IS NOT A CONTRACT. THE COST OF THIS POLICY CANNOT BE
COMPLETELY DETERMINED WITHOUT TAKING INTO ACCOUNT THE INTEREST THAT WOULD BE
EARNED ON THE PREMIUMS IF THEY HAD BEEN INVESTED RATHER THAN PAID TO THE
INSURANCE COMPANY.

decreasing interest. Interest credited in the first year is 12%. The rate decreases ½% per year to the level rate of 7½%.

To do this proposal, the "8) LEVEL OUTLAY" PROMPT is changed from "Y" to "N" or "No." Added PROMPTS ask the agent for the interest rates, what percentages to use and for which years. After typing the new input, the planned premium is projected as shown in Figure 5.3. The computer calculates the planned premium to be $581 which is only moderately less than the planned premium calculated using a level 7½% assumption ($631). (The premiums shown on the screen as the computer searches for the correct amount are $580.68 and $631.15, rounded to the nearest dollar.)

Consider another proposal, Figure 5.4. This proposal uses the optimistic assumption of continued interest at 12%. Simply type "12" next to the "15) ASSUMED % INTEREST" PROMPT. The planned premium is much lower, $341. In the Union Central policy, as with many other Universal Life policies using a high interest assumption, there is a significantly higher first-year premium ($541) to cover first-year expenses and mortality costs. This higher first-year premium is most common at the younger issue ages.

What will the insurance actually cost? It is apparent that the interest rate controls the answer. Another option of the program allows the agent to determine the effect of paying the $341 premium for a period of time, and then adjusting later premiums to make up for the lower interest rate. Using the decreasing interest rates in Figure 5.3, the cash value in the 10th year is $2,667. This is $479 more than the 10th year cash value of $2,188 using the 7½% level interest rate in Figure 5.4.

The agent then runs the "midstream" calculation shown in Figure 5.5. This special proposal can be run to study the change in interest rates as we have done here. Or, it can be used to update an in force Universal Life policy, which is the name given to the proposal in Figure 5.5.

Figure 5.4
HIGH CURRENT INTEREST RATE PROPOSAL

HIGH CURRENT INTEREST PROPOSAL   INITIAL SPECIFIED AMOUNT   100000
MALE, AGE 35

POLICY YEAR	AGE YR END	PLANNED OUTLAY*	CURRENT RATE 12.00%		ASSUMED RATE ***		GUART'D RATE 4.5%	
			CASH VALUE	**DEATH BENEFIT	CASH VALUE	**DEATH BENEFIT	CASH VALUE	**DEATH BENEFIT
1	36	541	11	100000	6	100000	5	100000
2	37	341	254	100000	237	100000	60	100000
3	38	341	514	100000	473	100000	107	100000
4	39	341	790	100000	712	100000	131	100000
5	40	341	1083	100000	952	100000	131	100000
		1906						
6	41	341	1396	100000	1196	100000	107	100000
7	42	341	1732	100000	1444	100000	46	100000
8	43	341	2091	100000	1691	100000	0	0
9	44	341	2474	100000	1940	100000	0	0
10	45	341	2884	100000	2188	100000	0	0
		3612						
11	46	341	3323	100000	2434	100000	0	0
12	47	341	3795	100000	2679	100000	0	0
13	48	341	4305	100000	2923	100000	0	0
14	49	341	4857	100000	3165	100000	0	0
15	50	341	5451	100000	3400	100000	0	0
		5318						
16	51	341	6090	100000	3626	100000	0	0
17	52	341	6778	100000	3839	100000	0	0
18	53	341	7518	100000	4034	100000	0	0
19	54	341	8313	100000	4207	100000	0	0
20	55	341	9164	100000	4350	100000	0	0
		7025						
25	60	341	14275	100000	4208	100000	0	0
		8731						
30	65	341	21201	100000	1473	100000	0	0
		10437						
35	70	341	30815	100000	0	0	0	0
		12143						
40	75	341	44478	100000	0	0	0	0
		13849						
50	85	341	100074	105078	0	0	0	0
		17262						

PRESENTED BY I M OPTIMISTIC   01/01/83

Figure 5.5
MID-STREAM PROPOSAL

MID-STREAM PROPOSAL   INITIAL SPECIFIED AMOUNT   100000
MALE, AGE 45

POLICY YEAR	AGE YR END	PLANNED OUTLAY*	CURRENT RATE 12.00%		ASSUMED RATE ***		GUART'D RATE 4.5%	
			CASH VALUE	**DEATH BENEFIT	CASH VALUE	**DEATH BENEFIT	CASH VALUE	**DEATH BENEFIT
11	46	3600	3270	100000	3136	100000	3061	100000
12	47	933	4341	100000	4016	100000	3520	100000
13	48	933	5523	100000	4944	100000	3943	100000
14	49	933	6829	100000	5925	100000	4330	100000
15	50	933	8272	100000	6957	100000	4678	100000
		7331						
16	51	933	9866	100000	8044	100000	4975	100000
17	52	933	11629	100000	9187	100000	5207	100000
18	53	933	13578	100000	10389	100000	5369	100000
19	54	933	15737	100000	11651	100000	5449	100000
20	55	933	18126	100000	12973	100000	5439	100000
		11996						
21	56	933	20771	100000	14355	100000	5313	100000
22	57	933	23699	100000	15794	100000	5064	100000
23	58	933	26942	100000	17291	100000	4670	100000
24	59	933	30542	100000	18846	100000	4112	100000
25	60	933	34545	100000	20461	100000	3352	100000
		16660						
26	61	933	39008	100000	22140	100000	2363	100000
27	62	933	43998	100000	23892	100000	1115	100000
28	63	933	49593	100000	25723	100000	0	0
29	64	933	55878	100000	27636	100000	0	0
30	65	933	62954	100000	29635	100000	0	0
		21325						
35	70	933	111502	123768	40992	100000	0	0
		25989						
40	75	933	191698	203200	55219	100000	0	0
		30653						
45	80	933	330904	347449	73154	100000	0	0
		35318						
50	85	933	565584	593863	100000	105000	0	0
		39982						

PRESENTED BY I M ADJUSTING   01/01/83

On these assumptions, the premium will need to be increased from $341 to $933, or 173%, beginning in the 11th year to mature the original Universal Life policy for $100,000 at age 85. If interest rates decrease and the premium is not increased, the coverage will expire, with no cash value left, at the insured's attained age of 70.

What is the most insurance I can buy for a given premium?
By making two changes to the input, the computer will quickly calculate the face amount. The "8) LEVEL OUTLAY" PROMPT is changed to the desired amount of premium. The "11) SPECIFIED DEATH BENEFIT" PROMPT is changed to "0". If desired, the frequency of premium payment may be changed by the "14) PAYMENT MODE" input ("C", for example, is the automatic monthly check plan).

Figures 5.6 A-C show the benefits purchased by an array of annual premiums at different ages. We have calculated these numbers using a male non-smoker plan, Options A and B, and a female, non-smoker, Option A.

Two interest rates are illustrated and the plan used is term to age 90. This helps illustrate the problem referred to previously. At a high assumed rate of interest, such as 12%, the low premium per thousand of specified death benefit builds inadequate cash values in the event interest rates decrease. When this happens, the insurance stops well before age 90. Also, the added death benefits under Option B become quite expensive for ages over 90. We would expect that a policyholder who keeps a policy with Option B in force for many years will consider withdrawing the cash well before this advanced age. The numbers shown include the 20th year cash value, for comparative purposes, and to allow easy calculation of cost indexes if the reader wishes to do so.

Figure 5.6A

SPECIFIED DEATH BENEFIT PURCHASED BY LEVEL ANNUAL RENEWAL PREMIUMS
MALE NONSMOKER - TERM TO 90 PLAN - OPTION A

$750 LEVEL ANNUAL RENEWAL PREMIUM

Issue Age	Age 25	Age 35	Age 45	Age 55
Specified Death Benefit (DB) assuming 12%	419230	229018	103057	46839
First Year Premium (Minimum)	2236	1281	797	level
SPECIFIED DB | Cash Value End of Year 20	8835	9314	7250	4557
AND 7.5% | Cash Value per 1000 Spec. DB	21.07	40.67	70.35	97.29
INTEREST | DB and CV stop before	Age 60	Age 70	Age 75	Age 80
Level Annual Premium per 1000 of Spec. DB	1.79	3.27	7.28	16.01
Specified Death Benefit (DB) assuming 7.5%	222590	126368	67056	34923
First Year Premium (Minimum)	1172	level	level	level
Cash Value End of Year 20 at 7.5%	18174	18402	15998	12917
Cash Value End of Year 20 per 1000 Spec. DB	81.65	145.62	238.58	369.87
Level Annual Premium per 1000 of Spec. DB	3.37	5.94	11.18	21.48

$1500 LEVEL ANNUAL RENEWAL PREMIUM

Issue Age	Age 25	Age 35	Age 45	Age 55
Specified Death Benefit (DB) assuming 12%	845313	462061	207881	95216
First Year Premium (Minimum)	4541	2617	1575	level
SPECIFIED DB | Cash Value End of Year 20	17838	18827	14665	9203
AND 7.5% | Cash Value per 1000 Spec. DB	21.10	40.75	70.55	96.65
INTEREST | DB and CV stop before	Age 60	Age 70	Age 75	Age 80
Level Annual Premium per 1000 of Spec. DB	1.77	3.25	7.22	15.75
Specified Death Benefit (DB) assuming 7.5%	449405	254896	135462	70907
First Year Premium (Minimum)	2399	level	level	level
Cash Value End of Year 20 at 7.5%	36682	37096	32319	26275
Cash Value End of Year 20 per 1000 Spec. DB	81.62	145.53	238.58	370.56
Level Annual Premium per 1000 of Spec. DB	3.34	5.88	11.07	21.15

$1000 LEVEL ANNUAL RENEWAL PREMIUM

Issue Age	Age 25	Age 35	Age 45	Age 55
Specified Death Benefit (DB) assuming 12%	561091	306660	137986	62955
First Year Premium (Minimum)	3003	1726	1056	level
SPECIFIED DB | Cash Value End of Year 20	11832	12484	9721	6106
AND 7.5% | Cash Value per 1000 Spec. DB	21.09	40.71	70.45	96.99
INTEREST | DB and CV stop before	Age 60	Age 70	Age 75	Age 80
Level Annual Premium per 1000 of Spec. DB	1.78	3.26	7.25	15.88
Specified Death Benefit (DB) assuming 7.5%	298176	169191	89844	46909
First Year Premium (Minimum)	1581	level	level	level
Cash Value End of Year 20 at 7.5%	24341	24629	21433	17366
Cash Value End of Year 20 per 1000 Spec. DB	81.63	145.57	238.56	370.21
Level Annual Premium per 1000 of Spec. DB	3.35	5.91	11.13	21.32

$2000 LEVEL ANNUAL RENEWAL PREMIUM

Issue Age	Age 25	Age 35	Age 45	Age 55
Specified Death Benefit (DB) assuming 12%	1129810	617570	277824	127495
First Year Premium (Minimum)	6081	3509	2094	level
SPECIFIED DB | Cash Value End of Year 20	23849	25173	19611	12303
AND 7.5% | Cash Value per 1000 Spec. DB	21.11	40.76	70.59	96.50
INTEREST | DB and CV stop before	Age 60	Age 70	Age 75	Age 80
Level Annual Premium per 1000 of Spec. DB	1.77	3.24	7.20	15.69
Specified Death Benefit (DB) assuming 7.5%	600714	340622	181086	94910
First Year Premium (Minimum)	3218	level	level	level
Cash Value End of Year 20 at 7.5%	49032	49566	43206	35188
Cash Value End of Year 20 per 1000 Spec. DB	81.62	145.52	238.59	370.75
Level Annual Premium per 1000 of Spec. DB	3.33	5.87	11.04	21.07

Figure 5.6B

SPECIFIED DEATH BENEFIT PURCHASED BY LEVEL ANNUAL RENEWAL PREMIUMS
MALE NONSMOKER – TERM TO 90 PLAN – OPTION B

$750 LEVEL ANNUAL RENEWAL PREMIUM

Issue Age	Age 25	Age 35	Age 45	Age 55
Specified Death Benefit (DB) assuming 12%	370299	189162	82240	36090
First Year Premium (Minimum)	1971	1052	level	level
SPECIFIED DB | Cash Value End of Year 20	10952	12231	10836	8507
AND 7.5% | Cash Value per 1000 Spec. DB	29.58	64.66	131.76	235.72
INTEREST | DB and CV stop before	Age 65	Age 75	Age 80	Age 85
Level Annual Premium per 1000 of Spec. DB	2.03	3.96	9.12	20.78
Specified Death Benefit (DB) assuming 7.5%	155828	86210	45404	23900
First Year Premium (Minimum)	811	level	level	level
Cash Value End of Year 20 at 7.5%	21002	21461	19201	15502
Cash Value End of Year 20 per 1000 Spec. DB	134.78	248.94	422.89	648.62
Level Annual Premium per 1000 of Spec. DB	4.81	8.70	16.52	31.38

$1500 LEVEL ANNUAL RENEWAL PREMIUM

Issue Age	Age 25	Age 35	Age 45	Age 55
Specified Death Benefit (DB) assuming 12%	746819	381674	166039	73337
First Year Premium (Minimum)	4008	2156	level	level
SPECIFIED DB | Cash Value End of Year 20	22115	24712	21907	17257
AND 7.5% | Cash Value per 1000 Spec. DB	29.61	64.75	131.94	235.31
INTEREST | DB and CV stop before	Age 65	Age 75	Age 80	Age 85
Level Annual Premium per 1000 of Spec. DB	2.01	3.93	9.03	20.45
Specified Death Benefit (DB) assuming 7.5%	314647	173941	91739	48503
First Year Premium (Minimum)	1670	level	level	level
Cash Value End of Year 20 at 7.5%	42397	43278	38797	31518
Cash Value End of Year 20 per 1000 Spec. DB	134.74	248.81	422.91	649.82
Level Annual Premium per 1000 of Spec. DB	4.77	8.62	16.35	30.93

$1000 LEVEL ANNUAL RENEWAL PREMIUM

Issue Age	Age 25	Age 35	Age 45	Age 55
Specified Death Benefit (DB) assuming 12%	495684	253297	110156	48495
First Year Premium (Minimum)	2650	1420	level	level
SPECIFIED DB | Cash Value End of Year 20	14670	16390	14525	11425
AND 7.5% | Cash Value per 1000 Spec. DB	29.60	64.71	131.86	235.59
INTEREST | DB and CV stop before	Age 65	Age 75	Age 80	Age 85
Level Annual Premium per 1000 of Spec. DB	2.02	3.95	9.08	20.62
Specified Death Benefit (DB) assuming 7.5%	208753	115437	60841	32095
First Year Premium (Minimum)	1097	level	level	level
Cash Value End of Year 20 at 7.5%	28130	28728	25728	20835
Cash Value End of Year 20 per 1000 Spec. DB	134.75	248.86	422.87	649.17
Level Annual Premium per 1000 of Spec. DB	4.79	8.66	16.44	31.16

$2000 LEVEL ANNUAL RENEWAL PREMIUM

Issue Age	Age 25	Age 35	Age 45	Age 55
Specified Death Benefit (DB) assuming 12%	998168	510112	221940	98183
First Year Premium (Minimum)	5368	2893	level	level
SPECIFIED DB | Cash Value End of Year 20	29566	33038	29293	23093
AND 7.5% | Cash Value per 1000 Spec. DB	29.62	64.77	131.99	235.20
INTEREST | DB and CV stop before	Age 65	Age 75	Age 80	Age 85
Level Annual Premium per 1000 of Spec. DB	2.00	3.92	9.01	20.37
Specified Death Benefit (DB) assuming 7.5%	420586	232446	122638	64910
First Year Premium (Minimum)	2243	level	level	level
Cash Value End of Year 20 at 7.5%	56671	57829	51867	42200
Cash Value End of Year 20 per 1000 Spec. DB	134.74	248.78	422.93	650.13
Level Annual Premium per 1000 of Spec. DB	4.76	8.60	16.31	30.81

Figure 5.6C

SPECIFIED DEATH BENEFIT PURCHASED BY LEVEL ANNUAL RENEWAL PREMIUMS
FEMALE NONSMOKER - TERM TO 90 PLAN - OPTION A

Issue Age	$750 LEVEL ANNUAL RENEWAL PREMIUM				$1500 LEVEL ANNUAL RENEWAL PREMIUM			
	Age 25	Age 35	Age 45	Age 55	Age 25	Age 35	Age 45	Age 55
Specified Death Benefit (DB) assuming 12%	657306	280150	134777	69165	1326685	565245	271845	139436
First Year Premium (Minimum)	2703	1474	999	883	5489	3007	1982	1552
SPECIFIED DB | Cash Value End of Year 20	9987	6880	6874	7222	20186	13916	13902	14613
AND 7.5% | Cash Value per 1000 Spec. DB	15.19	24.56	51.00	104.42	15.22	24.62	51.14	104.80
INTEREST | DB and CV stop before	Age 60	Age 70	Age 80	Age 85	Age 60	Age 70	Age 80	Age 85
Level Annual Premium per 1000 of Spec. DB	1.14	2.68	5.56	10.84	1.13	2.65	5.52	10.76
Specified Death Benefit (DB) assuming 7.5%	306677	159527	87857	49253	619272	322120	177465	99968
First Year Premium (Minimum)	1244	825	level	level	2545	1700	level	level
Cash Value End of Year 20 at 7.5%	19963	16522	15131	14637	40302	33355	30563	29758
Cash Value End of Year 20 per 1000 Spec. DB	65.09	103.57	172.22	297.18	65.08	103.55	172.22	297.68
Level Annual Premium per 1000 of Spec. DB	2.45	4.70	8.54	15.23	2.42	4.66	8.45	15.00

Issue Age	$1000 LEVEL ANNUAL RENEWAL PREMIUM				$2000 LEVEL ANNUAL RENEWAL PREMIUM			
	Age 25	Age 35	Age 45	Age 55	Age 25	Age 35	Age 45	Age 55
Specified Death Benefit (DB) assuming 12%	880246	375130	180448	92576	1773439	755509	363305	186334
First Year Premium (Minimum)	3631	1985	1326	1106	7349	4030	2637	level
SPECIFIED DB | Cash Value End of Year 20	13386	9226	9215	9684	26992	18611	18591	19544
AND 7.5% | Cash Value per 1000 Spec. DB	15.21	24.59	51.07	104.61	15.22	24.63	51.17	104.89
INTEREST | DB and CV stop before	Age 60	Age 70	Age 80	Age 85	Age 60	Age 70	Age 80	Age 85
Level Annual Premium per 1000 of Spec. DB	1.14	2.67	5.54	10.80	1.13	2.65	5.51	10.73
Specified Death Benefit (DB) assuming 7.5%	410831	213701	117714	66150	827790	430573	237235	133800
First Year Premium (Minimum)	1678	1117	level	level	3413	2283	level	level
Cash Value End of Year 20 at 7.5%	26738	22129	20272	19674	53874	44585	40860	39847
Cash Value End of Year 20 per 1000 Spec. DB	65.08	103.55	172.21	297.41	65.08	103.55	172.23	297.81
Level Annual Premium per 1000 of Spec. DB	2.43	4.68	8.50	15.12	2.42	4.64	8.43	14.95

What premium should I pay for a given amount of insurance?

We believe the client should be protected from large future premium increases by planning to pay a premium based upon a conservative estimate of long-term interest earnings. Our choice is to assume 7½% interest for most calculations, although we would not quarrel with using a rate which is plus or minus a percent.

If a large lump sum premium is to be paid in the early years of the policy (but not so much premium as to violate Section 101(f)), then future renewal premiums could be *reduced* dramatically because current high interest rates compound rapidly. Even under these circumstances, however, the agent will want to project future earnings on a realistic basis.

Figures 5.7A-C are tables of approximate annual premiums which will provide various amounts of whole life insurance using the Universal Life policy. Note the premium per thousand of maturity value which decreases for bigger policies. This represents a quantity discount. The amount of discount is directly related to the interest, mortality and expense charges of the policy. The actuarial structure of the policy we have been discussing is such that the discount continues to increase as the size of the policy increases. There is no need for banded premiums. Interestingly enough, the company's commission structure pays full traditional commissions on all planned premiums up to the premium the company currently charges for its most competitive, traditional product.

The discounts available to non-smokers are generally larger than traditional whole life policies because the problem of deficiency reserves (discussed in an earlier chapter) is not present. Planned premiums for smokers are somewhat higher, giving an equitable rate structure. The higher premiums and extra deaths at older ages attributed to smoking lead to the smoker's cash values in the early policy years being higher than those of non-smokers.

145

Figure 5.7A

LEVEL ANNUAL PREMIUM (AND 1ST YEAR MINIMUM) TO PROVIDE SPECIFIED DEATH BENEFIT
MALE NONSMOKER - ENDOWMENT AT 85 PLAN - OPTION A

$25,000 SPECIFIED DEATH BENEFIT

Issue Age	Age 25	Age 35	Age 45	Age 55
Level Annual Renewal Premium assuming 12%	49	90	195	429
First Year Premium (Minimum)	103	111	218	482
SPECIFIED DB — Cash Value End of Year 20	606	1111	2004	3540
AND 7.5% — Cash Value per 1000 Spec. DB	24.24	44.44	80.16	141.60
INTEREST — DB and CV stop before	Age 65	Age 70	Age 75	Age 85
Level Annual Premium per 1000 of Spec. DB	1.96	3.60	7.80	17.16
Level Annual Renewal Premium assuming 7.5%	97	165	308	596
First Year Premium (Minimum)	103	level	level	level
Cash Value End of Year 20 at 7.5%	2258	4045	6868	11945
Cash Value End of Year 20 per 1000 Spec. DB	90.32	161.80	274.72	477.80
Level Annual Premium per 1000 of Spec. DB	3.88	6.60	12.32	23.84

$100,000 SPECIFIED DEATH BENEFIT

Issue Age	Age 25	Age 35	Age 45	Age 55
Level Annual Renewal Premium assuming 12%	187	341	753	1660
First Year Premium (Minimum)	509	541	774	level
SPECIFIED DB — Cash Value End of Year 20	2197	4350	8093	14082
AND 7.5% — Cash Value per 1000 Spec. DB	21.97	43.50	80.93	140.82
INTEREST — DB and CV stop before	Age 65	Age 70	Age 75	Age 85
Level Annual Premium per 1000 of Spec. DB	1.87	3.41	7.53	16.60
Level Annual Renewal Premium assuming 7.5%	360	631	1192	2314
First Year Premium (Minimum)	509	level	level	level
Cash Value End of Year 20 at 7.5%	8828	16028	27436	47809
Cash Value End of Year 20 per 1000 Spec. DB	88.28	160.28	274.36	478.09
Level Annual Premium per 1000 of Spec. DB	3.60	6.31	11.92	23.14

$50,000 SPECIFIED DEATH BENEFIT

Issue Age	Age 25	Age 35	Age 45	Age 55
Level Annual Renewal Premium assuming 12%	96	175	382	842
First Year Premium (Minimum)	238	254	403	level
SPECIFIED DB — Cash Value End of Year 20	1124	2170	4026	7074
AND 7.5% — Cash Value per 1000 Spec. DB	22.48	43.40	80.52	141.48
INTEREST — DB and CV stop before	Age 65	Age 70	Age 75	Age 85
Level Annual Premium per 1000 of Spec. DB	1.92	3.50	7.64	16.84
Level Annual Renewal Premium assuming 7.5%	185	321	603	1169
First Year Premium (Minimum)	238	level	level	level
Cash Value End of Year 20 at 7.5%	4439	8032	13719	23892
Cash Value End of Year 20 per 1000 Spec. DB	88.78	160.64	274.38	477.84
Level Annual Premium per 1000 of Spec. DB	3.70	6.42	12.06	23.38

$250,000 SPECIFIED DEATH BENEFIT

Issue Age	Age 25	Age 35	Age 45	Age 55
Level Annual Renewal Premium assuming 12%	457	836	1864	4111
First Year Premium (Minimum)	1320	1401	1887	level
SPECIFIED DB — Cash Value End of Year 20	5490	10922	20292	35102
AND 7.5% — Cash Value per 1000 Spec. DB	21.96	43.69	81.17	140.41
INTEREST — DB and CV stop before	Age 65	Age 70	Age 75	Age 85
Level Annual Premium per 1000 of Spec. DB	1.83	3.34	7.46	16.44
Level Annual Renewal Premium assuming 7.5%	882	1559	2958	5749
First Year Premium (Minimum)	1320	level	level	level
Cash Value End of Year 20 at 7.5%	22032	40035	68597	119565
Cash Value End of Year 20 per 1000 Spec. DB	88.13	160.14	274.39	478.26
Level Annual Premium per 1000 of Spec. DB	3.53	6.24	11.83	23.00

Figure 5.7B

LEVEL ANNUAL PREMIUM (AND 1ST YEAR MINIMUM) TO PROVIDE SPECIFIED DEATH BENEFIT
MALE SMOKER - ENDOWMENT AT 85 PLAN - OPTION A

$25,000 SPECIFIED DEATH BENEFIT

Issue Age	Age 25	Age 35	Age 45	Age 55
Level Annual Renewal Premium assuming 12%	73	148	330	747
First Year Premium (Minimum)	107	level	level	level
SPECIFIED DB — Cash Value End of Year 20	951	1705	2019	0
AND 7.5% INTEREST — Cash Value per 1000 Spec. DB	38.04	68.20	80.76	.00
DB and CV stop before	Age 60	Age 65	Age 70	Age 75
Level Annual Premium per 1000 of Spec. DB	2.92	5.92	13.20	29.88
Level Annual Renewal Premium assuming 7.5%	136	244	465	919
First Year Premium (Minimum)	level	level	level	level
Cash Value End of Year 20 at 7.5%	3309	5714	8677	12314
Cash Value End of Year 20 per 1000 Spec. DB	132.36	228.56	347.08	492.56
Level Annual Premium per 1000 of Spec. DB	5.44	9.76	18.60	36.76

$50,000 SPECIFIED DEATH BENEFIT

Issue Age	Age 25	Age 35	Age 45	Age 55
Level Annual Renewal Premium assuming 12%	142	291	649	1469
First Year Premium (Minimum)	246	level	level	level
SPECIFIED DB — Cash Value End of Year 20	1832	3426	4068	0
AND 7.5% INTEREST — Cash Value per 1000 Spec. DB	36.64	68.52	81.36	.00
DB and CV stop before	Age 60	Age 65	Age 70	Age 75
Level Annual Premium per 1000 of Spec. DB	2.84	5.82	12.98	29.38
Level Annual Renewal Premium assuming 7.5%	263	478	917	1814
First Year Premium (Minimum)	level	level	level	level
Cash Value End of Year 20 at 7.5%	6547	11388	17348	24655
Cash Value End of Year 20 per 1000 Spec. DB	130.94	227.76	346.96	493.10
Level Annual Premium per 1000 of Spec. DB	5.26	9.56	18.34	36.28

$100,000 SPECIFIED DEATH BENEFIT

Issue Age	Age 25	Age 35	Age 45	Age 55
Level Annual Renewal Premium assuming 12%	276	572	1284	2911
First Year Premium (Minimum)	524	604	level	level
SPECIFIED DB — Cash Value End of Year 20	3655	6888	8170	0
AND 7.5% INTEREST — Cash Value per 1000 Spec. DB	36.55	68.88	81.70	.00
DB and CV stop before	Age 60	Age 65	Age 70	Age 75
Level Annual Premium per 1000 of Spec. DB	2.76	5.72	12.84	29.11
Level Annual Renewal Premium assuming 7.5%	516	943	1818	3603
First Year Premium (Minimum)	524	level	level	level
Cash Value End of Year 20 at 7.5%	13049	22750	34701	49339
Cash Value End of Year 20 per 1000 Spec. DB	130.49	227.50	347.01	493.39
Level Annual Premium per 1000 of Spec. DB	5.16	9.43	18.18	36.03

$250,000 SPECIFIED DEATH BENEFIT

Issue Age	Age 25	Age 35	Age 45	Age 55
Level Annual Renewal Premium assuming 12%	677	1412	3187	7236
First Year Premium (Minimum)	1358	1559	level	level
SPECIFIED DB — Cash Value End of Year 20	9170	17273	20472	0
AND 7.5% INTEREST — Cash Value per 1000 Spec. DB	36.68	69.09	81.89	.00
DB and CV stop before	Age 60	Age 65	Age 70	Age 75
Level Annual Premium per 1000 of Spec. DB	2.71	5.65	12.75	28.94
Level Annual Renewal Premium assuming 7.5%	1271	2338	4522	8969
First Year Premium (Minimum)	1358	level	level	level
Cash Value End of Year 20 at 7.5%	32601	56854	86765	123400
Cash Value End of Year 20 per 1000 Spec. DB	130.40	227.42	347.06	493.60
Level Annual Premium per 1000 of Spec. DB	5.08	9.35	18.09	35.88

Figure 5.7C

LEVEL ANNUAL PREMIUM (AND 1ST YEAR MINIMUM) TO PROVIDE SPECIFIED DEATH BENEFIT
FEMALE NONSMOKER – ENDOWMENT AT 85 PLAN – OPTION A

$25,000 SPECIFIED DEATH BENEFIT

Issue Age	Age 25	Age 35	Age 45	Age 55
Level Annual Renewal Premium assuming 12%	34	76	157	317
First Year Premium (Minimum)	72	102	212	463
SPECIFIED DB | Cash Value End of Year 20	483	800	1738	4342
AND 7.5% | Cash Value per 1000 Spec. DB	19.32	32.00	69.52	173.68
INTEREST | DB and CV stop before	Age 60	Age 70	Age 80	Age 85
Level Annual Premium per 1000 of Spec. DB	1.36	3.04	6.28	12.68
Level Annual Renewal Premium assuming 7.5%	78	143	260	482
First Year Premium (Minimum)	level	level	level	level
Cash Value End of Year 20 at 7.5%	1994	3317	5910	11618
Cash Value End of Year 20 per 1000 Spec. DB	79.76	132.68	236.40	464.72
Level Annual Premium per 1000 of Spec. DB	3.12	5.72	10.40	19.28

$100,000 SPECIFIED DEATH BENEFIT

Issue Age	Age 25	Age 35	Age 45	Age 55
Level Annual Renewal Premium assuming 12%	126	289	605	1235
First Year Premium (Minimum)	384	505	749	level
SPECIFIED DB | Cash Value End of Year 20	1685	2995	6968	17460
AND 7.5% | Cash Value per 1000 Spec. DB	16.85	29.95	69.68	174.60
INTEREST | DB and CV stop before	Age 60	Age 70	Age 80	Age 85
Level Annual Premium per 1000 of Spec. DB	1.26	2.89	6.05	12.35
Level Annual Renewal Premium assuming 7.5%	285	542	1001	1862
First Year Premium (Minimum)	level	level	level	level
Cash Value End of Year 20 at 7.5%	7756	13092	23585	46519
Cash Value End of Year 20 per 1000 Spec. DB	77.56	130.92	235.85	465.19
Level Annual Premium per 1000 of Spec. DB	2.85	5.42	10.01	18.62

$50,000 SPECIFIED DEATH BENEFIT

Issue Age	Age 25	Age 35	Age 45	Age 55
Level Annual Renewal Premium assuming 12%	65	148	308	625
First Year Premium (Minimum)	176	236	391	701
SPECIFIED DB | Cash Value End of Year 20	883	1503	3469	8721
AND 7.5% | Cash Value per 1000 Spec. DB	17.66	30.06	69.38	174.42
INTEREST | DB and CV stop before	Age 60	Age 70	Age 80	Age 85
Level Annual Premium per 1000 of Spec. DB	1.30	2.96	6.16	12.50
Level Annual Renewal Premium assuming 7.5%	148	277	507	942
First Year Premium (Minimum)	176	level	level	level
Cash Value End of Year 20 at 7.5%	3903	6567	11796	23249
Cash Value End of Year 20 per 1000 Spec. DB	78.06	131.34	235.92	464.98
Level Annual Premium per 1000 of Spec. DB	2.96	5.54	10.14	18.84

$250,000 SPECIFIED DEATH BENEFIT

Issue Age	Age 25	Age 35	Age 45	Age 55
Level Annual Renewal Premium assuming 12%	303	706	1495	3050
First Year Premium (Minimum)	1008	1312	1825	level
SPECIFIED DB | Cash Value End of Year 20	4211	7528	17477	43563
AND 7.5% | Cash Value per 1000 Spec. DB	16.84	30.11	69.91	174.25
INTEREST | DB and CV stop before	Age 60	Age 70	Age 80	Age 85
Level Annual Premium per 1000 of Spec. DB	1.21	2.82	5.98	12.20
Level Annual Renewal Premium assuming 7.5%	693	1337	2478	4620
First Year Premium (Minimum)	1008	level	level	level
Cash Value End of Year 20 at 7.5%	19351	32689	58967	116336
Cash Value End of Year 20 per 1000 Spec. DB	77.40	130.76	235.87	465.34
Level Annual Premium per 1000 of Spec. DB	2.77	5.35	9.91	18.48

There is another question about the premium the client should pay which is frequently asked during the sales process for Universal Life. The answer will help you understand the third part of this chapter. The question is,

What is the effect on my cash value if I pay a higher premium on Universal Life?

Most Universal Life policies provide for a lower load on higher premiums which works to the advantage of the client. The lower load is invariably applied to lump sum premiums but also applies to premiums above a specified level, frequently called the "target" or "design" premium.

The computer easily shows the impact. Figures 5.8 and 5.9 show proposals using 7½% and 12% interest rates. Figure 5.8 assumes a planned premium of $1,000; Figure 5.9 assumes a planned premium of $1,500. Cash values in all policy years are higher by at least 62%, well above the 50% increase in premium. Traditional policies do not show this kind of improvement unless they have banded premiums with a heavy discount or very large policy fees. The lower load on a higher Universal Life premium gives the client added leverage.

It would be possible to increase the planned premium even more. On most Universal Life policies being sold today, the load on $2,000 annually, compared to $1,500, is sharply lower. The extra $500 on the Union Central policy increases the first-year cash value by approximately $500. However, in the proposal shown in Figure 5.9, a $1,500 annual premium generates a *guaranteed* cash value of nearly $100,000 at age 85. Therefore, a higher planned premium of $2,000 a year would lead (in ten years or so) to an excessive premium, as discussed in Chapter 8, "TEFRA 1982—Tax Issues and Guidelines." At that time, under current law, a decrease in the premium paid or an increase in the death benefit would be needed.

Figure 5.8
STANDARD PROPOSAL—$1000 Premium

STANDARD PROPOSAL - $1,000 PREMIUM   INITIAL SPECIFIED AMOUNT   100000
MALE, AGE 35

			CURRENT RATE 12.00%		ASSUMED RATE ***		GUART'D RATE 4.5%	
POLICY YEAR	AGE YR END	PLANNED OUTLAY*	CASH VALUE	**DEATH BENEFIT	CASH VALUE	**DEATH BENEFIT	CASH VALUE	**DEATH BENEFIT
1	36	1000	214	100000	201	100000	196	100000
2	37	1000	1143	100000	1081	100000	890	100000
3	38	1000	2176	100000	2019	100000	1604	100000
4	39	1000	3323	100000	3017	100000	2328	100000
5	40	1000 5000	4596	100000	4079	100000	3064	100000
6	41	1000	6009	100000	5207	100000	3811	100000
7	42	1000	7580	100000	6408	100000	4560	100000
8	43	1000	9324	100000	7683	100000	5322	100000
9	44	1000	11264	100000	9039	100000	6087	100000
10	45	1000 10000	13422	100000	10481	100000	6845	100000
11	46	1000	15826	100000	12016	100000	7606	100000
12	47	1000	18508	100000	13653	100000	8361	100000
13	48	1000	21502	100000	15398	100000	9099	100000
14	49	1000	24848	100000	17262	100000	9820	100000
15	50	1000 15000	28586	100000	19250	100000	10523	100000
16	51	1000	32766	100000	21371	100000	11198	100000
17	52	1000	37443	100000	23634	100000	11833	100000
18	53	1000	42679	100000	26049	100000	12428	100000
19	54	1000	48546	100000	28628	100000	12971	100000
20	55	1000 20000	55125	100000	31381	100000	13459	100000
25	60	1000 25000	100908	122099	48202	100000	14532	100000
30	65	1000 30000	177909	206375	72145	100000	11491	100000
35	70	1000 35000	311905	346215	105715	117344	0	0
40	75	1000 40000	545631	578369	151648	160746	0	0
50	85	1000 50000	1635605	1717386	304324	319540	0	0

PRESENTED BY I M SAVING   01/01/83

Figure 5.9
STANDARD PROPOSAL—$1500 Premium

STANDARD PROPOSAL - $1,500 PREMIUM   INITIAL SPECIFIED AMOUNT   100000
MALE, AGE 35

	AGE		CURRENT RATE 12.00%		ASSUMED RATE ***		GUART'D RATE 4.5%	
POLICY YEAR	YR END	PLANNED OUTLAY*	CASH VALUE	**DEATH BENEFIT	CASH VALUE	**DEATH BENEFIT	CASH VALUE	**DEATH BENEFIT
1	36	1500	500	100000	476	100000	467	100000
2	37	1500	1975	100000	1866	100000	1650	100000
3	38	1500	3619	100000	3354	100000	2878	100000
4	39	1500	5451	100000	4943	100000	4140	100000
5	40	1500 7500	7492	100000	6642	100000	5440	100000
6	41	1500	9768	100000	8456	100000	6781	100000
7	42	1500	12306	100000	10396	100000	8152	100000
8	43	1500	15137	100000	12468	100000	9569	100000
9	44	1500	18298	100000	14683	100000	11023	100000
10	45	1500 15000	21828	100000	17052	100000	12505	100000
11	46	1500	25774	100000	19586	100000	14031	100000
12	47	1500	30189	100000	22301	100000	15592	100000
13	48	1500	35131	100000	25212	100000	17182	100000
14	49	1500	40669	100000	28333	100000	18804	100000
15	50	1500 22500	46874	100000	31680	100000	20462	100000
16	51	1500	53832	100000	35271	100000	22150	100000
17	52	1500	61638	100000	39125	100000	23863	100000
18	53	1500	70402	100000	43262	100000	25606	100000
19	54	1500	80100	101727	47707	100000	27373	100000
20	55	1500 30000	90183	113631	52484	100000	29170	100000
25	60	1500 37500	161416	195313	82467	100000	38455	100000
30	65	1500 45000	285414	331080	120389	139651	48059	100000
35	70	1500 52500	501197	556329	174085	193234	57672	100000
40	75	1500 60000	877581	930236	250403	265427	67318	100000
50	85	1500 75000	2632861	2764504	504113	529319	95370	100139

PRESENTED BY I M SAVINGMORE   01/01/83

How does Universal Life compare with traditional fixed premium life insurance?

There is a simple way to answer this question. Begin by picking the traditional policy that you wish to compare. Let us begin with a guaranteed cost whole life policy. Input the premium actually charged by the company. Type in the level death benefit in response to the "11) SPECIFIED DEATH BENEFIT" PROMPT. Type "A" next to the "12) DB OPTION-B ADDS CV" PROMPT. (This is an abbreviation for "Death Benefit Option—Option B Adds Cash Value to the Death Benefit." "A" selects a level total death benefit for the Universal Life policy.) The computer accumulates the premium and shows the cash value for Universal Life using whatever rate or rates of interest you select. These cash values can easily be compared with the traditional policy's cash values.[2]

A little tinkering will reveal that an interest rate between 5% and 8% will produce comparable values. To determine which policy appears to be the better value, a judgment must be made of the ability of the Universal Life company to credit higher interest than is guaranteed under the guaranteed cost policy.

The comparison just described is quite simple. Except for older policies, it is not often encountered in practice. To compare with more recent adjustable premium plans and participating plans, the flexible premium and benefit capabilities of the program are needed. One simple technique is to treat the current dividend projections as being paid in cash. Answer "No" to the "8) LEVEL OUTLAY" PROMPT, and input the premium less dividend for the first 10 or 20 years. Alternatively, the premium may be kept level and the death benefit increased to reflect the face amount of paid-up dividend additions.

Whatever tool an agent has available, the answer to the ques-

---

[2] FIPSCO and other companies offer programs which will do the comparison automatically *and* print disclosure information required by state replacement regulations. See marketing question *M 3* in Chapter 10, "Questions and Answers."

tion invariably hinges on the level of interest rates assumed. The cash value of the traditional policy with which Universal Life is compared should include the value of dividend credits. Allowances should be made on an estimated basis for other factors such as:

- A possible increase in the rate of dividend accumulations which may be credited on a participating policy, and
- The taxation of interest credits on accumulation, or
- The impact on dividends, including dividends on additions, of continued high interest earnings.

Actuarial guidance on these matters would be useful if available. A close reading of Chapter 13, "The Replacement Issue" is advised.

How can I keep my policy current with inflation?

Inflation is on the minds of most people but it can be overcome with a Universal Life policy. Figure 5.10 is a typical proposal using a cost-of-living increase rider. In this proposal, the agent has assumed that inflation will average 6% per year. He types "Yes" in response to the "217) AUTOMATIC INCREASE" PROMPT, selects the cost-of-living rider, and types "6" when asked for the "ANNUAL % INCREASE." The proposal provides for the same $100,000 of initial death benefit as Figure 5.2. The cost-of-living rider increases the death benefit at a 6% rate, compounding up to attained age 65.

Rather than recommend a planned premium for a level amount, the agent uses another program option. The input proceeds as follows:

Figure 5.10
INFLATION PROPOSAL

INFLATION PROPOSAL
MALE, AGE 35

INITIAL SPECIFIED AMOUNT   100000

	AGE		CURRENT RATE 12.00%		ASSUMED RATE ***		GUART'D RATE 4.5%	
POLICY YEAR	YR END	PLANNED OUTLAY*	CASH VALUE	**DEATH BENEFIT	CASH VALUE	**DEATH BENEFIT	CASH VALUE	**DEATH BENEFIT
1	36	1500	500	100000	489	100000	467	100000
2	37	1545	2014	106000	1965	106000	1677	106000
3	38	1590	3741	112360	3619	112360	2956	112360
4	39	1635	5702	119102	5464	119102	4293	119102
5	40	1680	7922	126248	7516	126248	5685	126248
		7950						
6	41	1725	10428	133823	9793	133823	7132	133823
7	42	1770	13253	141852	12314	141852	8614	141852
8	43	1815	16427	150363	15097	150363	10144	150363
9	44	1860	19990	159385	18164	159385	11701	159385
10	45	1905	23984	168948	21539	168948	13258	168948
		17025						
11	46	1950	28457	179085	25250	179085	14824	179085
12	47	1995	33465	189830	29325	189830	16369	189830
13	48	2040	39067	201220	33799	201220	17857	201220
14	49	2085	45333	213293	38705	213293	19267	213293
15	50	2130	52329	226090	44074	226090	20576	226090
		27225						
16	51	2175	60136	239656	49942	239656	21732	239656
17	52	2220	68840	254035	56347	254035	22673	254035
18	53	2265	78540	269277	63328	269277	23354	269277
19	54	2310	89342	285434	70926	285434	23694	285434
20	55	2355	101362	302560	79181	302560	23631	302560
		38550						
25	60	2580	184591	404893	131492	404893	12484	404893
		51000						
30	65	2580	324621	541839	205186	541839	0	0
		63900						
35	70	2580	571020	633832	310524	574349	0	0
		76800						

PRESENTED BY I M PREPARED   01/01/83

Creating The Proposal

INFLATION PROPOSAL   INITIAL SPECIFIED AMOUNT   100000
MALE, AGE 35

* INCLUDES THE FOLLOWING RIDERS:

    RIDER   BENEFIT

    COST OF LIVING   6 % FOR 30 YEARS
       INSURED ONLY

OUTLAY PAYABLE ANNUALLY
NEGATIVE FIGURES INDICATE PARTIAL CASH SURRENDERS
INDICATES FEDERAL PREMIUM GUIDELINE LIMITATIONS ARE EXCEEDED

UNION CENTRAL'S CURRENT INTEREST RATE OF 12.00% MAY INCREASE OR DECREASE BUT
NEVER BELOW 4.5%.   THE RATE   ON THE FIRST $1000 OF CASH VALUE IS 1.5%   BELOW
THE RATES SHOWN, BUT NEVER BELOW 4.5%. THE OWNER MAY ADJUST THE FACE AMOUNT,
PREMIUM AND   DEATH BENEFIT OPTION TO INCREASE OR DECREASE   THE   ILLUSTRATED
BENEFITS.

**DEATH BENEFIT   OPTION   ***INTEREST RATE   THRU AGE
SPECIFIED AMOUNT   A   10.00%   70

5% INTEREST ADJUSTED SURRENDER COST INDEX	10 YEARS	20 YEARS
CURRENT	- 1.02	- 6.35
ASSUMED	0.42	- 2.54
GUARANTEED	5.29	7.02

AT LEAST ONCE EACH YEAR,   UNION CENTRAL WILL SEND THE OWNER A REPORT SHOWING
THE CURRENT CASH VALUE,   AMOUNT OF INTEREST CREDITED,   PREMIUMS   PAID,   CASH
SURRENDERS,   MONTHLY   EXPENSE CHARGES,   AND COST OF INSURANCE DEDUCTED SINCE
THE PRIOR REPORT.

THIS ILLUSTRATION IS NOT A CONTRACT.   THE COST OF THIS   POLICY   CANNOT   BE
COMPLETELY DETERMINED WITHOUT TAKING INTO ACCOUNT THE INTEREST THAT WOULD BE
EARNED   ON   THE PREMIUMS IF THEY HAD BEEN INVESTED RATHER THAN PAID   TO   THE
INSURANCE COMPANY.

13) MODAL OUTLAY: "1500", first year planned premium

203) ANNUAL OUTLAY CHANGE: "Y" requests special option

INCREASE OR DECREASE: "I" to request annual increase

ANNUAL % CHANGE: "3" for 3% per year increase

OF YRS: "25" (or "A60") to stop increases

The agent selected a premium increase of 3% for 25 years (or to age 60), expecting that this slow annual increase would not be a burden on the client until he nears retirement. This is likely to be the case since continued inflation should mean that high interest rates will continue to be credited to the Universal Life policy. With inflation running at 6%, as this proposal assumes, it is reasonable to use an assumed interest rate of more than $7\frac{1}{2}\%$. The agent used 10% in Figure 5.9.

Let us look at the effect of using different interest assumptions. The death benefit reaches $574,329 at age 65 when the cost-of-living increases stop. At age 70, the cash values corresponding to different rates are:

Assumed	Cash Value	Assumed	Cash Value
$7\frac{1}{2}\%$	$128,801	10%	$310,524
8%	$156,109	11%	$424,381
9%	$223,087	12%	$571,020

At 12%, the cash value is slightly less than the death benefit. (Incidentally, the level premium to age 70, which is needed to give the 10% cash value of $310,524, would be approximately $1,871.) To increase the cash value at age 70 to the $574,329 death benefit, the planned level annual premium is $2,666.

3) Universal Life Product Comparisons

The first 100 companies which offered Universal Life to the public pointed the way for future product development. Just as traditional policies were developed to serve all markets and marketing organizations, Universal Life contract features and compensation methods have proliferated. At least one company has advertised that it offers five different Universal Life products, each designed for a specific set of circumstances.

In spite of their early attraction to the product, consumerists may come to abhor this diversity because it complicates the process of competitive comparisons. The situation in which more than one product is available to the same buyer from the same company will likely be viewed as especially troublesome. Nevertheless, this situation was to be expected. The competitive pressures, experimentation with alternative commission structures, and federal income tax uncertainties of the early 1980s encouraged a rush of different policy designs. The transparent operation of Universal Life policies does not make the decision of which policy to buy an easy matter.

Now that the reader has a better grasp of the benefit and cost relationships of Universal Life, let us discuss the considerations involved when a comparison of nontraditional policies is to be made.

The approach used for the rest of this chapter is to discuss three aspects of Universal Life comparisons: 1) the role of interest; 2) policy factors other than interest; and 3) the use of published comparisons, including an extensive example from various policies.

The Role of Interest

The first aspect of comparing nontraditional policies is to emphasize the importance of the interest rates which may be credited to the policy or policies under study.

If the agent and client believe that a product which utilizes an index approach will, in combination with other policy features, provide the best assurance of adequate interest earnings, then a decision may be made favoring a product which uses this approach. Those policies which allow more discretion on the part of company management must be analyzed with attention to the investment abilities and reputation of the company for fair dealing with its policyholders. Since performance records on Universal Life policies are limited, this analysis will be difficult.

One possibility is to examine the company's past results with respect to other interest sensitive products, such as IRAs. Another approach is to obtain data with respect to the investment returns on new investments made by the company in the current period of high interest rates.

Subjective evaluations for the future are important. What is the company's record of providing dividend increases on its traditional participating business? Will its past practices carry over to the Universal Life product line? It should be noted that the willingness of a company to credit the highest possible interest rates will be a function of its overall financial and competitive posture. The interrelationships of interest and other policy factors is important in the actuarial recommendations which must be made regularly to company management. Although we offer some further insights in the next part of this chapter, a thorough examination of all the possibilities is not practical.

Factors Other than Interest

An important aspect of any comparison is to evaluate the impact of mortality and loading factors on the client's cost. A fairly simple technique isolates the interest factor by comparing products using the same, or nearly the same, interest rate. (The reason for hedging with the words "nearly the same" is that different practices with respect to interest paid on the first

$1,000 of cash value result in a slightly different interest rate structure even when the computer is programed to use the same percentage. This variation is significant for smaller policies which have cash values of less than $3,000 or so for several years after issue.)

To accomplish this comparison, the agent needs access to a computer or proposal service, such as Computone or a home office service unit, for each of the products being compared. The agent can then fix the interest rate at a level consistent with long-term expectations and obtain proposals using the same planned premiums and equivalent death benefits. The specific proposals should be those which answer the client question or questions discussed earlier.

With the interest rate fixed, the policy which produces the highest cash value after a period of years is the policy which, in general, will be found to have the most favorable combination of mortality and loading. A number of precautions need to be kept in mind.

Variations by issue age, amount, or underwriting class can be critical. Don't be misled by general comparisons that are made in trade advertising materials. Companies invariably push the best features of their product line. Their comparisons may concentrate on a standard plan, say a non-smoker's $100,000 Option A at ages such as 35 or 45. The company may assert that this product is ranked near the top of all Universal Life policies. But all issue ages and underwriting classes are not created to be equally competitive. Indeed, a company which strains to meet a particular competitive goal will generally be less competitive elsewhere.

A classic example is the relative cost of insurance charges used for smokers as compared with non-smokers. A comparison of costs for smokers is complicated by the different patterns of cash values which emerge on Universal Life, and the fact that statistical services commonly do not give comprehensive information regarding this type of risk. As a second example, a high first-year cash value relative to the planned premium may be thought of as a positive factor, all other things being equal. But other things are seldom equal. Unless the policy has a very low load (and usually low commissions), a higher first-year value forces the company's actuary to be cautious in setting the renewal cost factors. The cash value in 10, or perhaps better, 20 years is a more helpful indicator of the client's cost. Of course, a client who surrenders his policy after one year is better off with a high first-year cash value. If such an early surrender seems likely, term insurance coupled with a money market fund is more suitable than any permanent insurance policy, traditional or Universal. In short, the agent who relies on information provided by the companies or oversimplified comparisons may well be led in the wrong direction.

Future benefit and premium increases cannot be ignored.

The Universal Life policy can function as a lifetime contract. A comparison of benefit increase options available without evidence of insurability is in order. Does the company offer a cost-of-living rider? Is guaranteed insurability available? Will the company underwrite planned increases at issue, or must evidence be provided when the increased benefits go into effect?

The impact of future charges when benefit or premium increases take place will be significant. This can be roughly evaluated by assuming simple patterns of future increases for each of the policies being considered. One suggestion is to prepare proposals with a 50% increase in both the specified death benefit and planned premium at the end of 5 and 10 years. Then one could compare the cash values at the end of 20 and 30 years, using constant interest rates. In addition to checking out these points, a direct comparison of loading charges may be helpful, especially if one or more lump sum premiums are anticipated.

Comparisons at equal interest rates are imperfect.

It is easy to assume that Company A and Company B will credit interest of, say, 8% over the next 20 years. However, when the actuarial approach to pricing the policies is considered, the correctness of this assumption is called into question. Consider the case wherein the interest earnings of both companies drop to 9%. Will both companies be likely to credit 8%? (We will ignore changes in the cost of doing business for purposes of this example.) Consider these hypothetical differences in pricing approaches.

Suppose Company A used a relatively low load at issue, relying on continued high interest rates to recapture its initial expenses of selling and issuing the policy. Company A must have a larger interest margin when rates drop, and could decide to pay 7½% instead of 8%. Suppose Company B used a relatively higher mortality table for its current cost of insurance, and that its future mortality experience looks promising to the actuary. Company B may be able to defer a decrease in its interest rate and still maintain a reasonable profit.

Recent Comparisons

For general comparisons, we have found the numbers in the book, *Interest-Adjusted Index* (published annually by The National Underwriter Co.) to be helpful. Upwards of 100 Universal Life policies are summarized in the 1983 edition. To emphasize the variation in policy factors other than interest, the following figures, adapted from this book, compare cash values at a constant interest rate of 8%.

We have compared 30 policies from 30 companies. Most, if not all, of these policies are available on a preferred risk or non-smokers basis in minimum specified amounts of $25,000 to $50,000. To facilitate comparison, the figures use Option A,

Why Universal Life

Figure 5.11A

AGE 25 - 8% Interest - $100,000 Specified Death Benefit - AGE 25
$750 ANNUAL PLANNED PREMIUM $1,250 ANNUAL PLANNED PREMIUM

Co. Code	CASH VALUES END OF YR 1	YR 10	YR 20	CV Ratio to Avg.	CASH VALUES END OF YR 1	YR 10	YR 20	CV Ratio to Avg.
104	243	8390	26543	1.13	567	15324	49158	1.05
101	355	8337	26303	1.12	850	15537	49332	1.05
102	109	7922	25889	1.10	474	14820	48185	1.03
103	480	8013	25311	1.07	983	15572	49609	1.06
107	169	7720	24881	1.06	669	15386	49137	1.05
109	567	8022	24727	1.05	1068	15509	48857	1.04
119	508	7998	24685	1.05	985	15273	48221	1.03
114	214	7765	24660	1.05	691	14835	47358	1.01
111	242	7639	24480	1.04	740	14905	47757	1.02
112	313	7631	24139	1.02	822	14787	47087	1.00
110	237	7569	24082	1.02	738	14879	47580	1.01
108	359	7561	24021	1.02	859	14878	47537	1.01
116	314	7672	23989	1.02	815	15019	47660	1.01
118	503	7867	23919	1.02	990	15152	47467	1.01
105	287	7344	23800	1.01	732	14801	47790	1.02
113	171	7423	23755	1.01	682	14906	47885	1.02
106	207	7345	23550	1.00	690	14605	46887	1.00
125	178	7485	23292	.99	674	14912	47327	1.01
115	112	7389	23281	.99	621	14816	47227	1.00
124	195	7205	22794	.97	677	14456	46194	.98
128	222	7275	22461	.95	722	14604	46214	.98
127	307	7253	22461	.95	781	14405	45566	.97
117	0	6897	22273	.95	315	14110	45553	.97
123	171	6794	22148	.94	656	14050	45513	.97
126	33	6813	21840	.93	462	13884	44762	.95
120	143	6773	21568	.92	623	14000	44906	.96
130	225	6845	21537	.91	702	14039	44790	.95
122	32	6666	21469	.91	512	13880	44758	.95
121	118	6725	21462	.91	598	13950	44795	.95
129	0	6669	21211	.90	454	14020	45098	.96

162

and a level death benefit of $100,000. Two annual premium levels, a low and a high, are included as follows:

Issue Age	Low Premium	High Premium
Male 25	$ 750	$1,250
Male 35	1,000	1,500
Male 45	1,500	2,000

Figure 5.11B should be studied first. This gives the comparison at issue age 35. In this figure, the policies are ranked by the 20th year-end cash values for the low annual premium amount of $1,000. For example, Company 101 has the highest 20th year-end cash value of $33,399. Company 102 has the next highest cash value of $33,382, and so forth. These rank numbers are kept the same for the other comparisons. By this device, a company which has a high ranking at a given age and premium level may more easily be seen to rank differently at another age or premium level.

Look at Company 106 for issue age 35. Using the same low premium and 20th cash value combination, the company ranks second for issue age 45; but its competitive position is just average for issue age 25. It may be that the company's mortality charge is relatively low for older issue ages, or its loading is relatively high for younger issue ages. Possibly a combination of such factors is at work. If the case is for $5,000,000, a detailed actuarial analysis would help discover the cause. The general comparison alerts the agent to the difference and could lead to a different purchase decision for different buyers.

These figures end our short course on "Creating the Proposal." We leave it to the reader to review those points which he finds most useful. To close, we offer the following observations.

- Note the variations in the cash value per dollar of premium. The leverage factor for higher premiums is apparent.
- Compare the cash value at the end of year 10 with 10

times the annual premium shown in the Figure headings. The client could have more cash than premiums paid into the contract after 10 years, using the middle interest rate of 8%. All 30 companies reach this level for the $1,250 annual premium at issue age 25. Only one company achieves this result using a $1,500 premium at issue age 45, reflecting the higher cost of insurance for this age.

- Compare the cash value ratios to the average 20th year cash value for each of the issue age and premium combinations. For example, in Figure 5.11B the competitive spread is from 14% above the average to 13% below it. Considering the comparison uses an 8% constant interest rate, the point made earlier that all Universal Life products are not designed to be equal is clear.

CHAPTER 6

Policyholders and Taxes—the Legal Background

The future of Universal Life depends upon whether it will be subject to the same tax treatment as any typical whole life insurance policy, i.e.:

1) whether the death benefit, consisting of the cash value plus pure death benefit, will be received, except in certain instances, income tax free under Section 101 (a) (1) of the Internal Revenue Code; and

2) whether the increments in cash value, even if borrowed, will not be taxed to the policyholder while the policy is in full force and effect.

The tax questions concerning Universal Life were largely resolved by The Tax Equity and Fiscal Responsibility Act of 1982 (TEFRA), as will be discussed in Chapter 8. However, the legislation affecting Universal Life insurance is only temporary.

167

It is scheduled to expire December 31, 1983. Thus, we believe it is important to understand the legal foundation upon which Universal Life is built as a life insurance product. If TEFRA is not continued past 1983 or some later extension, the tax discussion in this chapter will once again govern the tax treatment of Universal Life.

Basic characteristics of Universal Life have been discussed in earlier parts of this book. The tax discussion will assume the following additional facts most of which, we believe, are essential to the favorable tax treatment of Universal Life:

A) only one reserve is maintained by the insurer for the benefits provided by the policy;

B) the cash value of the policy is the same as the reserve under the policy;

C) the policy is a single integrated whole and does not consist of component parts available to the policyholder under a choice of several contracts, such as an annuity contract with term insurance riders;

D) the amount of pure death benefit is at least the greater of $10,000 or 10% of the cash value throughout the life of the insured. This is a change from at least one Universal Life contract which requires a pure death benefit of only $10,000 (not 10% of the cash value);

E) partial surrender of the policy cannot be made without the imposition of some surrender charges;

F) interest charged on borrowing under the contract is in excess of that credited on the borrowed amounts;

G) the contract contains the normal non-forfeiture provisions and has a standard suicide clause and incontestable language;

H) the policy reserves are treated as life insurance reserves by the insurer.

In our analysis, we will focus on established principles of law regarding the taxation of any life insurance contract to the policyholder. We will analyze in some depth the two main tax issues: whether the death proceeds of the Universal Life contract qualify as life insurance proceeds and whether the cash value build-up of the Universal Life contract occurs income tax free.

1. WHETHER UNIVERSAL LIFE QUALIFIES AS A LIFE INSURANCE CONTRACT UNDER SECTION 101 (A) OF THE INTERNAL REVENUE CODE.

Section 101 (a) (1) of the Internal Revenue Code provides that with certain exceptions, gross income does not include amounts received under a life insurance contract, if such amounts are paid by reason of the death of the insured. The answer to the question as to what constitutes life insurance for tax purposes is not well defined. Neither the Internal Revenue Code nor its regulations set forth with any precision a definition of life insurance. Consequently, our discussion of what constitutes life insurance must be based on the many court decisions and IRS rulings that have wrestled with this question.

In the leading case on the fundamentals of what constitutes life insurance, Helvering v. LeGierse, 312 U.S. 531, 539 (1941), the Supreme Court stated: "Historically and commonly insurance involves risk-shifting and risk-distributing." Later, the Supreme Court held in S.E.C. v. Variable Life Insurance Co. 359 U.S. 65 (1959) that a contract that has no element of fixed return has no true risk in the insurance sense and, therefore, cannot be classified as a life insurance contract.

The concept of risk shifting and risk distributing has received the most emphasis by the courts. As was quoted by Commissioner of Internal Revenue v. Treganowan, 183 F.2d 288, 291 (2d Cir. 1950): "Risk shifting emphasizes the individual aspect of insurance: The effecting of a contract between insurer and the insured each of whom gamble on the time the latter will die. Risk distribution, on the other hand, emphasizes the broader, social aspect of insurance as a method of dispelling of the danger of the potential loss by spreading its cost throughout the group ... " Note, The New York Stock Exchange Gratuity Fund: Insurance That Isn't Insurance, 59 Yale L.J. 780, 784.

In analyzing whether the Universal Life contract contains the proper elements of risk shifting and risk distribution to be a life insurance policy under Section 101 (a) of the Code, the following legal issues will be considered:

a. *Whether the contract can be split into two distinct and independent policies.*

The Universal Life policy could possibly be interpreted to be a combination annuity policy and term life insurance policy. If the policy were to be split for income tax purposes, in all likelihood, the portion attributable to an annuity would not be income tax free at death under Section 101 (a).

As an indication of the Service's position on split contracts, Private Letter Ruling 8047051 examined an individual, flexible consideration deferred annuity that provided for adjustable term life insurance coverage ranging from a minimum of $25,000 to a maximum of $150,000. Withdrawals were made from the annuity cash value to purchase a life insurance contract. Three options were permitted by the contract relative to the insurance coverage. One option permitted the term insurance to decrease to correspond to increases in the cash value of the annuity which made the contract look very similar to a typical whole life contract. In refusing to treat the combination policy as a life insurance policy for tax purposes, the Service based its decision on the following aspects of the policy:

i) The contract was clearly set up as a separate annuity contract and life insurance contract.

ii) The options permitted by the contract emphasized the fact that the annuity should be treated separately from the life insurance. In fact, the pure life insurance protection could be increased or decreased at the election of the policyowner. The Service noted that, in a typical endowment contract, the insurance protection relative to the investment element cannot be adjusted.

The Service also noted that, although the contract may not be severable under contract law, the severability of the contract is not conclusive as to how the contract should be treated for tax purposes.

In Mosely v. Commissioner, 72 T.C. 183 (1979), acq. 1980-1 C.B.1, the Court examined the distribution from a special reserve account of a life insurance policy which provided a specific death benefit. Under the policy, part of the premiums paid in years two through five were credited to the special reserve account. This special reserve account was combined with amounts paid by other policyholders in a fund which invested in common stocks. In the 20th year of the policy, distribution was paid on each policy if the following conditions were met:

I) The insured was then living, II) the policy was in full force on a premium paying basis, and III) all due premiums were paid.

The Commissioner had advanced the argument that the special reserve and death benefit provisions in the policy constituted two distinct and economically independent policies. The Commissioner argued that the distributions from the policy should be treated as income in the amount by which the distribution exceeded the amount of money that had actually been placed in the special reserve account. The Court held that the special reserve provisions were inseparable from the life insurance provisions of the policy and thus the taxpayer's basis in the policy was the total premiums paid. It noted that the company did not offer for sale a policy which contained only the special reserve provisions. Therefore, the taxpayer could not have purchased the special reserve benefits without the life insurance benefit.

The Mosely case is the leading case on the non-severability of a contract for tax purposes and is our primary authority for analyzing the severability of the Universal Life contract.

The Universal Life policy is not designed as a combination annuity, term life insurance contract. It is set up as a whole life insurance contract and, like any typical whole life insurance policy, only one reserve fund is maintained by the insurer for the benefits under the contract. Also, the policy has its own special provisions which distinguish it from other products typically offered by a life insurance company. These special provisions are the following:

i) The cash value accumulates at a higher interest rate than is available under other standard whole life policies.

ii) The cash value can be borrowed from the policy which cannot be done with most single premium deferred annuities.

iii) The pure death benefit can be varied which is not available under other typical whole life insurance policies.

These three characteristics, plus the basic structure of the Universal Life contract, prevent it from being considered as anything other than a single, integrated whole.

b. *Whether the Universal Life Policy has a sufficient amount of risk to qualify as Life Insurance.*

Once the determination is made that the Universal Life policy is a single policy that cannot be split into two or more parts, the determination still has to be made whether it qualifies as life insurance.

Most cases which have considered whether a policy constitutes life insurance have examined the combination purchase of an annuity and a life insurance policy. This combination purchase can be within a single policy as demonstrated by Old Colony Trust v. Commissioner (1st Cir. 1939) 102 F.2d 380; Revenue Ruling 75-255; 1975-2 C.B. 22 or, as has more generally been the case, through the purchase of separate contracts.

In Helvering v. LeGierse, supra, the Supreme Court considered whether Section 302 (g) of the Revenue Act of 1926 (which provided an exemption from federal estate taxation for the proceeds of life insurance less than $40,000.00) was applicable in a case where the decedent purchased a single premium life insurance policy at the same time she purchased an annuity from an insurance company. The Court refused to treat the life insurance contract as life insurance because the total premiums paid for the annuity plus life insurance exceeded the face amount of the life insurance policy. The Court noted that the purchase of an annuity and life insurance are opposites, and that in this combination one neutralizes the risk customarily inherent in the other. From the insurance company's viewpoint, insurance is related to longevity, annuity to transiency. Any risk that the prepayment in this case would earn less than the amount paid to respondent was an investment risk similar to the risk assumed by a bank, and thus was not an insurance risk.

LeGierse has been followed in other cases such as Keller v. Commissioner, 312 U.S. 543 (1941); Commissioner v. Meyer, 139 F.2d 256 (6th CA 1943); and Goldstone v. United States, 144 F.2d 373 (2d Cir. 1944). In all of these cases, the amount paid for the annuity and the single premium life insurance contract was *in excess of* the total amount of life insurance coverage. Thus, there was no risk other than an investment risk assumed by the insurer as long as the annuity contract was maintained in combination with the life insurance contract.

If a policy or combination of policies does not create an insurance risk, the proceeds paid upon death will not be excludable from income under Section 101 (a) (1) of the Internal Revenue Code, Kess v. United States, 451 F.2d 1229 (6th Cir. 1971); Revenue Ruling 65-57, 1965-1 C.B. 56.

Based on the foregoing discussion, the policy must exhibit, at the time the policy is issued, the proper risk-shifting and risk distribution to qualify for the favorable tax treatment afforded a life insurance policy under IRC Section 101 (a) (1). If the policy provides a significant, pure death benefit at the time of its purchase and spreads this risk over the insured group in accordance with proper actuarial standards, it falls outside of the non-risk situations analyzed by LeGierse and its progeny and should qualify as life insurance.

In the course of our investigation, we have talked with several officials at the IRS who were largely responsible for Private Letter Ruling 8116073 (the Private Letter Ruling on the E. F. Hutton CompleteLife Universal Life policy). One of the officials indicated the Service is reviewing its policy of what constitutes life insurance and is delaying the issuance of future private letter rulings. One of the questions presently being examined by the IRS is, "How much life insurance coverage is sufficient to make a policy that has an investment element a life insurance policy?" The Service has previously held that a death benefit of only 5% in excess of the cash value constitutes life insurance (LTR 8132119). However, as mentioned above, the IRS is not obligated to follow its prior private letter rulings.

If the amount of pure death benefit provided by the Universal Life policy is at least $10,000 or 10% of the policy's cash value, whichever is greater, then this should create enough of a mortality risk for the Universal Life policy to be determined to be a life insurance policy within the LeGierse holding. However, if the amount of life insurance coverage is a stated amount (such as $10,000) and does not depend upon the amount of cash value, situations can be envisioned where the policy would not qualify as life insurance—such as where the pure insurance coverage is $10,000 and the cash value is $1,000,000. Every time the insurance coverage is changed under the Universal Life contract, the determination as to whether a sufficient insurance risk exists must be made anew.

  c. *The effect of variable death benefits.*

The Universal Life policy, unlike most typical whole life insurance policies, may provide a total death benefit which increases or decreases during the life of the insured. Variable death benefits are present in many different types of life insurance contracts and do not destroy the life insurance nature of the contract. In Revenue Ruling 79-87, 1979-1 C.B. 73 variable life insurance death benefits that may increase or decrease, but not below a guaranteed minimal amount, depending upon the investment experience of the separate account of the prior year's net premiums, are classified as life insurance and proceeds therefrom are excludable under Section 101 (a) (1) of the Code.

Also, while private letter rulings cannot be used or cited as precedent, Private Letter Ruling 8116073 is evidence of the last known IRS position. This ruling examined the E. F. Hutton CompleteLife Universal Life policy that provided for flexible premiums payable during the lifetime of the insured and provided an adjustable death benefit payable at death prior to the maturity date and the cash value payable on the maturity date. Under this policy, the policyholder had the option to choose one of two death benefit options. Under Option 1, the amount of life insurance equaled a specified amount designated by the policyowner, or if greater, a level amount fixed in the policy (in this case $10,000.00), plus the policy's cash value at the date of death. Under Option 2, the amount of life insurance equaled a specified amount designated by the owner plus the policy's cash value on the date of death. The specified amount could be changed from time to time at the request of the policyowner, always subject to the minimum stated in the policy. Because the insurance policy always provided a specified amount of insurance and the cash value was equivalent to the cash value under a more typical or traditional life insurance contract, the IRS held in this private letter ruling that the death benefit plus cash value under the policy would constitute an amount paid by reason of death under a life insurance contract and would be non-taxable under Section 101 (a) (1) of the Code.

Private Letter Ruling 8120023 ruled favorably on a variable life insurance policy that used excess interest under the policy to purchase paid-up additions. The cash value of the variable insurance amount (the amount in excess of the initial insurance amount promised under the contract) was the net single premium for the amount of additional insurance. The Service relied on Revenue Ruling 79-87 in making its favorable determination.

Based upon the foregoing we conclude the possibility that the total death benefit provided by the Universal Life policy may vary does not cause it to be other than whole life insurance.

d. *Reserves under the Universal Life contract.*

Since the Universal Life contract is a life insurance policy, we can conclude that the cash value will qualify as life insurance reserves. The following discussion supports this conclusion.

Section 801 (b) of the Internal Revenue Code provides in relevant part:

> The term "life insurance reserves" means amounts
>
> (A) which are computed or estimated on the basis of recognized mortality . . . tables and assumed rates of interest, and;
>
> (B) which are set aside to mature or liquidate, either by payment or reinsurance, future unaccrued claims arising from life insurance . . . contracts . . . involving, at the time with respect to which the reserve is computed, life . . . contingencies.

With exceptions not here relevant, in addition to the above requirements, "life insurance reserves must be required by law."

The cash value (or reserves) under the Universal Life policy meet all three of the statutory requirements. First, as is true with many typical whole life insurance policies, the reserves under the policy are computed using a guaranteed rate of $4\frac{1}{2}\%$

or 5½% and using the Commissioners 1958 Standard Ordinary Mortality Table or another accepted mortality table.

Second, the reserves for the Universal Life policy will be set aside to provide for the payment of future unaccrued claims arising under the contract. As discussed above, the Universal Life contract is a life insurance policy. At all times with respect to which the reserves might be computed, the contract involves life contingencies because the benefit payable upon death is significantly greater than the surrender value.

Third, because the cost of insurance is calculated on the basis of the excess of the total death benefit over the policy reserves, the cost of insurance deductions from the reserves will be insufficient by themselves to fund payment of the total death benefit. These deductions will also be insufficient to fund payment of the policy's surrender value or of its projected benefit at maturity. The laws of all jurisdictions, therefore, require the insurance company to maintain for the Universal Life policy reserves that correspond to the reserves of a typical whole life policy. Consequently, the Universal Life reserves satisfy the statutory test for being life insurance reserves.

In Private Letter Ruling 8116073, the facts of which were reviewed above, the Service stated the following with regard to the reserves under the contract:

> If the cash value is nothing but a side fund, similar to a premium deposit account, then the amount of such cash value would not be an amount paid under a life insurance contract.

> However, if the cash value is, in fact, equivalent to the cash value or reserve under a more traditional life insurance policy, then the total death benefit can be compared with the death benefit equal to the face amount plus the cash value under such traditional life insurance policies.

> Under the policy, each net premium paid at the beginning of a period is considered to be a net single premium

which, together with the reserve at the end of the previous period, will purchase insurance coverage for a period of years and days, or for a period of years and a pure endowment at the end of the period.

Based on the foregoing, the IRS concluded that the reserves were computed on the basis of a mortality table and assumed rate of interest and they qualified as life insurance reserves.

e. *Continuation of the Universal Life Policy as a life insurance contract.*

Having concluded that a Universal Life policy is life insurance, we should examine whether it will continue to be a life insurance policy until its maturity. Revenue Ruling 66-322, 1966-2 C.B. 123 held that a contract which has a true insurance risk at its purchase and provides the insurance risk for many years does not lose its nature as an insurance contract at the time that the insurance risk disappears. This Revenue Ruling examined the distribution of retirement income contracts from a qualified plan and held that, until the retirement income contracts were actually converted into annuity contracts, they would be treated as life insurance contracts for income tax purposes. The distribution of a life insurance contract would cause the beneficiary to be taxed on the cash value of the contract at its time of distribution. This ruling was criticized in A. Rolph Evans v. Commissioner, 56 T.C. 1142 (1971), which held that retirement income contracts become annuity contracts at the time that the risk disappears.

Although Evans disagreed with Revenue Ruling 66-322, both authorities hold that if a contract is a contract of life insurance when purchased, it continues as a contract of life insurance until such time as the investment portion of the contract equals or exceeds the total benefits available at death.

Based on the foregoing authorities, if a policy is life insurance when it is purchased, it should continue as life insurance until such time as the cash value equals or exceeds the benefit provid-

178

ed at death under the policy. Thus, the Universal Life policy, if it qualifies as life insurance when it is purchased, should continue as life insurance until such time as the policy matures for its cash value. However, if the structure of the death benefit under the Universal Life contract dramatically changes, such as if the pure death benefit is reduced from $100,000 to $10,000, the policy would have to be subjected to a de novo test with regard to whether it qualifies as life insurance.

Section 72 (e) of the IRC governs the tax treatment of amounts received under an annuity, endowment or life insurance contract where such amounts are not received as an annuity. Chapter 8, "TEFRA 1982-Tax Issues and Guidelines," discusses the changes that have been made in the tax treatment of withdrawals and loans from annuity products. As previously discussed, the Secretary of the Treasury could, by regulation, cause withdrawals and loans from a Universal Life contract to be treated the same as withdrawals or loans from an annuity contract. We do not think this will or should happen.

Assuming the tax treatment of Universal Life is not changed by regulation, the law states and would continue to state that amounts received from a Universal Life contract would be taxed to the extent that they exceed the aggregate premiums paid. Clearly, this would apply to the surrender or partial surrender of the Universal Life policy.

2. WHETHER THE ANNUAL INCREASES IN THE CASH SURRENDER VALUE OF THE UNIVERSAL LIFE POLICY ARE TAXABLE INCOME TO THE POLICYOWNER.

Section 72 (e) of the Code determines the amounts received under an annuity, endowment, or life insurance contract to be included in gross income where such amounts are not paid as an annuity. Section 72 (e) (1) provides that where an amount is received before the annuity starting date, it shall be included in gross income, but only to the extent that it (when added to amounts previously received under the contract which were excludable from gross income) exceeds the aggregate premiums or other consideration paid. Section 72 (e) would apply to the surrender or partial surrender of the Universal Life policy.

In addition, amounts will be considered to be received under the Universal Life policy for purposes of Section 72 (e) if the taxpayer is determined to be in constructive receipt of the cash value build-up of the policy.

Regulation Section 1.451-2 sets forth the general rule with respect to the constructive receipt of income. This regulation provides that income is constructively received by a taxpayer

"in the taxable year in which it is credited to his account, set apart for him, or otherwise made available so that he may draw upon it at any time or so that he could have drawn upon it during the taxable year if notice of intention to withdraw had been given. However, income is not constructively received if the taxpayer's control of its receipt is subject to substantial limitations or restrictions."

The courts and the IRS have long recognized that the necessity to surrender a valuable right in order to obtain an amount prevents contructive receipt of that amount. Estate of W. T. Hales, 40 B.T.A. 1245 (1939), acq. 1940-1 C.B. 2, Rev. Rul. 58-230, 1958-1 C.B. 204; Cohen v. Commissioner, 39 T.C. 1055 (1963), acq. 1964-1 C.B. 4. There are only two ways to receive funds from the Universal Life policy before the policyholder's death - surrender (in whole or in part) of the policy or through policy loans. As the following analysis will show, each involves the surrender of valuable rights, and thus there is no constructive receipt by the policyowner.

a. *The surrender in whole or in part of the contract.*

If the policyholder completely surrendered the policy, he would be forced to forego the pure death benefit provided by the contract. It is well settled that when a policyholder can receive the cash surrender value of a policy only by forfeiting the right to receive a death benefit greater than such surrender value, the cash surrender value is not constructively received. Griffith v. United States, 245 F. Supp. 678 (D.N.J. 1965) aff'd per curia 360 F.2d 210 (3rd Cir. 1966). Furthermore, if the policyholder were to attempt to purchase a new contract, he would have to establish insurability, which might not be possible, and would have to pay new loading charges.

If the policyholder makes only a partial surrender of the policy, he is required to pay a surrender charge and to give up the favorable investment returns on the policy's cash value. Moreover, if the policyholder desired to repay the surrendered amount, it would be subject to new loading charges. Thus, there would be a significant decrease in the policy's cash surrender value attributable to the policyholder's surrender and subsequent repayment. The IRS has held in Rev. Rul. 68-482, 1968-2 C.B. 186 that a policyholder is not in constructive receipt of the build-up of cash under a policy if the cash value of the surrendered contract will not normally purchase a new policy of comparable or greater value. This principle should apply to partial or whole surrender of the Universal Life contract.

Under Private Letter Ruling 8111054 the Service examined a nonparticipating whole life policy that automatically provided paid-up additions of life insurance under specified conditions, at no additional premium. Included in the policy were two riders. One rider allowed an index addition to be converted to one year term insurance. The other rider allowed the index addition to be surrendered for its cash value. No part of the cash value of an index addition could be withdrawn except upon full surrender of the index addition. In such a situation, equivalent benefits could not be purchased from the insurance company because the purchaser would have to incur new loading charges. The Service relied on Revenue Ruling 68-482 discussed above and

Section 72 (e) of the Code in holding that neither the crediting of an index addition to the policy nor the increase in the cash value of the policy is included in gross income prior to the surrender of the policy.

Private Letter Ruling 8116073, as clarified by Private Letter Ruling 8121074, indicates the above discussion, in the eyes of the IRS, may not extend to the interest paid in excess of the minimum guaranteed under the contract. Arguably, the case precedent requires that the excess interest be subject to a different analysis since it is a pure investment return and is not part of the initial guaranteed life insurance reserve.

Even if the build-up of the excess interest is treated differently from the guaranteed interest, it should still be governed by the doctrine of constructive receipt. In the case of Universal Life, the excess interest under the policy is treated by the insurance company exactly the same to the policyholder as the guaranteed interest. Thus, the tax treatment of the guaranteed interest and of the excess interest to the taxpayer should be the same. Since there is a substantial limitation or restriction on receipt of the cash value, whether that cash value is attributable to the guaranteed interest or excess interest, the cash value increases attributable to the excess interest should also occur tax free.

Private Letter Ruling 8116073 mentioned above and the clarification of it in Private Letter Ruling 8121074 provide helpful information as to the tax treatment of excess interest credited to the cash value of a policy. Under these rulings the IRS noted the taxpayer would not be in constructive receipt of increases in reserve increments, since these reserve increments (in excess of what was guaranteed under the contract) were either attributable to an adjustment in the reserve requirement (if the policy were determined to be a nonparticipating policy) or were attributable to dividends (if the policy were determined to be a participating contract) in which case the dividends were used to purchase paid-up additions. In either case, the cash value build-up would not result in taxable income to the policyholder. In this Private Letter Ruling, the Service stated with regard to the possibility of the increased interest return being treated as a dividend:

> Policyholder dividends would not be considered to be income to the policyowner until the sum of all dividends received exceeds the sum of all premiums paid, pursuant to Section 72 (e) (1) (B) of the Code. Any such dividends, since they must be applied to purchase paid-up insurance under the policy, would be considered as premiums paid for such paid-up insurance.

Based on this discussion, the build-up of excess interest on the Universal Life policy should occur tax free.

The above discussion notwithstanding, if the IRS should determine that excess interest is a dividend to the policyholder, the implications are considerable. This is especially true if the dividend is considered a simple addition to the policy's cash value. Increases in the cash value in later years which arise from the dividend may be treated as a taxable accumulation similar to the interest credited on dividend accumulations under traditional participating contracts.

b. *Borrowing from the Universal Life Contract.*

Obtaining a policy loan also involves a penalty to the policyholder. First, the policyholder must pay interest on the amount borrowed. Second, the typical Universal Life contract pays no excess interest on the portion of the policy that is subject to a policy loan. This means the cash value of the policy increases at a slower rate if there is a loan outstanding. These factors involve such a substantial forfeiture of rights under the contract that the right to obtain a policy loan does not trigger constructive receipt.

Generally, interest paid on borrowing from a Universal Life

contract will be tax deductible under IRC Section 264 if four out of the first seven years premiums have been paid without the aid of any borrowing. However, there is an exception under IRS Section 264 if in any years (during the first seven or later) there is a *substantial* increase in premium. In this situation, the four out of seven year qualification period begins anew. Care must be taken with this contract that the policy is tax qualified before advice is given that the interest will be deductible.

There is another important issue with regard to the policyholder's ability to borrow from the Universal Life contract. Suppose a policyholder borrows from the Universal Life contract in an amount in excess of premium paid. Will the excess be taxed to him as ordinary income? The IRS may take the position that such loans are really distributions from the contract subject to possible taxation under IRC Section 72 (e). The IRS has made this argument with regard to loans made from Section 403 (b) annuity contracts.

Such "loans", according to the IRS, are not really loans but rather prepayments received under the contract. Revenue Ruling 81-126, 1981-17 I.R.B. *at* 6; Revenue Ruling 67-258, 1967-2 C.B. 68. The Service's position is based first on the fact that the contract requires the insurance company to make the loan so that access to the funds involved in the loan has been certain from the inception of the relationship between the insurer and the policyholder; and second on the fact that the loan need never be repaid out of the recipient's pocket, but rather may be repaid by a reduction in the amount which the insurer eventually must pay on the contract (Revenue Ruling 81-126). These same two factors are present in the Universal Life policy with regard to the ability of the policyholder to borrow from the contract.

The question of the tax treatment of borrowings from an annuity in excess of premium paid has been examined by the tax court's decision in Robert W. and Mary F. Minnis, 71 T.C.

1049 (1979) which held contrary to Revenue Ruling 67-258, the forerunner to Revenue Ruling 81-126, that the borrowing on an annuity contract was not a distribution subject to tax treatment under IRC Section 72 (e). In this case, the Tax Court held the borrowing constituted a bona fide indebtedness and consequently was not a distribution from the contract. The Court noted that policy loans have generally been regarded as a valid form of indebtedness for purposes of determining a taxpayer's federal income tax liability and that despite the insurance company's lack of recourse against the borrower, in most cases interest paid on a policy loan is deductible as was the case with the borrowing on the annuity policy before the Tax Court. Perhaps most relevant to the question of borrowing on a Universal Life policy, the tax court stated essentially that a loan is a loan is a loan and that it can not become income simply by rationalizing it as income. On page 1055 the Court recited:

> Finally, we think it appropriate for us to recognize that the transaction involved herein constituted a loan in ordinary parlance. In this context, the comment of the Supreme Court that "Common understanding and experience are the touchstones for the interpretation of the revenue laws" (see Helvering v. Horst, 311 U.S. 112, 117, 118 (1940) is highly relevant. See Primuth v. Commissioner, 54 T.C. 374, 381-382 (1970) (concurring opinion). *This is particularly true when one recognizes that loans have traditionally not been considered taxable income, even when the source of repayment is limited to particular property and involves no personal liability.* See Falkoff v. Commissioner, 62 T.C. 200, 206 (1974); 1 J. Mertens, Law of Federal Income Taxation, §5.12 (1974), and cases collected therein. (emphasis added)

Finally, the Court noted that if the proceeds of the annuity were not taxed at the time of the policy loan, the proceeds in all likelihood would be taxed at the time of the maturity of the policy. This later fact is not necessarily the case with a Universal Life policy.

The IRS chose not to acquiesce in Minnis, supra, and used Revenue Ruling 81-126 as its forum for stating its nonacquiescence. Nevertheless, the IRS position in Minnis, supra, has been codified in TEFRA.

Although a Universal Life policy is represented to be a policy of life insurance and not directly covered by either Revenue Ruling 81-126 or Minnis, supra, the IRS may challenge the borrowing from the Universal Life policy as a distribution governed by IRC Section 72 (e). The aspects of the policy that make it vulnerable are the following:

  i) the insurer is required to make a loan of the cash surrender value to the policyholder;

  ii) the policyholder is not required to repay the loan or any interest on the indebtedness;

  iii) there may be tax avoidance reasons to borrow from a policy if the interest is deductible under IRC Section 264; and

  iv) if the policy cash value increments are not taxed at the time of the borrowing in the policy, these increments will never be taxed if the policyholder retains the policy until the death of the insured.

If the IRS is successful in challenging the validity of the borrowing under the contract and the amounts borrowed under a Universal Life policy are treated under IRC Section 72 (e) as an amount not received as an annuity, the policyholder will be taxed as ordinary income on any amounts borrowed that exceed the policyholder's total premium payment—the same as would be true on a partial surrender of the contract.

Also, if the IRS rules adversely on loans and withdrawals from Universal Life contracts under TEFRA, such loans and withdrawals will be taxable to the extent of income within the contract, in the same manner as for annuity contracts.

Summary

The Universal Life policy is essentially structured like any typical whole life insurance contract and should be given the same tax treatment.

The more important issues regarding the tax ramifications of the Universal Life policy are:

1) whether the pure death benefit as a percentage of the cash value of the policy is sufficient to cause the policy to be treated as a policy of life insurance rather than as an annuity or other investment contract;

2) whether the cash value portion of the policy operates as an integral part of the policy or whether it is simply a side fund investment; and

3) whether policyholders will be permitted to borrow tax free from a policy in an amount in excess of the policy-holder's basis in the contract.

CHAPTER 7

Company vs. Company vs. IRS

The public has been bombarded with advertising and articles urging the investment of money at high interest returns. Money market products have proliferated since 1978, offering current interest rates that have gone as high as 18%. Tax free municipal bonds have been available at a return of 15%. Three-year certificates of deposit have offered 18%. Even the new all-savers certificate at its inception provided a tax free return in excess of 12%. It is not surprising that bundles of money have been moved from low return passbook savings accounts and transferred into higher return investments.

The life insurance industry has not been immune to the changes caused by high interest investment opportunities. In July of 1979, the FTC released a report asserting that consumers who purchased whole life insurance were losing billions of dollars each year because the Commission staff judged that the average return paid on savings associated with whole life policies was about 1.3%. (See our critical discussion in Chapter 1, "Origins of the Universal Life Policy.") In addition, the 185 page report criticized the insurance industry for its failure to inform consumers about "truth in purchasing life insurance." Even without this damaging report, the insurance industry would doubtless have been hurt by the repercussions of the wave of high interest rates.

Billions of dollars have been withdrawn from the cash value of policies to be placed in higher yielding investments. Traditional whole life insurance, because of its low interest return, has been losing its attractiveness, unless presented on a "minimum deposit basis" in which case it is planned that the investment dollars will be withdrawn from the insurance company after a period of time.

The life insurance industry has been forced to respond. Since investment opportunities offered by life insurance companies permit the build-up of interest on a tax free or tax deferred basis, the life insurance industry has always had a decided advantage in attracting and holding investment dollars. However, in an era of high interest rates, even the tax free nature of a cash value build-up is not enough to offset the relatively low interest returns available under traditional products.

The industry's response has been made, in part, through annuity products which have flourished. In 1981 alone, one company collected over 1.5 billion dollars *in premiums* on its single premium deferred annuity product. Other high yield life insurance products have been developed at an accelerating pace. Many of these products are discussed in some detail in Chapter 9, "How Others Expect to Compete." So in this regard, Universal Life is just one product of many that has been developed to respond to the wave of high interest rates.

Why has Universal Life developed as a major response to the public's quest for higher interest? First, as discussed previously, the consumer likes the product. It is easy to understand and offers a high rate of return. Second, and of prime importance, a rapidly growing number of insurance companies have identified a marketing thrust with Universal Life. Now these companies have an insurance contract that encourages the consumer to place his investment dollars with the insurance company and leave them there. After the initial loading charge of 7½% to 10% and a policy fee of up to $600, the cash value of the policy is credited with interest at a high current rate of, say 12%, tax deferred and tax free if the policy is maintained until the death of the insured. If money is borrowed from the policy, an interest rate of 5% to 8% is charged, and the borrowed funds are credited with only the guaranteed rate, say 3% to 5%. Overall there is a considerable incentive to the policyholder to leave his money with the insurance company. If the policyholder is in a 50% tax bracket, he would have to find a 24% before-tax investment return to compete with his 12% tax free return on the Universal Life policy.

How Long Can the High Interest Continue?

The question most often asked about the Universal Life policy is, "How long will the high interest continue?" The question is critical. Many approaches in the past have proven to be inadequate. The brief discussion below summarizes a general view, admittedly in an oversimplified way.

Interest rates fluctuate up and down depending on many things. Economic theories on cause and effect abound. In the long run, interest rates charged by lenders will vary directly with the inflation rate. This is because the inflation rate signals how much a consumer can expect a typical product to appreciate in price over time. If you borrow money at an interest rate equal to the inflation rate, you effectively pay no interest because whatever you have purchased increases in price by the amount of inflation.

Suppose you borrow $100,000 at 10% to purchase a home that will increase in value because of inflation to $110,000 at the end of the year. When you repay the $10,000 interest at the end of the year, you have effectively borrowed money at no net cost to you.

Thus, interest rates in the long run must exceed the inflation rate. Historically, the economists tell us the interest rate has been 2% to 3% in excess of the inflation rate over long periods of time.

Consequently, if and when the inflation rate comes down and stays down, all interest rates will drop, including the interest available under the Universal Life policy. However, the return available on typical whole life insurance, including dividends, will also be lower. If interest rates stay high for a long period of time, the return on whole life insurance will continue to increase. Therefore, the more meaningful question is, "Can Universal Life continue to offer an interest return on the policy's cash value which (1) will be in excess of the return available under typical whole life insurance, and (2) be competitive with after-tax interest rates available through other investments?"

Insurance companies have available to them the same types of investment opportunities that are available to other types of financial institutions. The primary charges insurance companies must incur are (1) commissions to agents, (2) administrative expenses, and (3) taxes including premium taxes. All three are incurred by all financial institutions in one form or another. Banks, for example, spend money on advertising and employ people who are responsible for new business instead of paying a direct commission on new business.

The cost that is not common to other financial institutions, mortality cost, is charged directly against the policyholder's cash value. After allowing for mortality cost, there is nothing about the makeup of insurance companies or of the Universal Life policy which prevents the interest return from being comparable to that available from non-insurance financial institutions. Whatever the difference, it should be more than offset by the tax free or tax deferred nature of the cash value under a life insurance product.

Nevertheless, there are two key characteristics of the Universal Life contract which can affect its future ability to return high interest. The first is the commission structure of the policy. The second is the insurer's treatment of the excess interest under the Universal Life contract.

Commissions paid for sales of the early Universal Life policies were generally lower than those available under a typical whole life contract. This did not make Universal Life contracts popular with some agents. For example, E. F. Hutton developed the CompleteLife Universal Life contract in the fall of 1980. This was a low commission product. Hutton then developed another Universal Life contract which provided higher commissions. All other things being equal, higher commissions will have to be charged over a period of time against the policy's cash value.

This must lower the effective rate or return to the policyholder. Consequently, the commission structure of each insurance company's Universal Life contract will have a significant bearing on the interest available under the contract. The variation in commissions available under Universal Life contracts pose an interesting dilemma for the agent. Should he sell a high commission, low cash value policy and charge no advisory fee, or should he sell a low commission, high cash value policy and attempt to collect an insurance advisory fee?

The insurer's treatment of the excess interest under the Universal Life contract is of primary importance to the high interest return on the Universal Life contract. The interest in excess of that guaranteed under the contract has been treated as a reserve increment, directly deductible against the insurer's profits. If, on the other hand, the excess interest has to be treated as

193

a dividend, the additional benefits will have to be charged against the insurer's after-tax profits. Depending upon the tax position of the company, this could substantially reduce the amount of excess interest that the insurer would be able to credit on the cash value. The same difficulty arises if the difference between current and guaranteed mortality costs is considered to be a dividend.

Mutual companies historically have only made payments in excess of guaranteed interest in the form of dividends. Thus, most mutual companies feel at a disadvantage when it comes to the treatment of the excess interest under the Universal Life contract. In fact, Massachusetts Mutual filed a ruling request in the summer of 1981 that the excess interest and reduction in costs on two Universal Life contracts, one offered by a stock company and the other by a mutual company, be treated exactly the same and that both be treated as dividends. As you can imagine, the Massachusetts Mutual ruling request was not embraced by many other insurance companies. Equitable Life Assurance Society of the United States has filed a rebuttal in which it strongly argues against the adoption of Massachusetts Mutual's requested rulings. Because of the importance of this issue we have included, at the end of this chapter, a complete discussion of the arguments made by each side.

Contrary to our predicted outcome in the first edition, the IRS did issue the rulings requested by Massachusetts Mutual. These rulings were quickly superseded by TEFRA. Nevertheless, the deductibility of excess interest continues to be an important question and there are several reasons why. First, the legislation affecting Universal Life is only temporary. Second, the legislation only creates a safe harbor. It does not resolve the issue of deductibility of interest not covered by the safe harbor. Third, the IRS rulings are not binding on any party other than the taxpayer requesting them. Because we believe the question will continue to be important, we have included our full discussion on the Massachusetts Mutual, Equitable ruling request battle in this chapter.

Indexing, which several Universal Life companies have already done, ties the total interest credited under the policy to some known rate. The first major company to use this approach was Life of Virginia which indexed to long-term U.S. government bonds. They were followed several months later by Transamerica Occidental which indexed to the 90-day T-Bill rates. If the Universal Life policy is indexed, the interest under the policy can only be credited on a prospective basis. The thinking is that excess interest guaranteed in advance cannot be treated as a dividend. Dividends are payments that are made on a retrospective ("looking backwards") basis and indexing would seem to make it impossible for the IRS to treat the excess interest credited on the policy as a retrospective payment. However, the IRS may argue substance over form. There is no assurance that indexing completely circumvents the problem.

Also, the indexing of a Universal Life contract may cause the contract to be treated for purposes of securities laws as variable life insurance. If this should be the case, the policy would have to be registered and could only be sold by a licensed security broker.

In November of 1981, the California Department of Insurance initiated regulatory discussion regarding special company reserve requirements for indexed policies. If an index is stated in the policy, New York insists that companies demonstrate the appropriateness of their investment strategies. The legal, actuarial and investment aspects of emerging new requirements will doubtlessly develop slowly over several years.

Mortality Charges—the Hidden Interest Cost

Any discussion of the interest credited under the Universal Life contract would be incomplete without looking at the importance of the mortality charges. Since the mortality charges generally reduce the cash value of the Universal Life contract before the current interest is credited, the mortality charges can have a substantial effect on the build-up of the cash value. Thus, the cost of the pure death benefit under a Universal Life contract which is at a rate unfavorable to the policyholder offsets to some extent the favorable high interest. A comparison of Universal Life contracts, therefore, involves more than simply a comparison of loading charges and interest rates. In fact, over a long period of time, the better whole life contracts, based on current dividend projections, will provide a higher cash value than some of the weaker Universal Life contracts, even with their high current interest projections. It is clear that low mortality costs under a Universal Life contract are an important part of the benefits offered to policyholders.

Company Tax and Universal Life

As discussed earlier in this chapter, Universal Life policies have been issued by stock companies which have treated the excess interest and reductions in cost of insurance as deductible expenses. Many mutual companies, which are locked into the specialized procedures for surplus distribution traditional to participating policies, object strenuously to the competitive disadvantage at which they find themselves. As is readily apparent, it is much preferable for a company to provide additional benefits to policyholders (excess interest) where those benefits are (essentially) fully deductible for company federal income tax purposes than to distribute dividends which are partially deductible.

Massachusetts Mutual Life Insurance Company (Mass Mutual) filed a ruling request with the Internal Revenue Service on or about July 1, 1981, which, we believe, is representative of the thinking of a number of mutual companies. In its request, Mass Mutual asked for a determination by the IRS that the excess benefits provided by a Universal Life contract be treated as dividends and not as expenses deductible to the insurer. In order to put itself in a position to make such a ruling request, Mass Mutual formed a subsidiary company domiciled in Delaware called MM Life Insurance Company. Mass Mutual then developed two typical Universal Life products, one offered by Mass Mutual itself called Policy M, the other offered by its stock subsidiary called Policy S. The only differences between the two policies were that Policy M had a participation right and Policy S did not; and Policy M also contained a disclosure that stated: "We do not expect a dividend surplus to be available for allocation to this policy." This disclosure was put in the policy to indicate that the insurer would not provide dividends in the traditional sense. Policy S excluded the disclaimer because the stock subsidiary could not issue participating policies.

As could be expected, not all insurance companies were overjoyed with Mass Mutual's ruling request. What is surprising is that the company which filed a lengthy rebuttal of Mass Mutual's ruling request is another mutual company, the Equitable Life Assurance Society of the Unitied States ("Equitable"). Equitable has a wholly-owned stock life insurance subsidiary. Equitable also has developed a nontraditional product, Variable Life (see Chapter 9, "How Others Expect to Compete"). Since the Service's position on the tax treatment to the insurer of the excess benefits provided by a Universal Life contract is of vital importance to the future of Universal Life, we feel it is desirable to discuss, in some detail, the pros and cons of the issues presented to the IRS by Mass Mutual and Equitable.

Even after the IRS makes its determination, we believe the legal issues presented herein will be of prime importance. The IRS is not a court of last resort. It is not a court of any sort. Its "final" determination is likely to be challenged in court, especially if that determination is adverse to Universal Life.

Mass Mutual has requested four rulings from the IRS. Only

Rulings 3 and 4 are objectionable to Equitable so it is these rulings on which we will focus, although the first two ruling requests deserve some mention. All headings and subheadings are from the draft of the Mass Mutual ruling request which have been made available to us.

RULING 1:

The Reserves for both Policy M and Policy S are "Life Insurance Reserves" as That Term is Defined by IRC Section 801 (b) and Treas. Reg. § 1.801-4.

We embrace this ruling and have presented a discussion of the policy reserves determination in Chapter 6, "Policyholders and Taxes—the Legal Background." Essentially, the reserves under each policy qualify as life insurance reserves because they are based on an assumed rate of interest and mortality cost and are a part of the total death benefit available to the policyholder in the event of the death of the insured.

RULING 2:

For Purposes of Life Insurance Company Income Taxation, Annual Interest Payments in Excess of the Policies' Minimum Interest Rate and Annual Reduction in the Cost of Insurance Below the Policies' Maximum Cost of Insurance Will Be Characterized In the Same Way Under Policy M As They Are Under Policy S.

A) In determining the tax treatment of participating and nonparticipating policies, Congress sought to strike an equitable balance based on the economic differences between the two policies.

Most participating policies are set up conservatively so the premium charged provides the insurer with a margin of safety. Dividends are then paid that represent both price reductions (deductible from income) as well as investment gains. To equalize the treatment to participating companies and nonparticipating companies, only the portion of the dividend that is deemed to come out of investment gains is treated as a nondeductible dividend to the insurer.

B) State law is concerned with formalistic concepts of Participation and Nonparticipation and therefore is not controlling for Federal Tax Purposes.

State law places certain requirements on policies issued by a mutual company that are not placed on policies issued by a stock company. However, state law may have little to do with the economic realities of benefits provided by the policies issued by a stock company which may, in certain circumstances, be deemed to be essentially a participating contract. Treas. Reg. §1.809-5 (a) (5) (ii). Thus, the determiniation of whether a policy is participating or not for federal income tax purposes can not be made on mere formalistic state law labels.

C) Economically, Policies M and S are Identical and Should Be So Treated for Federal Tax Purposes.

Mass Mutual structured its two policies to be economically identical. Thus, it would seen reasonable that the two policies would be treated the same for federal tax purposes. However, it is at this point that the interest of stock companies and mutual companies are at odds. Equitable did not challenge this point because, being a mutual company, it has little to gain by this dichotomy.

Rulings 3 and 4 will now be discussed together.

RULING 3:

Under both Policy M and Policy S, any difference between the policies' permanently guaranteed maximum cost of insurance and the amount actually charged by the company shall be treated as a policyholder dividend that was distributed to the policyholder and then immediately paid-back as a net premium to the insurance company.

RULING 4:

Under both Policy M and Policy S, any interest paid in excess of the minimum rate permanently guaranteed in the policy shall be treated as a policyholder dividend that was distributed to the policyholder and then immediately paid-back as a net premium to the insurance company.

A) An economic benefit provided to a policyholder should be characterized as a "dividend" if it possesses the distinctive economic characteristics of a dividend.

(Mass Mutual) Benefits available under policies take many different forms such as paid-up additions, cash, or reduced premiums. Even if policyholders do not have the right to receive cash, the benefit may still constitute a dividend. The form in which the benefit passes to the policyholder is not helpful in characterizing the benefit as a dividend or as something else. The key is whether an economic benefit is passed on to the policyholder.

(Equitable) A dividend is defined in the regulations as an amount returned to the policyholder where the amount is not fixed in the contract but depends upon the experience of the company or the discretion of the management, Treas. Reg. §1.811-2 (a). The state law concept of a dividend is that the policyholder must have the option to receive a dividend in cash. This ties in with the regulation which speaks of only amounts returned or refunded. Thus, the additional benefits provided by a Universal Life policy do not have the form of a dividend. If the policyholder wants the additional benefits in cash, he must surrender the contract. And a substantial limitation exists against the policy being surrendered for its cash value. (See discussion in Chapter 6, "Policyholders and Taxes—the Legal Background.")

(Mass Mutual) There is no practical difference between temporary guarantees of excess interest or the annual declaration of cash dividends. If a mutual company could avoid dividend treatment by replacing annual dividend declarations with annual guarantees, the limitation imposed in the deductability of policyholder dividends by Code Section 809 (f) would be circumvented, thereby contravening the policy of the 1959 Act.

(Equitable) The purpose of the 1959 Act was to equalize the tax treatment between stock companies and mutuals. If annual guarantees are not dividends to stock companies then they also should not be dividends to mutual companies. It begs the question to assume that annual guarantees must be treated as dividends by mutual companies and therefore should be treated as dividends by stock companies.

(Mass Matual) Under the regulations, dividends are described as periodic economic benefits passing from the insurer to the policyholder which have the following three attributes:

1) which are in excess of the benefits that are permanently fixed in the contract, either in amount or by formula, Treas. Reg. §1.811-2 (a);

2) which are made available to policyholders as a result of an exercise of discretion on the part of the management of the insurer, Treas. Reg. §1.811-2 (a); and

3) whose source is an undivided mixture of earnings from investments and earnings from underwriting, Treas. Reg. §1.811-2(a); Reg. §1.809-5 (a) (5) (ii); Republic National Life Insurance Company v. United States 594 F.2d 530 (5th 1979), aff'd in relevant part 77-1 U.S. T.C. (CCH ¶9133) 86,138 (N.D. Tex. 1976.)

The economic benefits of excess interest and reductions in the cost of insurance, as will be discussed below, have the above three attributes.

(Equitable) Definitionally, a dividend is not simply an economic benefit. It is an amount returned or refunded to the policyholder which is not fixed in the contract and which is a retrospective allocation of divisible surplus or depends upon the experience of the company, Treas. Reg. §1.811-2 (a). A dividend must be based on divisible surplus at the end of the year and an amount is not a year-end dividend if its calculation depends on experience factors after the close of the taxable year. Rev. Rul. 67-180, 1967-1 C.B.172. Rev. Rul. 79-260, 1979-2 C.B.262. Furthermore, a dividend is paid from divisible surplus, not just from general company profits. The regulations are very specific on the definition of a dividend and Mass Mutual is attempting to broaden these regulations beyond their intended scope.

B) Reductions in the Cost of Insurance Posses the Distinctive Characteristics of a Dividend.

(Mass Mutual) Both policies permit the insurer to grant reductions in the rates the company will charge for the pure death benefit provided by the policy. This reduction is at the discretion of the management and is made from earnings on investments and from underwriting. Since these reductions possess all three characteristics of a dividend, they should be held to be dividends.

(Equitable) The reduction in cost of pure death benefit extends to a future time and is not made from profits already earned. In fact, the company surplus may be negative when the policyholder receives the actual benefits. The reduction in cost of the pure death benefit as well as the excess interest is based on market conditions and, if a Universal Life policy is to stay competitive, it must base its guarantee for the current period primarily on prevailing market rates and only secondarily on anticipated company experience for such period. Thus, like the annual interest guarantees, the reduction in costs of the pure death benefit coverage are not dividends.

C) The Economic Benefit of Reductions in the Cost of Insurance Cannot Properly be Characterized Other Than As A Dividend.

(Mass Mutual) The reductions in the cost of insurance cannot be ignored. The policyholder is in the same position as if he had applied a formal dividend to purchase a paid-up addition. The reductions in the cost of insurance are not return premiums. This is because the insurer must rely primarily on the insurer's overall profit picture in deciding whether to declare a reduction. Republic National Life Insurance Co. v. United States 594 F.2d 530 (1979), aff'd in relevant part 77-1 U.S. T.C. (CCH ¶9133) 86,138 (N.D. Tex. 1976). Finally, the reductions in cost of insurance represent neither interest paid, since there is no indebtedness nor discounts on prepaid premiums since no premiums have been prepaid.

(Equitable) Again, there is no support for an "economic benefit" to be considered as a dividend unless it falls within the strict definition provided by the regulations. Here, the benefit does not qualify as a cash benefit. Also, the doctrine of receipt of economic benefit has never been applied in a case of a bargain purchase by a taxpayer from an unrelated party. Thus, there is no precedent for treating a reduction in cost of a policy as a dividend to the policyholder.

D) Excess Interest Possesses the Distinctive Characteristics of a Dividend.

(Mass Mutual) Excess interest is a discretionary benefit by which an insurance company conveys an economic benefit to policyholders. Since it represents a share of the company's earnings from both investment and underwriting, it satisfies the three-prong test set forth above for being a dividend.

(Equitable) The function of the excess interest, like the reduction in cost of the pure death benefit, is to guarantee to the policyholder in advance policy benefits which are expected to be provided by future earnings at the risk of the insurance company. In times of high inflation and volatile interest rates, annual advance guarantees involve very significant risks not present in dividend payments based on past performance. Also, unlike dividend payments which are credited on a policy's anniversary, annual advance guarantees accrue ratably and do not disappear if the policy is surrendered prior to its anniversary date.

E) The Economic Benefit of Excess Interest Cannot Properly be Characterized Other Than A Dividend.

(Mass Mutual) The crediting of excess interest is economically the same as if a cash dividend were conveyed to the policyholder who then used the benefit to purchase a paid-up addition. Because of the new contractual liability, the insurer must effect a corresponding increase in its reserve. This is a different situation than reserve strengthening whereby an insurer sets aside additional assets to cover its existing level of commitment to policyholders.

The increase in the insurer's commitment to the policyholder is indistinguishable from the purchase by the policyholder of additional insurance. Thus, the excess interest payment has the same benefit to the policyholders as a cash distribution and purchase of new insurance.

Stated more technically, a direct reserve increment would result in an imbalance between the prospective and retrospective methods of calculating reserves. If the excess interest were not treated as the payment of an economic benefit to the policyholder who then added that benefit to the policy, the retrospective reserve would exceed the prospective reserve.

Finally, the excess interest does not qualify as interest paid on indebtedness since there is no indebtedness and thus does not fall under IRC Section 805 (e) (i).

(Equitable) While the crediting of excess interest may take on the same form to the policyholder as though the policyholder had elected a paid-up addition, the effect is very different for the insurance company. As discussed above, the insurer takes on a risk that is not present with dividend payments and the payment is not made from divisible surplus.

The retrospective, prospective calculation only has merit where the plan of insurance (i.e. the amount of insurance, the period of coverage, the premium payment schedule, the cost of insurance, and the interest rate) is defined and fixed at issue.

Under a Universal Life policy these elements vary, and thus there is no reason to think that the retrospective reserve will equal the prospective reserve. In fact, all that the difference shows is that some benefit has been credited under the policy. It does not mean that an amount has been returned or refunded to the policyholder as must be the case with a dividend.

Even if Mass Mutual is right that excess interest and reductions in the cost of insurance constitute an economic benefit, these benefits, not being dividends, would be fully deductible under IRC Section 809 (d) (1).

Mass Mutual Response

Mass Mutual submitted a response to the Equitable comment, by letter, dated December 9, 1981. In its response, Mass Mutual reemphasized the following three points.

1) A dividend does not have to be a retrospective payment. Treas. Reg. §1.811-2 (a) provides a dividend is an amount returned to the policyholder when the amount is not fixed in the contract but depends upon the the experience of the company or the discretion of management. Thus, management discretion is sufficient to require excess interest and cost reductions to be treated as dividends. Moreover, the word "experience" does not relate only to past events. It can refer to what the company expects to happen in the future.

2) Prospective and retrospective reserve calculations for flexible life insurance policies must remain equal if all the relevant elements are properly taken into account. If the prospective and retrospective methods are not equal, it is because certain policy benefits are included in one calculation but not another. The only way to make them equal is by treating the excess interest and cost reductions as a dividend.

3) As a matter of policy, Congress intended that life insurance companies pay some tax on investment income distributed to policyholders. This policy extends to the taxations of distribution to policyholders of investment income. Excess interest and cost reductions are the same as the distribution of investment income.

Summary and Conclusions

If we may generalize, Mass Mutual is essentially arguing substance over form. Equitable, on the other hand, is arguing that the formalistic requirements of dividends must be adhered to and, in addition, that excess interest and reduction in cost of insurance are very different in *substance* from dividend treatment.

One of Mass Mutual's key assertions is that payments made at the discretion of the board of directors should be treated as a dividend. In fact, there are a number of payments made by insurance company boards of directors, at their sole discretion, which historically and traditionally have not been treated as dividends. These include the interest above minimum contract guarantees added to dividend accumulations, liberalized payments under nonguaranteed settlement options, interest paid on claims between date of death and final payment (required in some states but generally extended to all claimants), refunds of premiums paid beyond the date of death, and a variety of added credits in conjunction with group products.

We think the IRS was motivated to grant the Mass Mutual ruling request for two reasons. First, the Service would like to collect taxes from Universal Life contracts from some source, and it is not feasible to tax the policyholder. Second, the IRS has become more political in its approach, and the Mass Mutual rulings gave it an upper hand in negotiating to eliminate modified coinsurance in TEFRA.

The IRS followed its Mass Mutual rulings with a tax deferred annuity excess interest ruling (Revenue Ruling 82-133, 1982-28 IRB) that treated all excess interest on annuities as a dividend. This general ruling was issued at a time when annuity companies were battling with Congress over the tax treatment of withdrawals and loans from annuity products. By making the deductibility of excess interest an issue on annuities, the IRS was able to trade-off a previous non-issue in order to get its way on the tax treatment of annuity loans and withdrawals. These annuity loans and withdrawals are now taxed as income to the extent of interest earnings within the contract.

The IRS has played hardball in getting its legislation passed. Look for the Service to continue to be a formidable opponent on any proposals that tend to improve the existing tax characteristics of Universal Life.

CHAPTER 8

TEFRA 1982—Tax Issues and Guidelines

As we predicted in the first edition of *Why Universal Life,* the company vs. company vs. IRS battles have been resolved by legislation. The Tax Equity and Fiscal Responsibility Act of 1982 (TEFRA) has answered the key policyholder tax questions concerning Universal Life.

TEFRA created a firm foundation from which accelerated sales efforts for Universal Life can be launched. The key to passage of the life insurance portions of TEFRA was that mutual companies sacrificed the tax advantages of modified coinsurance (Mod-Co) in exchange for what they viewed as more equitable treatment in the deductibility of dividends on life insurance policies. The portion of dividends that are now allowed as a deductible expense are 77½% of dividends paid by mutual companies and 85% for stock companies. A 100% deduction is allowed for policies purchased within a qualified plan.

These new deductibility provisions apply for a two-year interim basis. The temporary nature of the law has led to it being termed "stopgap." (The repeal of Mod-Co is not part of the stopgap legislation.) The provisions are a safe harbor, or lower limits for the deductibility of excess interest on Universal Life policies, should the Mass Mutual ruling prove to be correct. There are a number of companies which continue to claim 100% deductibility of excess interest because their policies are indexed, or because they find fault with the Mass Mutual ruling.

From a practical standpoint, the change in deductibility means a reduction of interest rates credited to Universal Life ranging from 0% to perhaps $1\frac{1}{2}$%, depending upon the company's tax situation. Along with the passage of TEFRA there has come a sharp decrease in interest rates. Consequently, the effect of TEFRA on credited interest rates will be masked by this and other influences.

TEFRA defines the circumstances in which Universal Life policies (termed "flexible premium policies" in the legislation) will be treated as life insurance. These provisions are also part of the two-year stopgap measure.

We believe the tests concerning Universal Life are soundly conceived and defined to give considerable comfort to those who had reservations prior to TEFRA. This should come as no surprise since the Universal Life companies, acting with and through the ACLI, were largely responsible for the statutory language developed in 1982. There are two independent tests, defined in detail in a new section of the IRC Section 101(f). The second of these is a special purpose legislation, described in the footnote.[1]

---

[1] The second test is tailor-made for Adjustable Life policies of the type sold by Bankers Life of Iowa and Minnesota Mutual. The test is passed if, by the terms of the contract, the cash value will not at any time exceed the net single premium for the death benefit at such time. Additional rider benefits are ignored in the calculation.

Guideline Premium Tests

The first test defines two guidelines, both of which must be met in order that Universal Life will be automatically considered life insurance and entitled to the Section 101(a) exclusion of the death proceeds from Federal income tax. The death benefit guideline is the simpler of the two. In the first edition of this book, we included a chapter which proposed a minimum corridor death benefit higher than the prevailing industry practice. We suggested that, in order that the company's risk be substantive and consistent with traditional life insurance policies, a corridor related to the cash value was desirable and that the minimum death benefit should decrease with advancing age.

This is the approach adopted by TEFRA. A death benefit under Universal Life must be at least 140% of the cash value until the insured reaches age 40. The minimum percentage reduces 1% for each year of age after 40 but is always at least 105%. This provides a corridor of 5% for ages above 75, and requires that Universal Life policies will always offer a minumum amount of pure insurance protection.

The second guideline limits the sum of premiums paid. The legislation, praticularly the calculation rules, clearly indicate that the intent of Congress was to limit the use of Universal Life for investment purposes. The maximum premium allowed is an approximation to the premiums which have been commonly available on non-participating whole life policies. The legislation attempts to avoid loopholes which would permit much higher, investment-oriented premiums such as those typical of traditional endowment and retirement income contracts. The rules carefully delimit the benefits and assumptions which may be used. Single premium policies are permitted as part of the guidelines.

The sum of the premiums paid can never exceed *the greater of:*

- the single premium necessary to fund future benefits under the contract, based on 1) maximum mortality rates fixed in the contract, 2) other charges fixed in the contract, and 3) interest at an annual rate which is the greater of a) the rate guaranteed in the contract, or b) 6%.

- the sum of level annual amounts which are: 1) payable over the life of the contract, but not for less than 20 years; and 2) computed on the same basis as the single premium guideline except that the interest rate guaranteed in the contract is 4%.

There are three calculation rules that apply to all policies. We paraphrase these rules in italics, and follow with a brief commentary.

1) *The pure death benefit assumed to exist at any future time cannot exceed the benefit when the contract is issued.* This prevents increasing the guideline by projecting large future benefits which may subsequently be reduced.

2) *The maturity date of the contract cannot be less than 20 years after issue (or age 95 if the insured's issue age is over 75).* This prevents a short funding period for any guaranteed endowment benefits which would have the effect of substantially increasing the guideline.

3) *The amount of any endowment benefits payable at maturity cannot exceed the smallest contractual death benefit assumed in the calculation.* This directly prohibits a guideline premium based on the traditional retirement income product design. (It is worth noting that the clear purpose of this test may well carry over to future legislation or regulations restricting traditional retirement income policies. See our discussion of Revenue Ruling 66–322 and Evans v. Commissioner in Chapter 6, "Policyholders and Taxes—the Legal Background."

Another TEFRA provision allows for a change in the guideline premiums when the benefits change although authorities disagree on the calculations required. Still another provision defines supplemental benefits under the guidelines. Life insurance on persons other than the insured is referred to as "family term insurance." This leads to a cautious interpretation by many companies that business partners or others cannot be covered by a rider in a Universal Life policy without jeopardizing the Section 101(a) exclusion.

In reflecting upon these guidelines, we believe that Universal Life companies are ecstatic that they have received special mention in the revised Internal Revenue Code. The guidelines are strict, but fair.

Other Considerations Related to TEFRA

The legislation provides, among other things, that failure to meet the guidelines can be avoided by refunding excess premiums (with interest) within 60 days after the end of a policy year in which an excess premium was paid.

It is important to note that a violation will result in disqualification of death proceeds from the Section 101(a) exclusion, apparently forever. We expect that companies will routinely revise their policy forms and procedures to avoid such a severe penalty. The Union Central policy, shown in Chapter 5, "Creating the Proposal," provides that,

> The death benefit must be at least 140% of the cash value until the annual date (defined as the policy anniversary in the policy) when the insured is age 41. Beginning on this date, this percentage reduces in steps of 1% on each annual date to no less than 105%. The specified amount will be automatically increased to maintain these percentages. . . . The Company may limit the amount of any increase in premiums. In order for this policy to continue to be qualified as life insurance under any applicable law or regulation, the Company may refuse to accept premium payments or may return premium payments with interest.

We expect this type of wording to be the standard approach beginning in 1983.

Another avenue is to add an annuity feature. Annuity premiums would consist of the excess Universal Life premiums and any interest or withdrawals which might be required under Section 101(f).

What is a Universal Life contract if it does not fall within the safe harbor test? TEFRA does not answer this question. We believe that, based on the extensive legal analysis in prior chapters, a good case could be made that such a contract still qualifies as life insurance. In any event, the worst possible case would have to be treated as a combination annuity and pure term product, and the portion of the contract attributable to the pure insurance amount would be treated as life insurance under Section 101(a).

TEFRA includes special treatment for annuities. If certain conditions are met, 100% of the excess interest is now deductible ($92\frac{1}{2}$% in the case of mutual companies). There is a 5% penalty on withdrawals that occur within the first ten years of the issuance of an annuity, unless it is in the event of death or disability or involves periodic payments.

In addition, the taxation of withdrawals from new annuity policies will now be on a lifo rather than a fifo basis. This means that such withdrawals (or loans) from an annuity will be taxed as income to the extent that there is income in the annuity contract. This provision applies only to annuities issued after August 13, 1982, or investments made within previously issued contracts after that date.

One of the interesting offshoots of the annuity tax rules is a special provision which exempts life insurance and endowment contracts from the annuity treatment of taxation on withdrawals or loans, *except as determined by the Secretary of the Treasury.* (We understand that the Secretary insisted on this authority.) It is possible that the Treasury will use this authority to cause withdrawals or loans from certain existing single premium policies, or even Universal Life contracts, to be treated as distributions from annuities. However, it is expected that the guidelines applied by the Secretary will not be any more stringent than those required for Universal Life. (See our notes above in connection with the guideline premium calculation rules.)

It is our opinion that, if a Universal Life contract qualifies as life insurance for purposes of Section 101(a) treatment, it will also qualify as life insurance for purposes of Section 72 of the Code. This means that loans from or secured by Universal Life policies will continue to be treated as true loans and not treated as taxable income. Other contracts, such as the single premium whole life policy discussed in a later chapter, may not fare as well.

TEFRA's Future

Since the deductibility of excess interest is temporary legislation, we feel certain that it will become increasingly controversial as new insurance tax legislation is considered during 1983. Pessimists have suggested that the Secretary of the Treasury will hold Universal Life hostage in an attempt to achieve other ends, principally that of raising more tax revenue from the life insurance industry.

On its merits, we believe the treatment of the deductibility of excess interest will prove to be quite satisfactory, and, with the exception of fine-tuning amendments, will continue as the law of the land. To raise revenues, it is possible the IRS will seek to reduce the percentages below the 85% level for stock companies and 77½% for mutual companies. The guideline premium provisions need some clarification. The death benefit corridor provisions for Universal Life were so well thought-out that they will be continued practically as is. The logic on which they are based may even be extended to all life insurance policies.

CHAPTER 9

How Others Expect to Compete

We suspect every major insurance company by now has either commenced the development of its own Universal Life contract or has issued an internal "white paper" discussing Universal Life, or both. The most unusual progress report we have heard to date was from one company that has chosen the development route. It has only decided on the name of its product—"Eternal Life"! The rest, it thinks, will come easily.

Acknowledged Problems with Universal Life

For the companies that have chosen to fight the Universal Life concept, there have been two main thrusts to their attacks. First, they maintain that the high interest paid under the contract cannot continue because interest rates are coming down. Second, they maintain that, if the high interest does continue, other companies will soon be able to pay a comparable high interest and, therefore, there will be no advantage to purchasing Universal Life.

The resolution of the issue regarding the deductibility of excess interest has put Universal Life companies in a strong position because they are able to maintain that their policy is a valid and effective contract. Universal Life companies do not dispute the fact that interest under their contracts may come down or that the interest payable under other types of contracts may go up. Nevertheless, they point to the discrepancy in the interest rates that are presently being paid and, based upon projection of their current rates into the future, point out the apparent superiority of their product. To the extent that Universal Life has lower loads and may, in some instances, operate with a smaller margin of profit, it can provide insurance at a lower cost.

Dissenters point out a number of weaknesses, or potential weaknesses, in the Universal Life contract. Several of these figured prominently in a partial moratorium on approval of Universal Life policy form approvals imposed by the New Jersey Department of Insurance in January, 1982. The Department's Chief Actuary, William A. White, commented as follows in an internal communication to his associate actuary:

"It had been my hope—reflected by our current approvals practice—that we would be able to 'make up the rules as we went along (with respect to the review and approval of Universal Life policy forms).' This hope was based on the assumptions:

1) that consistent patterns of policy forms and premium/benefit arrangements would emerge from the companies entering this market;

2) that time and staff expertise would be available within the Department to manage both the day-to-day review

of forms and the formulation of principles and guidelines for that review; and

3) that the NAIC and other states that have access to professional actuarial resources would contribute to the development of responsible, defensible, and useable guidelines for review.

Unfortunately, none of these hopes has materialized."

After describing the scope of the three month moratorium, White commented:

"It should be emphasized that this moratorium does not reflect any criticism of the direction that a substantial part of the life insurance industry is taking in designing policy forms of this type; on the contrary, there is general agreement that this form of coverage may be the only rational response to the unusual and uncertain economic climate—particularly with respect to inflation and interest rates—that prevails today. The New Jersey Department is aware of and concerned with the sense of urgency that attaches to making available of these kinds of coverage to the citizens of this state."

White then outlined his concerns in "highly summarized and possibly incomplete form." The following points are weaknesses of the product which the authors have identified as significant. Because White makes several key points so articulately, the material in quotes is extracted from his communication. The interested reader may wish to read the specifics of the New Jersey Department's study, including the record of hearings in New Jersey.

1) *Sales illustrations for Universal Life focus on figures that assume the high excess interest will continue indefinitely.*
   "As regulatory practices now stand, there is nothing to prevent a company from selling a policy on the basis of

wildly optimistic assumptions and projections as to interest and mortality and then, almost immediately, reverting
to overly conservative and high-cost guarantees in the
actual setting of interest and mortality factors." Everything is a matter of degree. What is one person's "wildly
optimistic assumption" is another person's dispassionate
assessment of the likely course of events. Absent a rigid
price fixing mechanism, the best course would seem to be
disclosure of intermediate interest rates and guarantees in
such a way that the customer can, if he reflects on the
matter, assess the likelihood of performance at a level less
than the current assumptions used.

2) *The interest paid under Universal Life will be sensitive so
market conditions and could fluctuate greatly.* All agree
with this self-evident statement. The disagreement is over
the extent to which the customer should be cautioned or
warned of the impact on his life insurance program. This
argument has been around since the first public discussion
of the use of new money in the pricing of individual life
insurance. In general, the disclosure of relatively technical
numbers, such as interest-adjusted surrender cost, has not
been overly effective in enlightening the buyer. The
authors' despair of finding the magic words which will edu-
cate effectively on a matter so difficult to illustrate during
the course of a sales interview. The best response of the
Universal Life companies, we suspect, is that it is in their
best interest to cushion the fluctuations in interest credits
and encourage understanding of this feature of their policies in order to promote reasonable persistency. Mean-
while, the companies which continue to credit a portfolio
rate of interest will continue to suffer. Perhaps these companies can come up with a formulation for improved disclosure which will improve the buyer's understanding of
this important issue. This is a formidable challenge.

3) *Unwarranted replacements are taking place with an increase in customer costs a likely result.* "A major concern of companies that do not market Universal Life policies is that they will suffer unprecedented replacements of existing business at the hands of those companies and agents that do offer the product. 'Replacement' is becoming increasingly respectable and accepted, but twisting is still illegal. Carried to extremes, replacement could jeopardize the continued existence of many major life insurance companies." Current regulations do not provide a comprehensive guide for the client to determine if replacement is in his best interest. The state Insurance Departments must be concerned with solvency, but, "This issue will have to be carefully developed to distinguish between open competition, anticompetitive regulatory measures, and the relative public interests." In the meantime, it is to be hoped that the sales efforts of Universal Life agents will accentuate the positive in their presentation of the product. Out of context quotes from the Federal Trade Commission Staff Report and reprints of inflammatory newspaper articles are not the stuff from which fair competitive practices emerge.

4) *The flexibility of Universal Life premiums may be oversold.* In addition to the possible reliance on high yields illustrated over long periods of time, the client may not recognize that failure to build the cash value fund will lead to sharply increased insurance costs at ages of 60 and older. Universal Life companies point to the transparency of the contract and the details of the Annual Report as the means for avoiding this problem. It would be helpful to know that a projection of future costs and values would be available on request. Some companies guarantee the future availability of such projections in their con-

tracts. Other companies do not. There is another point which is primarily a marketing concern.

5) *The policy may be difficult to use in a minimum deposit situation.* Sales which rely on the deductibility of policy loan interest, accompanied by the increase in dividend values in traditional policies, do not work as well using Universal Life. This is so because the typical Universal Life contract does not credit excess interest on borrowed funds. However, the dollars and cents value of a "minimum funds" approach using Universal Life should be compared to the more complex numbers of the minimum or variable deposit types of traditional par product sales before a firm conclusion on marketability is reached. To complicate this type of comparison further, a few companies are now coming on the market with variable loan rate participating policies which have higher dividends to reflect the improved net return to the company when earned policy loan interest is permitted to rise toward current market interest levels. As the number of states which pass enabling legislation increases, more policies of this type will be available.

The key points of the "attack approach" used by competitors of Universal Life can be summarized as follows. The opponents of Universal Life question the ability of the contract to provide meaningful benefits to the consumer in the long run. Other points of contention are based on questioning the integrity of the product and the companies which offer it. Can Universal Life continue to provide the high interest currently offered under the contract?

In addition, it should be noted that, if interest rates in the economy decline, Universal Life may well continue to offer better value to the public than many traditional life insurance policies. This will be the case if (a) the return on new money pass through is still above the general account earnings of major companies (with the drag earnings from 8% policy loan rate reduced), or (b) if the Universal Life contract is available with lower sales costs and premium loadings, or (c) if market of Universal Life attracts larger premiums, thus reducing the unit costs for the insurance company.

Product Competition

An increasing number of companies have determined that the best defense is a good offense. They have turned to product innovation in the hope of retaining market shares, or, in the case of a number of smaller companies, as a strategy to achieve improved industry recognition and accelerate growth.

The product competitors of Universal Life fall into essentially three categories: current or new money nontraditional products, approaches which package a buy term and invest the difference approach, and variations of traditional insurance plans, some of which are merely examples of target marketing which attempts to avoid the competition by competing in areas where current market place forces are less intense. Our objective for the second part of this chapter is to discuss the fundamentals of these products or combination of products and speculate on the quality of each.

Current Interest or New Money Products

The life insurance industry has been offering new products at an unparalleled pace. Many of these utilize specific investment approaches and are designed to be sold with an appeal which expands on the customary selling of insurance needs. The following products are given major attention because, like Universal Life insurance, they provide greater flexibility for the policyholder and are designed to return a better return on the policyholder's investment dollar. We have included an analysis

of key characteristics of each of these for ease of comparison with Universal Life insurance. They are:
1) Variable Life
2) Adjustable Life
3) Current Value Life
4) Universal Life with Indexed or Alternative Investments
5) Excess Interest Whole Life

1) VARIABLE LIFE ("VLI")

This is a whole life insurance product which invests the cash value of the contract in equity accounts. The objective of the contract is to provide insurance benefits for the policyholder to keep up with inflation. Because the contract is part life insurance, part securities, it has been registered with the Securities and Exchange Commission. The death benefit increases or decreases annually depending upon the investment results. However, it will never decrease below a guaranteed amount.

This product has competitive potential with Universal Life due to the anticipated higher return that can be obtained with an equity investment vs. an interest type return. The agent can illustrate, for example, the past performance of the company's equity fund (example: 21% per year over the last five years) compared to an interest return of 12% on the Universal Life. This potential return will appeal to certain risk taking clients. From past experience in reviewing a cross section of the buying public, it appears the smaller buyer is attracted to guaranteed returns, while the larger buyer is often willing to take a greater risk in attempting to earn higher returns.

The Universal Life Companies are already talking about Phase II Universal Life, which may offer stocks, bonds, real estate, money markets, as well as indexed interest and guaranteed interest. Phase II Universal Life will probably offset any current advantages offered with Variable Life.

Equitable of New York, John Hancock and others are beginning to make a comeback with the VLI plan developed in the 1960's. Equitable has had back-to-back years of high return on their VLI separate account and has launched a national advertising campaign to publicize it.

This product may well share in the excitement over index linked plans. Should the Reagan economic policies stimulate a boom in equity markets, a resurgence of VLI is not only possible, but likely. The policy is not as flexible in current designs as Universal Life insurance, but this tends to be forgotten when the high returns of the underlying investments are the primary sales incentive.

a) Current Investment Return. The performance of the equity portfolio held determines the return. It may be negative, subject to minimum guarantees. The return may also be highly positive, for example, 40% for Equitable in 1980.

b) Low Load on Savings Element. VLI can be sold with a wide range of field compensation patterns. The small sample available is insufficient to judge trends of the 1980's.

c) Reasonable Mortality Cost. Obscured by the actuarial design.

d) Flexibility of Premiums. Generally there is none. However, the larger the portfolio gains, the more cash value is available for premium loans.

e) Flexibility of Benefits. Benefit changes are largely a function of the investment performance.

f) Clarity of Policy Wording. Obscurity would be a better word for both policy wording and, to a considerable extent, sales illustrations as well. The SEC required prospectus is no help.

2) ADJUSTABLE LIFE

Under this policy, policyholders may increase or decrease the amount of premium payments, pure death benefit and periods of protection. Coverage can even move between term and whole life coverage to meet the policyholder's changing needs. The policyholder has his option of types of insurance coverage. He can elect to buy term protection, or he could elect protection that expires at the end of the premium payment period. The latter protection is similar to level term. Like Universal Life, this product requires individualized illustrations for the client and computer resources for the insurance company's administration for the tailor-made insurance programs.

It is difficult to see any benefits offered by Adjustable Life that are not also available in Universal Life. The Adjustable Life is more complicated to understand and administer and, in the future, most Adjustable Life policies will probably evolve into true Universal Life products.

Adjustable Life has been marketed with good success by Bankers Life of Iowa and Minnesota Mutual. College Life entered the market about 1980. The product was conceived, in part, as a way around the restrictive legal interpretations of the insurance departments. It provided flexibility before the retrospective concepts of Universal Life insurance were acceptable. It seems unlikely to attract more advocates because of the huge investment required for internal systems.

However, because the plan operates in close analogy to traditional forms, and does not use a fund approach nor excess interest, it seems comparatively safe from tax problems. At such time as the interest rate credited by its sponsors is competitive with new money or indexed Universal Life insurance plans, it could become the product of choice for those able to afford the computer hardware and software.

The descriptive material which follows is brief because the policy is not likely to be a serious competitor except for the companies already set up to administer it.

    a) Current Investment Return. Bankers of Iowa and Minnesota Mutual operate on a portfolio return basis. Their return is not quoted separately and is not currently competitive with new money products.

b) Low Load on Savings Element. The load is close to the average of traditional permanent forms.

c) Reasonable Mortality Cost. Obscured by the actuarial design of traditional forms.

d) Flexibility of Premiums. Substantial, subject only to the plan minimums.

e) Flexibility of Benefits. Similar to the basic Universal Life insurance benefit flexibility.

f) Clarity of Policy Wording. The policies are essentially traditional with fairly complex wording to describe the multitude of change options available.

3) CURRENT VALUE LIFE

This variation on Universal Life insurance receives separate attention even though there is only one such form known to have been filed with any state insurance department. This product is similar to Universal Life in that it uses current investment return. The board of directors of the insurance company annually declare the formula basis used to compute an annual endowment. This current investment return is issued if the client selects from a series of options in the policy, to use current interest.

The policy differs from Universal Life and approaches a traditional product when the insured selects an option in the policy based on guaranteed premiums and guaranteed returns. In many respects the product is designed and administered as a traditional product, falling between traditional and nontraditional policies. It should be noted that every option in the contract provides for coverage to age 95. This guarantees that the company will receive premium income equivalent to a whole life plan while the policy is in force and also guarantees the salesperson a commission based on a higher premium per thousand that may be the case with Universal Life.

The form takes a different approach to premium flexibility, emulating the options available under traditional permanent plans. (See item "d".) In addition, it uses a unique "annual renewable endowment feature" in lieu of excess interest.

a) Current Investment Return. Basically the same as Universal Life insurance. The board of directors annually declares the formula basis used to compute the annual endowments under policies of the Current Value type.

b) Low Load on Savings Element. The load is at the high end of the Universal Life insurance range. The product is intended to be marketed by successful agents tied reasonably close to the company. In many respects the product is designed and administered as a transition product between traditional and nontraditional permanent policies.

c) Reasonable Mortality Cost. Same as Universal Life insurance.

d) Flexibility of Premiums. The present form is substantially different from Universal Life insurance in that it will only function as a permanent policy. There are a series of options, described in the policy form, which allow the policyowner or agent to select benefits and premium payments based on either the current or guaranteed assumptions.

e) Flexibility of Benefits. Same as Universal Life insurance.

f) Clarity of Policy Wording. The wording is somewhat more obscure because of the unfamiliar endowment language. Also, the half-dozen options are imposing to read and compare. Nevertheless, the drafting of all general provisions and the clarity of the company's sales illustrations are expertly and cleanly done. The total effect is one of reasonable clarity.

It should also be noted that the company allows completely flexible illustrations on renewal. The policyowner or agent may request benefit changes at any policy duration. It is even possible to specify interest and other assumptions different from the company's current basis in order to gauge the effect of a change in economic conditions.

4) UNIVERSAL LIFE INSURANCE WITH INDEXED OR ALTERNATIVE INVESTMENTS

Very few of these products have been marketed so far. An investment return based on the index may be guaranteed in the provisions of the policy contract, or it may be set by action of the insurance company's Board of Directors using a formula approach. A so-called "directed investment" contract is another type. The T-Plan offered by Transamerica Occidental of California and "The Challenger" offered by Life of Virginia are the primary examples which have been brought successfully to market thus far. We believe a dozen or more similar products will be available by the end of 1982 and that several of these will be sold by companies which are among the top 100 in assets.

As a harbinger of things to come, the chief insurance officer of Equitable has said that his company will have a new life insurance product that will go "beyond Universal Life." It will be a "multiple fund vehicle" offering alternative investments to policyholders, including stock, real estate, and money market funds. Think of this policy as "second generation Universal Life."

a) Current Investment Return. The Life of Virginia and Transamerica Occidental plans have been described in several articles by Samuel H. Turner, President of Life of Virginia, and the Chief Marketing Officer of Transamerica, David R. Carpenter. Several other companies have followed with their own version of an indexed policy.

There are many possible variations of this design. Competitive activities in Europe strongly suggests that these variations will proliferate. The marketing mechanisms may be a function of the index approaches taken. The regulators have, so far, taken a relatively relaxed view.

b) Low Load on Savings Element. Although no trends can yet be projected, it seems likely that products which are tied closely to different investment media will have rather low load factors. Certainly this will be the case if the marketing effort is directed at or through security brokers.

c) Reasonable Mortality Cost. Similar to Universal Life insurance.

d) Flexibility of Premiums. Similar to Universal Life insurance, although somewhat larger minimum premiums are likely to avoid unreasonable handling time by sales people who will expect to be dealing in volume.

e) Flexibility of Benefits. Similar to Universal Life insurance.

f) Clarity of Policy Wording. Clarity is reduced by the need to build careful protective wording around the index feature. It is also likely that transfer options to other forms, either traditional policies or Universal Life insurance variations linked to alternative investments will be provided. Many words are needed to describe these options, further reducing clarity.

5) EXCESS INTEREST WHOLE LIFE

Excess Interest Whole Life is a whole life policy with added features, usually associated with Universal Life. The features of the product are: level premium; level death benefit; endowment at age 95; guaranteed cash values; whole life commissions; cost of protection based on net amount at risk; current term rates for amounts at risk; cash values credited with high current excess interest; premium payment features using cash values without borrowing; automatic premium loans and cash value loans.

The Excess Interest Whole Life policy uses a fixed and level premium payment until maturity, usually age 95. The policy generally does not allow for a change in the fixed level premium, but it can have an automatic premium deduction provision. This provision allows the policyholder to automatically deduct the gross premium from the excess of the net accumulation account (accumulation account minus surrender charge) and the guaranteed cash value. This provision is available after a limited number of years, such as five, if the net accumulation account will become sufficient to eliminate the need for continued premiums to keep the policy in force. In effect, this creates the vanishing premium without policy laons.

The first year premiums are subject to a high expense charge, such as 50%, plus an annual policy fee, typically $25.

There are two accounts related to cash values in Excess Interest Whole Life, namely the guaranteed cash value and the accumulation cash value account. Guaranteed cash values are traditional whole life guaranteed cash values and are stated in the policy. The accumulation value is based on the current interest rate applied to the net premiums less mortality charges. The net premium is the premium due less the policy fee and any additional charges for riders, benefits, and class of risk. In addition, the first-year-premium is reduced by the first-year expense charge.

There are two sets of term rates, those which are guaranteed and stated in the policy and the current term rates which are subject to change prospectively. The current term rates are the rates actually used in determining the term charges and can never exceed the guaranteed term rates. Once the gross premium is paid, the net premium is determined, and a deduction is made for mortality charges on the net amount at risk. The balance earns the current interest rate. There is a minimum interest guarantee, usually 4% or $4\frac{1}{2}$%.

If the policy is surrendered during a defined number of years, which range from 10 to 25, a surrender charge is applied to the accumulation account. The following is a sample schedule of surrender charges.

Figure 9.1

Year	Surrender Charge as a percentage of the Accumulation Account	Year	Surrender Charge as a percentage of the Accumulation Account
1	100%	9	20%
2	80	10	15
3	60	11	10
4	50	12	8
5	40	13	6
6	35	14	4
7	30	15	2
8	25	16	0

If the deduction of the surrender charge from the accumulation value account results in an amount less than the guaranteed cash value, the policyholder receives the guaranteed cash value.

If the policyholder has not paid the premium by the end of the grace period, and if the net accumulation account minus the guaranteed cash value does not result in sufficient money to pay the premium, an automatic premium loan is available. The loan will be made from the guaranteed cash value at 8% interest.

There is a corridor amount of insurance of at least 5% of the accumulation value.

Buy Term and Invest the Difference

Rather than product competition, the following are more correctly referred to as "program" competition. Buy term and invest the difference has always been a competitor of traditional whole life insurance policies, whether an actual competitive situation existed or whether it was an option in the back of the mind of the prospective customer. In fact, Universal Life is itself an answer to buy term and invest the difference. It differs from the following programs in that it is one integral policy and is entirely life insurance.

1) Single Premium Whole Life and Decreasing Term
2) Term and Annuity Riders
3) Term and Individual Retirement Accounts
4) Term with Extra Term Protection
5) Group Term Insurance
6) Retired Lives Reserve
7) Deposit Term

1) SINGLE PREMIUM WHOLE LIFE AND DECREASING TERM

A few companies have designed a high interest contract with a small corridor of death benefit always increasing ahead of the cash value, and classify the contract as "Single Premium Whole Life" (SPWL). This contract offers value competitive with Universal Life since the policy earns high rates of interest, such as 13%, and has no loads or charges for the pure death benefit. Under the SPWL, the entire cash value accumulation plus pure death benefit will be paid out income tax free at the death of the insured. The SPWL combined with a decreasing term policy to either age 65 or 100, competes effectively for the large insurance purchaser.

The keys to this combination are no load on the SPWL and low cost term. If the issuing companies start to build in loads to pay higher commissions to the sales force, the attractiveness of the product will be reduced. The disadvantage to the sales force is lower commissions. Finally, some policies of this type have a minimum premium requirement such as $5,000.

2) TERM AND ANNUITY RIDERS

The term can be level term or decreasing term. The annuity can be either a single premium or annual premium annuity. The annuity is usually either no load or has a modest load, thus generating high early returns. Generally, the annuity will return a high rate of interest. The specific rate varies each year.

The combination, with interest projected over many years, generates very large values when compared with traditional products. If the cost of the term is low and the no load (or low load) annuity pays a high rate of interest, this product can illustrate numbers which compare favorably to the cash value accumulation of the Universal Life product.

One negative factor is the increasing cost per thousand of the level term or the termination of the death benefit of the decreasing term policy in the future. A second negative factor is the taxation of the annuity at the insured's death. Where a Universal Life policy death benefit is paid income tax free to the beneficiary, the death proceeds of an annuity which exceed the cost basis of the annuity are taxed as current income. This can decrease substantially the net proceeds available to the beneficiary, a fact which is often glossed over in the sale of the combination.

3) TERM AND INDIVIDUAL RETIREMENT ACCOUNTS

One of the more competitive of all products available in the future will be the Term Life Insurance (or low cost permanent life insurance) in conjunction with an Individual Retirement Account. The IRA has the distinct advantage that the contribution is tax deductible and the interest or dividends paid within the IRA accumulate on a tax deferred basis. The key factor is the tax deductibility of the contribution to the IRA, since the interest in the Universal Life policy is accumulated on a tax deferred basis which can be tax free if the policy is held to the death of the insured. We must again consider the escalating cost of level term insurance and the termination of decreasing term insurance, but the tax shelter offered by the IRA is powerful.

However, there are three limiting factors to an IRA. At present, the maximum contribution to the IRA is $2,000. Many people desire a larger cash value or savings accumulation per year. For those clients wanting substantial cash value build-up, both the IRA and Universal Life policy can be used. However, for the average client whose need for life insurance includes post-retirement estate liquidity, the cost of term insurance is a significant consideration.

The second limitation of the IRA is that the cash build-up can not be withdrawn without penalty before age 59½, whereas the cash value of the Universal Life is immediately available.

The third limitation to the IRA is the unfavorable tax treatment at death of the IRA proceeds compared to Universal Life. Life insurance is paid free of income tax to the beneficiary whereas IRA proceeds are taxed as current income when received.

4) TERM WITH EXTRA TERM PROTECTION

This is a relatively new concept and provides a term to 65 policy with a decreasing term rider. As the decreasing term reduces, the dividends of the policy purchase paid-up insurance. The term to 65 stops at age 65 and, at this point, the paid-up additional insurance is the death benefit. At early purchase ages, the paid-up additions are substantially more than the initial death benefit. The policy has no provision for policy loans and thus offers a totally new concept in traditional life insurance. The initial premium is low and thus the client is offered a pure death benefit contract, on a level premium basis at modest cost.

5) GROUP TERM INSURANCE

Many traditional companies are increasing their activity in the area of marketing jumbo group term policies as a way of competing with flat or declining whole life sales. Group term guarantee issue limits are rising and it is not uncommon to see each life insured for $500,000.

6) RETIRED LIVES RESERVE

Many companies are issuing, in conjunction with group term life insurance, a Retired Lives Reserve fund. The RLR fund is established to provide a means of funding group term premiums after retirement. The attractive feature of RLR from an insurance company viewpoint is that monies in the fund are locked in and can not be withdrawn nor borrowed. Thus, the insurance company has solved the problem of policy loans. The RLR is very competitive relative to other products in that the contributions are tax deductible to the corporation and are not reportable to the insured as income. The death benefits from the RLR fund are paid income tax free to the beneficiary. A second version of the RLR is to provide a RLR Wrap Fund and not issue the group term insurance. The agent merely wraps the RLR fund around some other carrier's group term and funds the death benefit at a future retirement date. Since the insurance company is not on the risk until a future date, substantial amounts of guarantee issue are available. It is not uncommon to see guarantee issue in amounts of $500,000 per insured at age 65.

7) DEPOSIT TERM

This product is a 10-year level term insurance product which requires a one time deposit in the first year which averages about $10.00 per $1,000. At the end of 10 years, if all premiums have been paid, the deposit (plus tax free interest) is supposed to be refunded. However, if the policy lapsed before the expiration of the 10-year period, the deposit is *not* refunded either in whole or in part. This feature locks the policyholder into the contract. Opponents of the policy maintain the yearly renewable term insurance is less expensive and does not require the policyholder to commit himself to the same insurance company for a 10-year period. Deposit term has been severely criticized because of its ability to mislead the consumer and has been outlawed in several states.

Deposit term has a particular appeal to the agent. Generally, the agent is well paid for selling the product in that he gets from one to three times the term premium as commissions for selling the product. The first year deposit is almost like a built-in fee for selling the contract. The insurance company likes the product because it can keep the first year deposit if the insured drops the policy in the early years. It is not generally a good buy for the insured because he can usually buy cheaper term, without the deposit. Therefore, the insured is putting up money on the deposit that is not necessary. This product will continue to compete because the agent likes the commissions, but the policy has none of the flexibility of Universal Life. When the public understands the advantage of Universal Life, the popularity of deposit term will probably start to decline.

Variations of Traditional Insurance Plans

A number of products and target marketing approaches have been designed to provide flexibility to an otherwise rigid whole life policy. Sometimes the flexibility is more in the underwriting of benefits or the convenience of administration than in the more fundamental product features such as premium and death benefit flexibility. To the extent that these products successfully simulate the flexibility of Universal Life or fit a need not addressed by traditional products and methods, each of these demonstrates another means by which others expect to compete.

1) Increasing Whole Life
2) Indexed Benefit Life
3) Salary Savings

4) Substandard Policies
5) Easy Issue Life Insurance
6) Guarantee Issue
7) Mass Merchandised Products
8) Tax-leveraged Participating Policies

1) INCREASING WHOLE LIFE

This policy is designed to provide a death benefit that will increase at a predetermined rate to keep pace with inflation. Once the initial individual requirements are satisfied, no further evidence of insurability may be required. The premiums for the policy are actually computed to provide the increasing death benefit and may be level or increasing premiums. Also, dividends can be used to purchase paid-up additions to further increase the total death benefit. Example: A $50,000 policy is purchased at age 30 which will increase to $150,000 by age 45 and to $300,000 by age 60.

This product is a high premium, high cash value policy. The contract is usually sold on a leveraged basis with four out of seven premiums being paid to tax qualify the contract and then maximum loans being taken to pay premiums. The tax deductible interest generated by the loans is attractive to high income taxpayers, whether they are individuals or corporations. It is possible to pay four out of seven premiums and withdraw the net interest after taxes from the policy cash values and dividends. If the policy values are sufficient, it is possible to achieve a zero cash outlay. The policy only is applicable to a small segment of the buying public due to the large initial deposits and the large interest deposits that have to be deposited in later years. The product has excellent features, but may find very strong competition from high interest yielding Universal Life products. Assuming that a traditional company issuing Increasing Whole Life credits lower than current interest, it is hard to see how this contract can compete with Universal Life.

2) INDEXED BENEFIT LIFE

This policy is designed to enable the death benefit to keep pace with inflation. Under some policies the amount of death benefit will increase automatically each year while under other policies the policyholder will have the option to increase his death benefit each year to correspond with the percentage increase in the consumer price index. Again, evidence of insurability will generally *not* be required after the initial issuance of the policy.

This contract has potentially good features. Its acceptance by the public has been limited and some companies have withdrawn their products. However, many people are very concerned about inflation, and this policy form could have great appeal. The key to its success will be the cash values, interest or cash values credited, and total return generated. If it is issued as term insurance, the term insurance cost per thousand will be of great significance.

This product will be strongly challenged by Universal Life through its level death benefit plus cash value death benefit option. This option adds the cash value to the level death benefit, and assuming the premium deposit is large enough to generate an increasing cash value, the death benefit will increase similarly to the Indexed Benefit Life.

3) SALARY SAVINGS

Due to the high cost of marketing individual whole life policies a new emphasis is being put on the voluntary salary savings program market. This market generally deals in policies issued with less than $25,000 death benefit and can compete successfully with Universal Life, since Universal Life usually has a minimum death benefit of $25,000 or more. The Salary Savings is usually sold on a payroll deduction basis, with contributions of $2.00 to $10.00 per week. The small contributions, and small amounts of insurance, do not usually attract sophisticated buyers and hence small guarantee issue (or simplified issued) traditional whole life policies are attractive. In the past year however, Universal Life companies have reduced their minimum size policies to lower amounts and may try to capture part of this large market.

4) SUBSTANDARD POLICIES

A number of companies are today issuing substandard risks at approximately standard rates. This is a difficult product to beat on the front end because the client can usually purchase the product at a lower premium. Psychologically, the client is attracted to the "Standard Issue" stamped on the policy. However, substandard companies may be faced with more competition from Universal Life companies since the rated individual does not necessarily have to deposit more premium. He can pay the same premium and get less cash value. More and more Universal Life companies are going after the substandard business.

5) EASY ISSUE LIFE INSURANCE

A new competitive product being used today is a policy that requires only a few simple health questions, no medical and possibly no attending physician statements. All risks up to four or more tables are accepted standard. The ease of purchase, fear of rejection, or desire not to divulge personal or medical history are substantial reasons for the client to purchase these products. Companies generally reduce the quality of the product by increasing premiums, providing few optional benefits, providing a low rate of return, but people still like and buy these products.

6) GUARANTEE ISSUE

The last type of contract that will be discussed is a different type of product but truly competitive for the simple reason that anyone can buy one and there are no health questions. The insured is usually not covered for the death benefit for the first two years of the policy. Full death benefits are provided in the third year and thereafter. If death occurs during the first two years, the insured's premiums are refunded plus 10% interest. For a totally uninsurable person, this is an appealing contract. He can be assured of being accepted and insured after two years. If he dies during the first two years, his family gets his premiums deposited plus 10%. The disadvantage to the contract is its high premium and low rate of return.

7) MASS MERCHANDISED PRODUCTS

Many traditional companies have gone to mass mailing, credit card life insurance, cut out coupons in newspapers and magazines, and telephone solicitation. All of these market techniques are effective and produce sales using traditional products such as term, guarantee issue life, IRAs, etc. The main drawback is that no professional advice is usually given by a qualified agent and the products are not always the most competitive in the market place.

8) TAX-LEVERAGED PARTICIPATING POLICIES

TEFRA provides an important safe harbor for favorable tax treatment of excess interest credited by stock life insurance companies. At the worst, 85% of the excess interest will be deductible to most of these companies. At the same time, the liberalized deduction for dividends is of major importance to mutual companies. Since the passage of TEFRA, mutuals have been taking an aggressive approach to the Universal Life competition.

In addition to the competition, which has been building among nontraditional policy types, several mutual companies now combine a high dividend rate, such as $11\frac{1}{2}\%$, with a variable loan rate. These policies are designed to take maximum advantage of the U.S. tax system by creating a high tax deduction for the taxpayer for the interest paid on borrowed monies.

241

At the same time, these policies credit a high rate of interest on the borrowed funds. For example, if a policyholder in the 50% tax bracket borrows from a policy at 14% interest, that person's net after tax cost of borrowing is 7%. If the contract earns $11\frac{1}{2}$% on the monies that are borrowed, there is a net gain of $4\frac{1}{2}$% each year.

One company has taken the approach that the lending rate will be indexed to corporate bond rates (as defined in the model act written by the NAIC), but the amount credited on the borrowed amount will be $\frac{3}{4}$ of 1% below the interest paid on the borrowed amount. This type of policy will credit a high rate of interest on the borrowed amounts even though it may be significantly higher than that credited on the existing cash value. Again, this policy is designed to exploit our present tax laws which, with some limitations, permit the deductibility of interest paid on life insurance loans and to give the policyholder the benefit of tax-free buildups along with deductible interest payments.

Insurance companies have been favored by the tax treatment allowed for the deductibility of interest. This did not have a major impact on government revenues when the interest credited on cash values was 5% and the loan interest rate was 8%. The net spread for the 50% taxpayer was only 1%. However, when the spread becomes much larger, insurance companies will begin selling tax benefits aggressively and pay less attention to death benefits. (This is another in the long list of distortions in the U.S. economy caused by the combination of high inflation, interest rates, and income taxes.) The creation of these types of policies may very well cause the IRS and Congress to look doubly hard at the deductibility of policy loan interest. This product competition could eventually reduce, if not eliminate, the favorable tax benefits attributable to borrowing. For a discussion concerning minimum deposit policies see Chapter 12, "Marketing Universal Life."

The One Product Category—Adjustable Premium

Finally, there is one product that is a competitor to Universal Life but which does not fall under any of the categories discussed above. This is the so-called adjustable life or indeterminate premium product. This plan was introduced well before the initial Universal Life policy of E. F. Hutton found its way to market. Crown Life of Canada was an early innovator. Since the early 1970s Life of Virginia has marketed contracts with adjustible premiums which reflect ranges of long-term bond interest rates. Attention to this type of contract was heightened with the successful introduction of the Aeconomaster by Aetna Life in 1979.

For a period of time in 1980, it appeared that this would become the staple product of the stock companies. It offers a low going in premium for permanent insurance, albeit with the possibility of a rate increase after the first few years. As the reader may know, stock companies generally offer nonparticipating or guaranteed cost contracts. This means that the policyholders do not share in the company's profits as is the case with participating products offered by mutual companies. (Some stock companies sell participating plans.)

In order to more effectively compete with the mutual companies, the indeterminate premium policies typically provide for a low "current premium" which, except for some initial period, is not guaranteed and may be decreased or increased after such period. The "current premium" is a function of the company's assumptions as to future experience as regards investment, mortality and expense. If these assumptions were comparable to those used by mutual companies in setting dividends, the ultimate net cost of the insurance would be expected to be quite similar to the participating policies. Usually the "current premium" is guaranteed for the first two years of the contract after which time it may be adjusted to reflect the updated assumptions as to future experience, but may not be increased above a stated maximum.

The product is exciting to the more traditional life insurance buyer. He has a level premium product, which is guaranteed for one to five years. Of course, he must be willing to pay a higher premium in the future, up to the stated maximum in the policy, if lower interest rates are reflected in the company's assumptions and it has to increase their premium rates. However, he is currently getting his lower "current premium" and the policy has the advantage of giving him the benefit up-front. On the negative side, this product can be viewed as an early, modified version of Universal Life. As the public gains sophistication and a better understanding of Universal Life, the adjustable or indeterminate premium life will probably be replaced by Universal Life. For the present, it is a transitional product and will continue to be sold, but, we expect, in decreasing amounts as Universal Life is sold by an increasing number of stock companies.

In many respects, it was (and is) a competitive response to the enhanced protection policies sold by many mutual companies in the mid-1970s which cut the rate per thousand by 25% and more from the prevailing levels of straight participating whole life.

The states have ruled that the lack of guarantees is sufficient to limit the deficiency reserve requirements imposed on companies when their premiums are less than the required valuation or net premiums. The same is true of the new breed of low-cost term insurance which has come to be known as re-entry term.

The state of New York has had more to say on this policy. On December 19, 1980 the Insurance Department of New York distributed a Circular Letter which established several rigid guidelines for approval of life insurance policies with projected indeterminate or adjustable premium rates less than or equal to maximum guaranteed premium rates. The Department said that, "While the Department recognizes this projected premium approach may be beneficial to policyholders, it is necessary to establish the following guidelines for approval of such policies to *prevent possible unfairness and misunderstanding to policyholders.* (Emphasis added.)

Among other things, New York required an actuarial memorandum describing the calculation of premiums which included the company's assumptions as to investment earnings, mortality, persistency and expense and a comparison of these assumptions for comparable nonparticipating and participating guaranteed premium policies. When premiums are changed, updated comparisons are required and a "justification for the action that will be taken on (the company's) indeterminate or adjustable premium policies." This is as close to rate regulation as a major insurance department has been in recent years. Many companies do not wish to disclose the competitive details of their policies for sound business reasons. New York indicated that the guidelines would be reviewed for possible amendment as experience develops. One wonders if they will have enough takers to develop the experience.

Regardless of the above, Universal Life offers an enhanced degree of premium flexibility and, under the current regulatory interpretation, the same relief on deficiency reserves that made indeterminate premium plans popular for a brief span of years. It appears that they have served their purpose as a transition product and will have less impact on the permanent market with the continuing growth of Universal Life.

Summary

Universal Life combines many of the attractive features that have been incorporated into product approaches discussed in this chapter. Public interest has added to the name recognition accorded the product, even while the acknowledged problems have been spotlighted by those who have not moved into a similar nontraditional product development.

Changes and modifications in Universal Life are surely to be expected. Some will be shaped by new ideas which prove themselves in the market. The new version of the Standard Nonforfeiture Law may allow additional enhancements to the product. Clearly, one or more adverse tax rulings could force Universal Life into shapes so far unimagined and, heretofore, unnecessary. Overall, the driving force is the interest of the consumer in a more responsive product to meet the challenge of inflation.

For this overriding reason, the more constructive competitive approach may be away from destructive criticism and toward further product innovation. Each company is working through its choice as this book goes to press. The authors believe in the long-term benefits of vigorous competition to benefit the public and the companies. We will follow the news and the production figures with the same intense interest as our readers, knowing that, in the final analysis, the market will tell us which is the best approach.

CHAPTER 10

Questions and Answers

Preamble

It would have been possible to write an entire book on Universal Life out of questions and answers. However, to have done so would have detracted from the detailed discussion that many aspects of the Universal Life contract deserve.

The following questions and answers deal with some of the knottier issues concerning Universal Life. This chapter assumes a working knowledge of the prior chapters and should not be tackled until the reader is prepared to voice his or her own answers to the questions. The answers to a number of questions go further into the subjects addressed than does the text of the book. The intent is to add substance on subjects which could not be covered conveniently in a short book on a major subject.

We assume full responsibility for matters of importance which are omitted.

The questions have been grouped together into several categories in order to make this chapter more readable. The categories and the letter legend that identifies each category are as follows:

A) Agency related questions and answers.
M) Marketing related questions and answers.
C) Cost disclosure related questions and answers.
I) Insurance company home office related questions and answers.
P) Product design related questions and answers.
L) Legal and tax related questions and answers.

AGENCY QUESTIONS

A 1. Can an agent make a living selling Universal Life?

Yes, the simplicity of Universal Life makes it possible to attract larger sales and premiums. We expect this to more than offset the decreased commission percentages offered by some of the Universal Life companies. The early experience of several companies reinforces this expectation.

A 2. If my client accepts the idea of Universal Life, should he replace other policies he now has?

Sound practice requires that this answer be determined in view of all the circumstances. There are, as the FTC correctly asserted, substantial numbers of older policies, many of them nonparticipating, which provide a poor return to policyholders. However, there are also many policies which provide reasonable current value and on which the initial cost of selling and issuing the policy has been paid and amortized by the company.

If the company has good investment and expense experience and is passing on the benefit of this experience to policyholders, careful analysis is needed to determine if replacement is warranted. Often a replacement which combines several very small policies will be worthwhile to the policyholder. Such a replacement simplifies future updating of his insurance program and may save on expense charges built in through annual policy fees and the expense charges which are a part of the formulas used to determine dividends. This is not to say that every small policy should be replaced. Policies with companies which pass on a high interest return in their dividends will often provide good current value. They should not be lumped in with other policies and replaced merely to simplify a client's program.

Very old policies on which the amount at risk is minimal are good candidates for proper replacements. It is easy to find examples where the current value of such contracts will, in a very few years, accumulate to more than the amount insured if the maximum value is borrowed and invested in tax sheltered investments. We do not believe that the need to reestablish incontestability and suicide periods is a factor of importance in most cases. For a useful discussion of replacement regulations and other factors, please refer to Harold Skipper, Jr.'s article in the *CLU Journal* October, 1981.

A 3. What compensation are companies willing to pay on replacement of their own traditional policies?

Many companies have not as yet addressed this question. It can be an expensive proposition to replace existing business and reincur part of the sales expense. On the other hand, if companies do not act to keep their current assets, they take the risk that another, more aggressive company will replace their business. Those companies who have decided to pay for self-replacement have settled on a formula which generally requires a doubling of insurance in force with an increase in the same anticipated premium income before and after the replacement. We expect a proliferation of such rules.

A 4. If two policies available through a company differ only in that one has higher commissions and lower early cash values, which of the two should the agent sell and why?

Clearly the agent should sell the policy which is the better value for the client. Anyone who doubts this may want to review the pledge of the Chartered Life Underwriter and similar ethical constraints common among organizations of life insurance underwriters. If the commission paid is not enough to compensate the agent for his services, he has no alternative but to charge an appropriate fee for his services as an underwriter as part of the client's financial and estate planning team. Since the laws in some states frown on the fee approach, we hope to see a series of changes in these laws. Surely this approach is better than repeal of the anti-rebate laws which has been proposed by the insurance commissioner in Wisconsin. To the extent that lower commision contracts capture the market, the pressure to move in this dirrection will build as the number of agents who can make a reasonable living with life insurance diminishes.

A 5. Will the flexibility of Universal Life premium options result in little or no renewal premium income with a proportionate drop in agents' renewal commissions?

No, we believe that Universal Life may be the only policy needed by the client (assuming that the company performs reasonably well). Regular increases in benefits and premiums will be a regular service provided by the agent. This will parallel the new policy sales activity of the past.

In addition, the new Cost-of-Living Adjustment rider (COLA) offered by some Universal Life companies will increase agents' commissions. Under the terms of this rider, the policyholder will automatically have his insurance increased by the percentage increase in the Consumer Price Index. Thus, if the CPI goes up 7%, the death benefit of a $100,000 policy will increase 7% to $107,000. A similar increase occurs each year up to the limits allowed by the company. No action need be taken by the policyholder. Substantial added commissions may be paid with limited effort on the part of the agent.

Some companies pay additional sales compensation based on the mortality charge in the Universal Life contract, even if there is no renewal premium paid to the company.

A 6. Will the simplicity of Universal Life lead to an increase in productivity as measured by the number of cases sold?

Yes, an agent who works at his business should close more cases for each hour invested. Of course, as Universal Life business becomes widespread, many of these sales will be adding benefits to policies already on the books.

A 7. Will it be necessary for each agent to have access to a computer to sell and service Universal Life?

The agent must have a computer to illustrate the full flexibility of Universal Life. Rate books are not applicable to Universal Life products. Rates and values will be derived by the computer and, after an initial adjustment period, proposals will be easily obtained by the agent.

A 8. Why should an agent sell Universal Life rather than a term and annuity combination?

Universal Life is a complete product in which the cash accumulation will not incur an income tax at death. The annuity part of a combination sale will always be taxed. See, also, the questions below on the extent to which the new IRA products may affect the market for Universal Life.

A 9. Will a newly recruited agent be able to successfully market Universal Life?

Yes, we think a new agent will be more successful than has been the case with traditional products. Universal Life is simple. The premiums and benefits can be made to fit an unlimited range of needs. This is preferable to the agent learning the details of a ratebook and then trying to "find a suit on the rack which fits the client." The sales illustration, such as that produced by a microcomputer, can be run in the field office in less than five minutes.

MARKETING QUESTIONS

M 1. Will Universal Life restore a portion of the savings dollar to the life insurance industry?

Most definitely. Only a major effort by other financial institutions or the Congress which strikes at the basic tax shelter of all permanent life insurance products would jeopardize this favorable result.

M 2. Where is Universal Life an inappropriate product?

Regulations on products such as Section 79 and Retired Lives Reserve were developed with traditional products in mind. It can be awkward trying to fit Universal Life to these regulations with confidence that the results will be those intended. The agents would be wise to consult competent counsel before assuming that a use of Universal Life is appropriate for these and other applications which may be handicapped by such regulations.

Also, if a buyer has no spare cash with which to take advantage of the favorable policyholder tax situation on Universal Life, pure term insurance is likely to be the preferred product. In addition, the current minimum face amount limits of many Universal Life companies rule out the purchase of small Universal Life policies.

M 3. What is the current thinking about replacement regulations? How do these affect Universal Life?

The intent of the state replacement regulations is to protect the public against inappropriate replacements. The current regulations fall far short of accomplishing that laudable goal. Among other deficiencies, such regulations as are in effect do not provide a meaningful test of the comparative financial value of the original policy compared with the suggested replacement.

In some states, the authorities are coming to believe that

replacement regulations are counterproductive. These regulations may actually expedite and encourage replacement whether or not replacement is warranted. Several computer services are available which mechanically reproduce the required disclosures, thereby complying with the letter of the regulations without providing information adequate for the consumer to make an informed judgment. Anyone who has seen the flimsy verbal justifications for replacement on the replacement forms would have grave doubts that the regulations are effective.

The regulations in effect at this time have limited effect on Universal Life. The NAIC has made limited progress in establishing disclosure requirements for sale of Universal Life and other nontraditional products. The states will need to make much more progress to protect the public interest.

M 4. What is the market for juvenile sales of Universal Life?

Possibilities are excellent. Term costs within Universal Life are low. Premiums paid by a parent or grandparent rapidly accumulate substantial cash values which reduce the insurance cost as the juvenile reaches adulthood. The flexibility of premim payments has clear advantages over traditional policies where equal gifts to several juveniles are desired. And the ability to modify premiums to fit a changing tax law can also be useful.

COST DISCLOSURE QUESTIONS

C 1. Should sales proposals show an intermediate interest rate between the guaranteed and the current rate?

Yes, as discussed in Chapter 7, "Company vs. Company vs. IRS," it is unlikely that the high pass-through offered in 1982 will continue indefinitely. Disclosure of an intermediate interest rate prepares the purchaser of Universal Life for the probability that he will not get what he sees in an illustration of cash values using the current high rate. With an intermediate rate, such as 8%, he may assess realistically the need to increase premiums should the accumulation of cash value be insufficient to continue insurance or allow the planned withdrawal of funds at retirement. Specific examples of this are given in Chapter 11, "Marketing Ideas and Case Studies."

C 2. When interest rates eventually drop, will Universal Life policies be subject to high lapse rates?

No, we believe that the interest rates passed through by Universal Life companies will remain reasonably competitive. However, if sales emphasize high return as the only or primary reason for the purchase, a Universal Life company may well experience a loss of cash values as Universal Life policyholders switch to another company.

It is quite possible that companies which continue to pay participating policy dividends on the basis of portfolio investment yields (as compared with new money methods) will eventually be able to credit a higher return than Universal Life policies. This time will be hastened by traditional products which provide for policy loan interest to be payable under the new variable loan rate regulations. However, the replacement of then existing Universal Life policies will involve the same penalties to the policyholder that exist when Universal Life policies replaces whole life today. That is, the cost of sales and home office issue must be paid again.

One other point should be made in answering this very complex question. At such time as new Universal Life contracts are offering two or three percent less than portfolio products, there will certainly be a negative effect on Universal Life sales. In addition, those who already own Universal Life policies will make more frequent use of the option to suspend or reduce premiums.

C 3. If a strong emphasis is placed on the interest return during the sale of Universal Life, will the Securities and Exchange Commission require the agent to obtain a security broker's license?

The answer to this question is unclear. The agents and their companies are well aware of the potential controversy. At the time of this writing, the SEC is accumulating sales and other material from more than a dozen Universal Life insurers. (See the discussion in Chapter 1, "Origins of the Universal Life Policy.") The industry experience with variable Life insurance in the 1970s clearly shows that federal regulation will be invoked where there is clear evidence that the risk of investment loss has been passed on to the policyholder. Nevertheless, it is clear that the pass-through of double digit interest rates should not, in and of itself, create a special problem for Universal Life.

C 4. Will future disclosure requirements for Universal Life be changed?

Yes, we think so. The current NAIC model cost disclosure regulation and the Buyer's Guide did not contemplate the sale of Universal Life. In addition to the 8% projection discussed above, proposals have already been made to caution policyholder and prospective buyers in writing about the difference between excess interest return under Universal Life and the dividend projections of traditional policies.

The use of 5% interest in the surrender cost indices does not work well for Universal Life. It produces negative costs in many illustrations. Something can and surely will be done to update the regulations. Given the slow motion activity of the states, however, we would be surprised to see an effective regulation before 1984.

C5. Is it in the comsumer's best interest to replace existing cash value policies with a Universal Life policy in the same company?

No unequivocal answer is possible. A thorough analysis is needed to evaluate the pros and cons. If all other factors seem favorable to the exchange, careful study of the projected cash values under the Universal Life policy is indicated.

We suggest that the interest rate used should be graded from the current level down to a long-term level judged to be realistic by both client and agent. It appears that a long-term rate, which is expected to be 1% or 2% above the policy, will often favor the Universal Life policy. However, even this rough rule of thumb may not apply if the company offers an updated program within a few years. A more detailed discussion concerning replacement can be found in Chapter 13.

INSURANCE COMPANY QUESTIONS

I 1. Why are life insurance companies offering Universal Life?

There are two types of reasons, offensive reasons and defensive reasons. On the offensive side, there are a growing number of companies who believe that the product offers improved value which appeals to the public and which will return savings dollars to the companies. The simple business truth that early entry into this market will increase their market share is appealing. The additional cash raised promises higher profits than are likely at a time when term insurance competition is intense and inflation is squeezing profit margins.

We suspect that some small companies are offering Universal Life as a means of survival. Only by attracting agents with an exciting new product will these companies be able to build sales. The costs today of recruiting, financing, training, and retaining an agency force are exceedingly high.

In some cases, a major market may be seen in the replacement of traditional business. A significant number of the early Universal Life companies have been well positioned to innovate, since they have only limited amounts of traditional policies on the books.

Defensively, some companies believe, very simply, that they must be able to match the offerings of other companies or they may lose the agent's confidence and his future new business. They don't expect to push for Universal Life sales, but they want to have the product to keep pace.

Currently, there are more companies acting from defensive reasons than offensive. They are greatly concerned with constant increases in policy loans and surrenders. They know that funds have left them for money market investment or, with increasing frequency, have shifted to companies with new money approaches using Universal Life and various annuity or single premium products. Although these companies may not be satisfied with the arguments favoring Universal Life's tax positions, they seek to protect themselves against favorable tax rulings on Universal Life which would cause an immediate decrease in the attractiveness of their traditional products.

Consequently, mutual companies which did not have stock subsidiaries established have moved quickly to purchase or establish them. Prices for inactive companies with certificates of authority to do business in several states have gone up sharply. The number of Universal Life policies being filed in the insurance departments is growing daily in order that the defensive companies will be ready to match the nontraditional policies.

I 2. Why are some companies holding back?

There are several key reasons. Please refer to Figure 1.2 which summarizes the Tillinghast, Nelson & Warren, Inc. questionnaire. Tax uncertainties, addressed in Chapters 6 and 7, are important, also.

The administrative reasons are of roughly equal concern to many home offices. Many companies consider Universal Life to be an undertaking equivalent to entering a totally new line of business such as variable annuities or dental insurance. Thus, unless there is, in their opinion, an overriding marketing reason, they are unable to justify disrupting the data processing work in progress.

There is, as well, a reluctance and perhaps even an inability to change. The evils of inflation, with destructive effects on sales organizations and home office expenses, have created distractions for company managers which are unparalleled in the experience of many of them. Then, when serious discussion of new product options is on the agenda, a bewildering array of options are presented. Many of the product options are untested in the marketplace over different economic cycles. The complexity and risk of the situation creates hesitancy and delay. Life (insurance) is not as comfortable as it used to be.

I 3. Can companies with large amounts of traditional permanent products on the books allow an exchange of these policies for Universal Life?

Probably not. The problem faced by the large companies is the impossibility of changing their interest earnings from the current portfolio of long term bonds and mortgages to current higher yielding securities. Selling the old assets at current depressed prices would, in most cases, result in insolvency. If a company simply made the exchange and promised to pay the higher interest rate on the exchanged Universal Life policy, the result would be the same within a few years. The company's surplus would have to be used to pay the difference between the Universal Life interest credited and the interest previously paid out in the form of cash value increases and dividends. Surplus would last two or three years at the most, unless interest rates came down dramatically in the meantime.

I 4. Will companies allow a policyholder to exchange his traditional policy or policies for Universal Life?

Yes, it appears that companies have little choice but to allow such an exchange. As we will discuss in Chapter 13, "The Replacement Issue," the specific terms of the exchange are important to determine if replacement is likely to be beneficial.

I 5. Will companies allow an exchange of blocks of traditional policies issued in connection with qualified retirement plans for Universal Life?

Yes, individual life insurance pension trust business is well-suited to an exchange program. This business involves a large number of policies, many of them relatively small policies purchased to increase benefits when an insured employee receives an increase in compensation. It is common for one person to have a dozen or more policies on his life after a number of years in such a plan. There is a clear advantage to all parties in replacing these policies with a single, flexible policy, though there may be a significant increase in the interest cost to the company.

New England Mutual Life Insurance Company became the first company to institute such a selective program during 1982. Phoenix Mutual also has initiated a program of this type.

I 6. What impact on profits will there be for a company selling Universal Life as compared to past profits on traditional policies? (Note that, in the case of mutual insurers, the word "profits" might more properly read "contributions to surplus.")

It seems safe to say that profits for a given amount of life insurance are in a state of decline or shortly will be. Competition from nontraditional policies, low cost term insurance, and the problems of replacement, surrenders, and policy loans have already had a significant effect. The constant increase in investment earnings (less federal tax) has enabled many companies to show good earnings in the late 1970s and early 1980s. When interest rates decline, as they eventually must, the level of profits on existing business will clearly decrease.

We expect that the competitive pressures will continue. Laying aside the cost of vigorous competition for market share, the transparency of Universal Life suggests that companies will have to pass-through a currently competitive rate of interest if they wish to attract agents and their clients' business. Current mortality rates can easily be compared from one contract to another. Non-smoker and other preferred rates are a part of many Universal Life policies now being issued. We expect the competition in this part of policy design to intensify.

But profits on a given amount of insurance are not the whole story. There is another question of great importance. Will enough additional insurance be sold by the industry to make up for the smaller profits on a given amount of insurance? We think so, for reasons discussed throughout this book. The overall result of vigorous competition should eventually be a better value for policyholders, an increase in the public's level of savings with life insurers, and a financially sound private insurance business.

I 7. Will companies be able to afford new administrative and computer costs?

Yes, without question. Home office computer systems for Universal Life are relatively inexpensive. The price tag for some so-called stand-alone computer packages is under $100,000. There are roughly a dozen independent firms already serving this market.

This is not to say that all companies will want to buy such a package and move ahead. Many companies have consolidated systems which have been developed at a cost of millions of dollars. They often prefer to add new products by fully integrating their billing, premium accounting, commission payments, and other computer-based services into these large systems. The time and cost of this approach is quite substantial.

Fifty or more small companies have already committed to smaller systems. The large companies will take this expedient route, if they must, to offer Universal Life on a timely basis.

I 8. How will companies invest Universal Life premiums?

Short-term, at least shorter than has been the case historically. The maturity of investments will generally be for periods of less than five years. The reasons are discussed more fully in Chapter 1, but focus on the realization that the statutory requirement for specified cash values is a "demand liability."

I 9. Will companies segregate the assets they have from Universal Life? If they do, how will this affect traditional policies, in particular, the dividends on participating policies?

They will likely segregate assets in one way or another. Since excess interest paid on Universal Life depends upon current high returns, the investments purchased will result in blocks of assets fundamentally different than those purchased with premiums of traditional policies. In order to adjust the excess interest payments on a timely basis and measure the profits from Universal Life, separate accounting is needed.

The situation in New York is of special interest. This state requires a company licensed there to obtain special approval if the company wishes to use new money accounting methods. New York is the only state which has not approved the contract. When if finally allows the Universal Life policies—an event we expect in the fall of 1982—there will likely be an extension of their new money requirements to accommodate the companies. Most of the largest life insurance companies have sustantial business in New York. These companies will then be able to segregate or "segment" their investments and compete for Universal Life business. See also the answer to question "P 8" below.

To the extent that Universal Life funds are segregated, the potential for earnings to existing policyholders may be lowered. This conclusion is pure speculation, however, since the failure of the company to offer Universal Life may result in poor future earnings if the company's market share subsequently declines.

I 10. What will mutual companies do to thrive in a Universal Life marketplace?

As we discussed in Chapter 9, mutual companies are increasing the interest return on cash values (including dividends) to make their policies more comptetive on an absolute basis. Moreover, they are hitting hard on the tax leveraging advantages by creaditing high interest on borrowed amounts. For policyholders in a 50% tax bracket, some of the revised mutual company contracts will be very attractive.

We question how long the advantages gained by borrowing to pay premiums will last. Congress will no doubt take an interest in policies that gain a competitive edge at the expense of the federal government.

There are a number of other possibilities. A general update program, similar to the highly advertised program put into effect by Northwestern Mutual during 1979, may be instituted. At least one smaller mutual company instituted such a program in 1982 and granted increased death benefits on existing policies, which averaged 30% to 40%. (This type of progam was generally more attractive prior to the passage of TEFRA.)

New dividend options have been devised to purchase more insurance for a given dollar amount of dividend. Interest rates on dividend accumulations have been steadily increasing for several years and now average 7% or more. This rate competes favorably with short-term government securities being earned in, for example, early 1983. Variable loan interest rate contracts are increasing in number, and several companies have begun to pay higher dividends on policies which do not have policy loans.

PRODUCT DESIGN QUESTIONS

P 1. To what extent will the new IRA products affect the market for Universal Life?

A healthy competition between these types of products has already begun. Both products have the appeal of tax favored high return to the policyholder. In fact, IRAs have an initial advantage becasue IRA contributions are directly deductible for individual federal income tax purposes.

Some buyers can afford both an IRA and a Universal Life policy. Others, with a primary concern for retirement, will put their money into an IRA, and not be able to afford the permanent insurance benefits of Universal Life. They will accept the "lock-in" of their money until retirement as a reasonable trade-off in return for the tax advantages of an IRA.

Many people with a need for life insurance and limited available funds will prefer Universal Life over an IRA. The product provides flexible benefits. Premiums can be varied according to a change in their circumstances as shown in Chapter 2, "One Policy for Life." Importantly, there is no "lock-in." Values may be withdrawn at any time and with no adverse tax consequences as long as the amount withdrawn does not exceed the premium basis in their Universal Life policy.

P 2. How do current interest rates affect the return on Universal Life?

In general, current high interest rates are passed through to Universal Life policyholders at a rate which is guaranteed one year at a time. When current rates decline, the pass-through will also decline. In the next few years, a Universal Life policy and other new money products will be a better buy than the purchase of a new traditional whole life policy. New money is discussed further in Chapter 7 and in the answers above.

P 3. In the long run, will interest passed through to policyholders on Universal Life policies be similar to interest paid through dividends on traditional permanent policies?

By the "long run" we mean 15 to 20 years. The history of interst rates over many hundreds of years points to a future decrease in the prevailing level of interest rates in the United States. In more stable economic times, long-term rates exceed short-term rates because a borrower will be asked to pay more for the use of money over longer periods of time.

When this time comes, policies based on longer term investments will be a better buy than the Universal Life policy of today. By then, we expect to see a variety of flexible policies on the market. Some of these will involve investment in longer term securities or investment trusts for real estate and other forms of real property.

P 4. Will Universal Life be the predominant cash value product by the end of the 1980s?

We hope the reader will reach his own conclusion on this key question after reading this book. Here are the critical condiderations in summary form.

The Universal Life Policy can be structured to provide benefits and/or premiums comparable to almost any traditional policy: endowment, whole life, limited pay life, term or any combination of these. All other things being equal, a policyholder should prefer to add the flexible features of Universal Life to his insurance program.

To the extent that Universal Life companies are able to offer a higher pass-through of interest than traditional policies (and a reasonable level of mortality charges), Universal Life will assume a dominant role at an early date. If traditional products are updated to offer comparable value, they will maintain a major position in the marketplace. Obviously, we cannot predict the outcome of this unprecedented competition in these unprecedented economic times. A number of Universal Life companies are beginning to make a substantial mark. But the others are hard at work improving and conserving the traditional business in which they have a huge investment.

Some believe that flexibility and higher current interest return will be of most interest to the higher income or sophisticated buyer. We think that these features, since they are reasonably priced and simply explained, assure the marketability of Universal Life at all income levels where people need and can afford personal insurance.

P 5. Now that the stopgap legislation has passed Congress and the taxation of excess interest has been determined, will Universal Life policies continue to pay high interest rates?

Yes, in direct proportion to the interest rates that companies can earn on their investment portfolio. As earned interest goes up and down, the interest paid within the Universal Life policy will be adjusted accordingly. At present, the portion of excess interest paid as dividends that is allowed as a deductable expense if 77.5% for mutual companies and 85% for stock companies. A 100% deduction is allowed for policies purchased within a qualified plan. These percentages are reasonable enough that most early Universal Life companies were not forced by the new legislation to reduce the interest they had been crediting.

Also involved in this question is the impact of the margin which companies have had between the interest they guarantee and the amount which they actually earn to provide the excess interest payments to policyholders. Universal Life returns of 11% or so can be met without great diffuculty or risk when secure, short-term investments are returning 14% and more. As rates come down, profit margins and competitive consider- ations begin to conflict, and the high rates may need to be reduced quite independently of the change in the taxation of dividends.

P 6. Are back-end loaded products, which make a surrender charge against the accumulated cash value, worthy of consideration?

Yes, but careful study using the right numbers is required. Advertisements which state that there is "no direct expense charge to the persistent policyholder" are, we think, an artfully worded come-on. Unless the company has actually reduced field compensation or other policy costs, it must arrange its surrender charges to provide roughly the same values to its policyholders as any similarly situated company.

Persistent policyholders may benefit from this product design but the history of policies with deposit features provides no con- vincing proof that this occurs. And, given the fact that a partic- ular policyholder cannot know when a surrender will occur, he may be buying into a surrender charge which reduces his range of options as his circumstances change.

There is another type of special charge that is being used by some companies. This provides that a portion of the excess interest may be held back in the event of surrender. The idea behind this charge is to give the company protection against disintermediation. The details of the charge may or may not be described in the policy contract.

We expect that product designs with surrender charges will become more common. Undoubtly, there will be some types of back-end load products which are better than others. An adequate understanding of how each new product works will be important to the agent since policyholders can misunderstand the unusual provisions of this type of product. Depending upon the way these policies are advertised and sold, it is possible that new regulations will evolve. Comparisons with the more straightforward Universal Life designs should help you understand the differences.

P 7. Is a policy which links the interst return to an investment index more or less marketable than a declared rate product?

One way or another, a competitive return must be offered. If the indexed product's return is above current market interest rates, the product will sell. If not, the agent's job is made more difficult.

Products which rely on a single index can be expected to have a short life span. If a company chooses to use a policy design with an index, it is likely that the company will eventually want to offer several such policies as the relative level of expected return changes from one type of investment to another.

P 8. What will be tomorrow's Universal Life product design?

Universal Life products with directed investments are being developed. The cash value accumulation will vary with the type of investment in which the premiums are invested. Separate accounts are going to be used in a manner related to the variable life insurance policies developed in the early 1970s. In these designs, the policyholder carries a substantial part of the investment risk and, of course, shares in favorable returns. A group of companies have already worked on changes to the model legislation which deals with variable life insurance in an attempt to prepare the way for "variable Universal Life insurance."

In another interesting development, Equitable Life Assurance of New York has received approval from the New York Insurance Department for an investment approach which uses the company's general account. Equitable has defined a "segmentation" approach which allows it to separately keep track of income and investments for a specified block of individual policies. The objective of this segmenting of its business is, presumably, to allow for a new generation of products which will pass through earnings based on investments quite different from those in which the company is currently invested.

P 9. Are products which require a minimum annual premium preferable to Universal Life with a full stop-and-go premium option?

It may be that the discipline of regular premium payments is important to assure that the policyholder's plan for savings and insurance protection is realized. This is one of the advantages claimed for traditional policies. From the agent's point of view, minimum annual premiums are desirable in that they assure some level of renewal commissions. On the other hand, the stop-and-go option is an important part of Universal Life flexibility which helps to sell the policy in the first place. The trade-off is not easy to evaluate. On balance, we think that keeping maximum flexibility is desirable, and that the discipline of keeping the policy in operation as planned should result from the annual report and the agent's regular service of his client.

P 10. How do Universal Life mortality charges compare with low-cost term premiums?

Some mortality charges are much higher than low-cost terms. Others are quite competitive with the best of the annually renewable term policies. Few, if any, Universal Life companies have attempted so far to match the very low premiums under various select and ultimate term contracts which require periodic reunderwriting to enjoy the lowest possible premium rates. (A number of authorities have offered their opinion that these very low cost products may prove to be unprofitable. Some of them are clearly sold with considerable assistance from major reinsurance companies, assistance which will diminish when and if profits fail to materialize.)

In summary, Universal Life does not match the cheapest term available, but the best of the Universal Life contracts provide the pure insurance benefits at a reasonable cost.

P 11. Are Universal Life products being designed to automatically keep pace with inflation?

Yes, several Universal Life policies now have COLA riders which enable the death benefit to increase each year with inflation. We think these will be attractive to people who are concerned with inflation. It should be pointed out that any increase in the death benefit effects an increase in the mortality cost which means there will be a less rapid increase in the cash value. COLA riders are best sold with the idea that planned premiums will be incresed to maintain the cash values. See our example in Chapter 5, "Creating the Proposal"

P 12. Will Universal Life replace the traditional rate manual?

No. Some buyers will continue to prefer traditional policies. Fixed benefits and fixed premiums will be sought after for many years to come. Even companies which are totally commited to Universal Life have found that their agents wish to sell traditional life insurance along with nontraditional. In the spring of 1982, for example, Life of Virginia, a leader in the Universal Life business, was still selling half if its new business on policies other than Universal Life.

New forms of rate charts are in use by Universal Life companies. These are short-cuts to the running of computer illustrations as discussed in Chapter 4, "New Technology and the Sales Process." The charts list the level premiums needed to provide the equivalent of whole life insurance. Usually, the premium based on current assumptions is given. Another chart can show the premium based on the guarantees in the contract. Thus, a form of simplified rate book will exist as a sales aid even for companies which may eventually rely entirely on Universal Life.

LEGAL AND TAX QUESTIONS

L 1. With respect to taxes, will Universal Life policyholders be treated differently than traditional products policyholders?

We think not, because Universal Life contracts are essentially structured in the same way as whole life. The passage of TEFRA has clarified the answer to this question, since the law defines the circumstances in which Universal Life policies (termed "flexible premium policies" in the legislation) will be treated as life insurance. These provisions are part of the two-year stopgap legislation we discussed in detail in Chapter 8, "TEFRA 1982 - Tax Issues and Guidelines."

L 2. Why shouldn't borrowings in excess of aggregate premiums be taxed to policyholders?

Historically, life insurance policyholders have never been taxed on borrowings in excess of their cost basis. There are a number of traditional whole life policies in force today where the borrowings exceed the policyholder's cost basis because of minimum deposit approaches. An administrative nightmare would be created if the rules of the game were changed.

In technical terms, borrowings have always been treated as an advance against benefit proceeds to be received on death or surrender. Under normal circumstances where the policy has not been transferred for value, death benefits are received free of income tax. In the event of policy surrender, Universal Life policies will be taxed to the extent that net cash proceeds plus previous borrowings exceed the cost basis. This is the same rule which applies to traditional policies.

L 3. How will Universal Life deal with the hypothetical case *in which the cash value is large and death benefit small, say, for example $1,000,000 premium and $10,000 death benefit?*

The statutory language in TEFRA has established a carefully crafted death benefit corridor and guideline premium tests. These were designed to resolve the problem of too little death benefit. If the policy adheres to these guidelines, it will continue to qualify as life insurance under IRC Section 101. Most, if not all, Universal Life companies will restructure their computer proposal methods so the agent will not run illustrations that fall outside the guidelines. In any event, most companies will administratively alert the policyholder if the guidelines may be violated, allowing an opportunity to adjust premiums or benefits.

L 4. What legislation can we expect to be passed in 1983 (or later) concerning Universal Life products?

First, we believe the legislation defining the death benefit corridor and guideline premiums will be extended in essentially the same form. The TEFRA parameters are reasonable, workable and satisfactory to all concerned.

The stopgap legislation concerning excess interest is a different matter. We think the form of the legislation concerning the deductibility of excess interest paid as dividends is sensible. However, in spite of the legislation, a number of companies are claiming 100% deductibility of excess interest. Simultaneously, the industry has experienced operating losses from causes such as increased claims and expenses in group health insurance. Government revenues will surely be less than estimated during the hurried development of stopgap.

Consequently, there is a real possibility that two changes will occur. First, the limits of deductibility may become absolute limits, not merely a safe harbor. Excess interest credited in excess of the policy's guarantee will not be deductible by the Universal Life company under any circumstances. Second, the portion of dividends which is deductable may be lowered as

Congress does its annual balancing act between revenue and the government's operating deficit.

Finally, a general reform of the insurance company tax law is unlikely before 1984 or 1985. Indications are the law will be considered in the wide context of all financial institutions. Preoccupied with recession and unemployment, Congress will need time.

L 5. Do high interest rate life insurance products that are not flexible premium products have to comply with the parameters that have been established for Universal Life?

IRC Section 101 (f) specifically states that the guidelines apply only to flexible premium products; that is, to products for which premiums are not fixed as to timing or amount. There are an increasing number of high interest life insurance products that provide for premiums that are fixed as to the timing and amount; these clearly are not covered by Section 101 (f). These products are generally covered by the rules pertaining to life insurance as discussed in this book.

It is likely that Congress, with prodding from the IRS, will consider extending the logic of the rules for Universal Life insurance to all life insurance products. If this happens, the single premium whole life policy mentioned in Chapter 9, "How Others Expect to Compete", will have to dramatically increase its amount of pure death benefit.

L 6. What is the future for products that offer a high interest return on total cash value (including borrowed funds) and charge variable loans rates?

The immediate future for these products is bright because of the tremendous tax advantages. In the long run, the outlook is dim. We believe that limits will be imposed on the deductibility of interest paid on borrowing, and that these products will lose their attractive tax leverage. This is a case of just too much of a good thing. Among the many approaches the government may take is one of imposing a maximum on the interest that can be deducted in connection with life insurance policy loans.

L 7. Is there a possibility that Universal Life policyholders will be taxed on the interest credited to the cash value?

Yes, there is such a possibility—especially if Congress is frustrated in its ability to collect sufficient taxes from life insurance companies. (A proposal to tax cash value increases was considered and partially enacted in Canada during 1982.) We certainly do not favor this type of taxation. It would be damaging to the purchase of life insurance policies and would be extremely unpopular. Nevertheless, the gaping federal deficit may provoke irrational thinking and ill-concieved legislation.

L 8. What will happen if the stopgap legislation for Universal Life insurance is not continued?

The industry would be thrown back to the pre-1982 legislation. As discussed in an earlier chapter, Universal Life apparently qualified as life insurance under the older law because it offered mortality benefits and caused risk shifting and risk distribution. Universal Life would continue to be sold. We would expect the companies to continue to comply with the parameters of Section 101 (f) even though this section of the IRC would no longer apply.

With respect to the deductibility of excess interest, the answer becomes much more involved. The industry would be thrown back to the Mass Mutual adverse ruling in which the IRS basically held that excess interest credited on Universal Life would be treated as a dividend. Litigation on this point would undoubtly develop. In any event, because the safe harbor would be lost, some companies would drop the interest rate credited because of concern for the tax liability, which would then be unknown. In the case of mutual companies, the old tax law had such a negative effect that high interest rate life insurance products developed by the mutuals might well be taken off the market.

CHAPTER 11

Marketing Ideas and Case Studies

With the background of the previous chapters, let us now look at the various applications of Universal Life. In the first part of this book, we discussed a typical family situation. Many of the obvious situations were covered in Figure 2.1. The case studies here illustrate other uses of the Universal Life policy to meet family and personal life insurance needs.

Personal Life Insurance

1) Gifts of Universal Life to children and grandchildren can be made by parents or grandparents. Under the gift program the premium paying period can be shortened or lengthened to fit the age of the donor and donee, as well as changing circumstances.
2) Universal Life insurance can be purchased in irrevocable

trusts for estate tax purposes. The size of the policy can be adjusted as situations change and the need for estate liquidity varies.

3) Split-Dollar Contracts can be established where the owner controls the cash value (standard Universal Life Option B, cash value plus death benefit) and the son or daughter has the benefit of the death benefit. If sufficiently large deposits are made, the tax-sheltered interest may pay for the entire cost of the death benefit.

4) Universal Life may eliminate the need for jumbo term policies. Since the cash value can always be withdrawn from the Universal Life contract, it is easily converted into a term policy. Clients will, in general, be more willing to pay money into permanent Universal Life insurance if they know they can get the money back for emergency needs and capital expenses.

5) Universal Life can be used for substandard insurance. In many substandard situations, the Universal Life policy requires no additional out-of-pocket premium. In other situations, the Universal Life premium will often be no more than the basic premium plus the extra premium on a traditional permanent product.

Business Life Insurance

In the business insurance market, the possibilities are unlimited. The availability of the "other insured rider" (a rider allowing more than one person to be insured under one policy) makes the Universal Life policy an excellent product for business insurance situations. Nearly all types of business needs can be satisfied by one policy form. The following are some of the applications.

1) Buy-Sell. Not only can more than one person be insured under the policy, but the problem of the disparity of pre-

miums for stockholders, young partners, and older partners who join the firm at a later time are easily resolved. Using Universal Life, one can arrange for the premium to be equal for any or all of the parties involved.

2) Split-Dollar. This application is discussed above in the individual or personal insurance setting, but an additional point of interest is the withdrawal of the companies' contributions in the eighth year. Since it is a withdrawal and not a loan, there is no interest due. If large enough premium payments are made in the early years, no further premium payments may have to be paid.

3) Qualified Plans. These are ideally suited for Universal Life. A major nuisance in defined benefit plans has been the large number of policies that accumulate on the life of each participant due to salary increases. This problem is now solved since the flexible death benefit of the one policy originally taken out is just increased or decreased for adjustments in salary. The combinations of death benefit and cash values are unlimited.

4) Key-Man Insurance. Not only can the size of the policy be adjusted as the needs of the company change, but (if the policy permits) the key people insured under the policy can be changed as they come and go and the cash value is undisturbed.

5) Deferred Compensation. The size of the policy and cash value can be adjusted each year to meet the terms of the deferred compensation agreement. The company can adjust the payments to pay up the policy at age 65 (or actual retirement). Partial withdrawals can be made at the key-person's retirement to fund his benefits, and the death benefit of the policy can be kept in force until the key-person's death.

The charge against corporate earnings has always been a problem in selling deferred compensation cases. Since the cash value is high in the first and subsequent policy years, there is very little charge against the company's earnings. The corporate financial people like Universal Life because they can more easily justify this low charge to earnings.

These are just a few of the applications where the Universal Life policy is useful. In most markets, the Universal Life policy is more efficient than the specific products that were designed for that market. The skillful use of the policy's flexibility, augmented by the powerful illustrations available through the new technology, will satisfy all manner of life insurance needs. The agent will think of other ideas as he discusses the product with his clients and some new ideas will be mentioned by the clients.

Case Studies₁

₁ These illustrations have not been changed from the first edition and do not meet the TEFRA Corridor requirements at all ages. However, this in no way diminishes the illustration of the policy's flexibility. The TEFRA corridor requirements are fully discussed in Chapter 8, "TEFRA 1982—Tax Issues and Guidelines."

Ledger Sheet   Case Study 1

Facts:
David is age 36, married and has four children. He would like to buy a Universal Life policy which is similar in premium structure to the traditional whole life policy his father purchased 25 years ago. David wants to compare the cash values and death benefits at age 65 and age 75 to see if there are significant reasons to purchase Universal Life rather than a whole life policy.

Plan:
The agent runs a $100,000 Universal Life illustration, male, age 36. It shows guaranteed interest at 4% and current interest at 12.36%. Since the current rate could change significantly, an additional column, assuming 8% interest is illustrated. The illustration is based on a premium of $2,000 per year.

Comments:
The $2,000 premium is sufficient to continue the policy at the 4% guaranteed rate, 8% illustrated rate, and the current 12.36% rate. The cash value and death benefit increase greatly with the increase in interest rate. At the 12.36% current rate, David has $1,323,790 in cash value and $1,456,170 in death benefits at age 75.

Ledger Sheet   Case Study 1

AGE	YEAR	ANNUAL PREMIUM	4.0% BASIS (guaranteed) CASH VALUE	DEATH BENEFIT	8.0% BASIS (illustrative) CASH VALUE	DEATH BENEFIT	12.36% BASIS (current) CASH VALUE	DEATH BENEFIT
36	1	2,000	904	100,000	980	100,000	995	100,000
37	2	2,000	2,556	100,000	2,767	100,000	2,860	100,000
38	3	2,000	4,257	100,000	4,688	100,000	4,944	100,000
39	4	2,000	6,010	100,000	6,752	100,000	7,277	100,000
40	5	2,000	7,812	100,000	8,970	100,000	9,887	100,000
45	10	2,000	17,598	100,000	22,877	100,000	28,539	100,000
50	15	2,000	28,753	100,000	42,964	100,000	61,858	100,000
55	20	2,000	41,397	100,000	72,517	100,000	121,984	146,984
60	25	2,000	55,899	100,000	116,099	141,099	229,024	254,024
65	30	2,000	73,211	100,000	179,046	204,046	418,581	460,439
70	35	2,000	93,589	118,589	269,649	296,614	749,962	824,958
75	40	2,000	115,423	140,423	398,344	438,178	1,323,790	1,456,170

Tax Free Loan   Case Study 2

Facts: Harold is age 48 and has a son, age 25, who is single and making $28,000 per year as an engineer. Harold would like to loan his son $100,000 on an interest free basis for 8 years and then receive the money back. The son decides to invest the money to generate interest which will be income tax free.

Plan: After discussing the idea with their life insurance agent, Harold decides to pay a $100,000 single premium into a Universal Life policy. The $100,000 single premium will purchase as much insurance as is provided in the contract. After eight years, a partial withdrawal of $100,000 will be made to repay Harold, and the son will then have a fully paid life insurance policy on his father's life. His cash value will continue to grow on a tax free basis.

Comments: If Harold dies the first year, his son has $126,282 tax free to repay the $100,000 loan and $26,282 to add to his own estate. If Harold dies at age 75, his son has already paid back the $100,000 in the eighth year and has $1,097,690 cash at current interest rates. Since the son has already repaid the $100,000 to Harold, the cost basis of the policy is zero. Therefore, any further withdrawals will be taxable interest. In the future, it might be preferable to make policy loans, which would not be taxable to the son. The Universal Life contract makes provisions for both policy loans and partial withdrawals.

Tax Free Loan

Case Study 2

AGE	YEAR	ANNUAL PREMIUM	4.0% BASIS (guaranteed) CASH VALUE	4.0% BASIS (guaranteed) DEATH BENEFIT	8.0% BASIS (illustrative) CASH VALUE	8.0% BASIS (illustrative) DEATH BENEFIT	12.36% BASIS (current) CASH VALUE	12.36% BASIS (current) DEATH BENEFIT
48	1	100,000	93,743	118,743	97,378	122,378	101,282	126,282
49	2	0	97,300	122,300	104,990	129,990	113,575	138,575
50	3	0	100,981	125,981	113,198	138,198	127,373	152,373
51	4	0	104,790	129,790	122,050	147,050	142,862	167,862
52	5	0	108,729	133,729	131,595	156,595	160,251	185,251
53	6	0	112,802	137,802	141,889	166,889	179,773	204,773
54	7	0	117,013	142,013	152,989	177,989	201,689	226,689
→ YEAR 8: $100,000 PARTIAL WITHDRAWAL								
55	8	0	16,592	100,000	56,772	100,000	113,935	138,935
56	9	0	16,045	100,000	60,860	100,000	127,673	152,673
57	10	0	15,352	100,000	65,285	100,000	143,085	168,085
58	11	0	14,493	100,000	70,083	100,000	160,375	185,375
59	12	0	13,444	100,000	75,293	100,293	179,772	204,772
60	13	0	12,175	100,000	80,917	105,917	201,530	226,530
65	18	0	1,190	100,000	115,828	140,828	356,724	392,396
70	23	0			165,298	190,298	628,028	690,831
75	28	0			235,770	260,770	1,097,690	1,207,460

Personal Split-Dollar   # Case Study 3

Facts:
DiAnn is age 50 and has a daughter, Sally, age 25. Sally has married a real estate salesman named Frankie, age 27. Frankie has had limited business success in recent years. DiAnn has inherited $300,000 and is worried that her daughter's family will not be able to sustain their standard of living if Frankie dies.

Plan:
DiAnn decides to set up a personal split-dollar policy. Frankie will be the insured. He is willing to pay the cost of pure protection under the policy in the future, but has no available funds at the present time. DiAnn is willing to pay the entire premium on $250,000 of life insurance in the amount of $5,000 per year. She would like to (a) receive her premiums back if Frankie dies, and (b) have the flexibility to recover her premiums at some future date, if he lives. An endorsement split-dollar arrangement is set up, with all premiums being paid by DiAnn. Sally is given the right to change the beneficiary. The option in the policy to pay a death benefit of the cash value plus the face amount of $250,000 is elected.

Comments:
The $5,000 per year premium is sufficient to provide benefits to age 75 at 4%, 8%, and 12.36% interest. Objectives (a) and (b) will be accomplished. Note that, if Frankie dies in 20 years and the policy interest rate is the equivalent of 8% interest, DiAnn would receive $194,330 and Sally the face value of $250,000. DiAnn's total premiums over 20 years would have been $5,000 x 20 or $100,000. DiAnn has a $94,330 profit over her deposits, and Sally gets $250,000 tax free.

Personal Split-Dollar

Case Study 3

A G E	Y E A R	ANNUAL PREMIUM	4.0% BASIS (guaranteed)		8.0% BASIS (illustrative)		12.36% BASIS (current)	
			CASH VALUE	DEATH BENEFIT	CASH VALUE	DEATH BENEFIT	CASH VALUE	DEATH BENEFIT
27	1	5,000	3,338	253,338	3,528	253,528	3,654	253,654
31	5	5,000	21,723	271,723	24,774	274,774	27,822	277,822
36	10	5,000	48,729	298,729	62,217	312,217	78,918	328,918
41	15	5,000	80,414	330,414	116,306	366,306	169,396	419,396
46	20	5,000	116,675	366,675	194,330	444,330	329,812	579,812
51	25	5,000	157,092	407,092	306,107	556,107	613,890	863,890
56	30	5,000	200,345	450,345	466,033	716,033	1,117,750	1,367,750
61	35	5,000	243,733	493,733	694,183	944,183	2,012,190	2,262,190
66	40	5,000	282,090	532,090	1,017,330	1,267,330	3,595,150	3,954,660
71	45	5,000	306,052	556,052	1,472,510	1,772,510	6,356,970	6,992,670

Irrevocable Trust   Case Study 4

Facts:	Fred, age 55, and Margaret, age 53, are husband and wife. Fred is concerned about the estate taxes that will be due at his and his wife's deaths. Their combined estate is $3,500,000, tied-up completely in a business that Margaret inherited five years ago.
Plan:	Fred's attorney suggests that Fred and his wife each establish an irrevocable trust, and that each trust purchase $500,000 of life insurance on the grantor of the trust. The irrevocable trusts will be beneficiaries and owners of the policies. Two Universal Life policies are bought. Annual premiums of $30,000 are planned, $15,000 to each trust. To offset inflation, the policies are set up so that the death benefit of each policy will be the cash value plus the $500,000 face value of each policy. Fred feels that it would be wise to fund Margaret's trust over a short period. He, therefore, asks to review an illustration on his wife with premiums limited to ten years. To complicate matters, Fred has high blood pressure readings during his physical and his policy is issued with a Table 2 rating. The agent now needs to illustrate the same plan, with the same $15,000 premium including the rating.
Comments:	Fred's policy appears to be adequately funded at $15,000 premium per year. However, when the Table 2 rating is added, the policy becomes level term to age 72 at 12.36%, level term to age 69 at 8%, and level term to age 62 at the 4% guaranteed interest rate. It is important for the agent to point out that, with the rating, no additional cash is needed immediately, but cash must be added in the future if the policy is to continue.

Irrevocable Trust
Fred (Standard Issue)

Case Study 4

AGE	YEAR	ANNUAL PREMIUM	4.0% BASIS (guaranteed)		8.0% BASIS (illustrative)		12.36% BASIS (current)	
			CASH VALUE	DEATH BENEFIT	CASH VALUE	DEATH BENEFIT	CASH VALUE	DEATH BENEFIT
55	1	15,000	6,418	506,418	8,899	508,899	9,324	509,324
56	2	15,000	13,633	513,633	19,289	519,289	20,595	520,595
57	3	15,000	20,460	520,460	30,071	530,072	32,811	532,811
58	4	15,000	26,816	526,816	41,225	541,225	46,035	546,035
59	5	15,000	32,616	532,616	52,705	552,705	60,313	560,313
64	10	15,000	49,447	549,447	112,590	612,590	149,060	649,060
69	15	15,000	31,934	531,934	167,893	667,893	271,750	771,750
72	18	15,000			193,493	693,494	367,006	867,006

Irrevocable Trust — Fred (Table 2 Rating)

AGE	YEAR	ANNUAL PREMIUM	CASH VALUE	DEATH BENEFIT	CASH VALUE	DEATH BENEFIT	CASH VALUE	DEATH BENEFIT
55	1	15,000	3,114	503,114	6,230	506,230	6,596	506,596
56	2	15,000	6,584	506,584	13,415	513,415	14,474	514,474
57	3	15,000	9,176	509,176	20,383	520,383	22,516	522,516
58	4	15,000	10,758	510,758	27,012	527,012	30,635	530,635
59	5	15,000	11,190	511,190	33,134	533,134	38,696	538,696
64	10	15,000			47,843	547,843	70,635	570,635
69	15	15,000			8,992	508,992	60,848	560,848
72	18	15,000					14,937	514,938

Irrevocable Trust — Margaret (10 Premiums)

AGE	YEAR	ANNUAL PREMIUM	CASH VALUE	DEATH BENEFIT	CASH VALUE	DEATH BENEFIT	CASH VALUE	DEATH BENEFIT
53	1	15,000	7,492	507,492	10,205	510,205	10,658	510,658
54	2	15,000	15,927	515,927	22,143	522,143	23,570	523,570
55	3	15,000	24,140	524,140	34,708	534,708	37,742	537,742
56	4	15,000	32,065	532,065	47,922	547,922	53,302	553,302
57	5	15,000	39,629	539,629	61,795	561,795	70,377	570,377
62	10	15,000	68,958	568,958	141,620	641,620	184,391	684,391
63	11	0	58,182	558,182	145,036	645,036	199,042	699,042
67	15	0			156,879	656,879	272,976	772,976
70	18	0			165,332	665,332	352,625	852,625

Gift to Minor   Case Study 5

Facts: Julie is born, and Mom and Dad want to pro-
                 vide for her future college education. They
                 believe she will need about $20,000 per year to
                 go to college. Since they would like her to be a
                 professional, graduate school could add four
                 years to her schooling. Mom and Dad both work
                 and feel they could pay $800 per month into a
                 college fund for the next five years.

Plan: A Universal Life policy is established for
                 $100,000 on Julie's life. Premium payments are
                 planned to be $9,600 per year for five years. A
                 partial withdrawal of $20,000 per year for 8
                 years will be made starting at Julie's age 18.

Comments: This case shows the earning power of com-
                 pound interest. At 12.36% interest, the objec-
                 tives are accomplished plus Julie has a death
                 benefit of $23,100,800 at age 60 and
                 $72,178,300 death benefit at age 70. However,
                 at 4% interest, the plan can not continue past
                 age 19 due to a lack of cash value.

Gift to Minor   Case Study 5

AGE	YEAR	ANNUAL PREMIUM	4.0% BASIS (guaranteed)		8.0% BASIS (illustrative)		12.36% BASIS (current)	
			CASH VALUE	DEATH BENEFIT	CASH VALUE	DEATH BENEFIT	CASH VALUE	DEATH BENEFIT
0	1	9,600	7,696	100,000	9,983	100,000	8,291	100,000
1	2	9,600	16,940	100,000	17,873	100,000	18,903	100,000
2	3	9,600	26,588	100,000	28,590	100,000	30,865	100,000
3	4	9,600	36,642	100,000	40,181	100,000	44,324	100,000
4	5	9,600	47,117	100,000	52,723	100,000	59,474	100,000
5	6	0	48,930	100,000	56,840	100,000	66,691	100,000
6	7	0	50,821	100,000	61,296	100,000	74,815	100,000
7	8	0	52,792	100,000	66,116	100,000	83,945	108,947
8	9	0	54,846	100,000	71,326	100,000	94,209	119,209
9	10	0	56,986	100,000	76,961	101,961	105,738	130,738
10	11	0	59,214	100,000	83,047	108,047	118,693	143,696
11	12	0	61,533	100,000	89,620	114,620	133,249	158,249
12	13	0	63,946	100,000	96,720	121,720	149,603	174,603
13	14	0	66,457	100,000	104,383	129,383	167,976	192,976
14	15	0	69,070	100,000	112,660	137,660	188,620	213,620
15	16	0	71,789	100,000	121,596	146,596	211,812	236,812
16	17	0	74,619	100,000	131,247	156,247	237,870	262,870

➡ **YEARS 18 THROUGH 25: $20,000 PARTIAL WITHDRAWAL**

AGE	YEAR	ANNUAL PREMIUM	4.0% BASIS (guaranteed)		8.0% BASIS (illustrative)		12.36% BASIS (current)	
17	18	0	56,730	100,000	120,067	145,067	244,674	269,674
18	19	0	38,092	100,000	107,989	132,989	252,315	277,546
19	20	0	18,671	100,000	94,945	119,945	260,900	286,990
20	21	0			80,857	105,857	270,546	297,600
21	22	0			65,622	100,000	281,381	309,520
22	23	0			49,140	100,000	293,554	322,910
23	24	0			31,309	100,000	307,229	337,952
24	25	0			12,019	100,000	322,592	354,851
25	26	0			12,787	100,000	362,318	398,550
26	27	0			13,618	100,000	406,946	447,641
30	31	0			17,678	100,000	647,757	712,532
40	41	0			35,366	100,000	2,071,560	2,278,720
50	51	0			73,027	100,000	6,614,440	7,275,890

Leveraging Home Equity   Case Study 6

Facts:
Douglas is age 39 when he sells his home. At the closing, he receives a check for his equity of $100,000. He moves to Philadelphia and decides to pay half the proceeds as a down payment on his new home and invest the other $50,000.

Plan:
While talking to a Philadelphia insurance agent, Doug is shown a Universal Life illustration. He likes the idea of life insurance to cover his new $150,000 mortgage. He further likes the idea that he can make a single premium payment and that the interest accumulates tax free. Currently, Doug is paying $450 per year for term insurance. After the new Universal Life policy is issued, he terminates the term insurance and puts the $450 per year in the Universal Life policy, in addition to the $50,000 initial premium payment.

Comments:
This case illustrates the flexibility of Universal Life. Substantial cash values are available for withdrawal or policy loans. Douglas can stop paying the $450 any time he likes. The cash value would be sufficient to carry the policy without these premiums.

Leveraging Home Equity

Case Study 6

AGE	YEAR	ANNUAL PREMIUM	4,0% BASIS (guaranteed)		8,0% BASIS (illustrative)		12,36% BASIS (current)	
			CASH VALUE	DEATH BENEFIT	CASH VALUE	DEATH BENEFIT	CASH VALUE	DEATH BENEFIT
39	1	50,450	46,624	150,000	48,487	150,000	50,425	150,000
40	2	450	48,548	150,000	52,498	150,000	56,767	150,000
41	3	450	50,524	150,000	56,826	150,000	63,896	150,000
42	4	450	52,554	150,000	61,497	150,000	71,914	150,000
43	5	450	54,638	150,000	66,539	150,000	80,938	150,000
44	6	450	56,779	150,000	71,983	150,000	91,087	150,000
45	7	450	58,975	150,000	77,860	150,000	102,517	150,000
50	12	450	70,807	150,000	115,178	150,000	185,060	210,060
55	17	450	84,120	150,000	170,415	195,415	332,437	365,681
60	22	450	99,218	150,000	250,996	276,096	594,143	653,557
65	27	450	116,929	150,000	367,645	404,410	1,055,980	1,161,580
70	32	450	138,525	163,525	534,137	587,551	1,863,040	2,049,350

Change of Lifestyle   Case Study 7

Facts: David (Case Study 1) is now age 46. He decides
                   to leave his regular job at the home office of an
                   insurance company to become a life insurance
                   agent. He needs capital to start his agency and
                   decides to use the value of his Universal Life
                   policy. He further decides to stop premiums for
                   the next five years.

Plan: David makes a partial withdrawal from his Uni-
                   versal Life policy which he bought 10 years ago
                   at age 36. The cash value at age 46 is $22,877
                   (assume 8% interest was credited.) David with-
                   drawals $20,000 and skips premium payments
                   for the next five years. After the five years, he
                   feels he is able to once again deposit the $2,000
                   per year.

Comments: This is a continuation of Case Study 1. It shows
                   the versatility of Universal Life. David can
                   withdraw money when he needs extra funds.
                   No interest need be paid. He can use the stop-
                   and-go premium feature and maintain his cover-
                   age at the initial $100,000 death benefit level.
                   After his business gets started, the policy may
                   be continued as desired.

Special Note: In this case, the $20,000 cash withdrawal equals
                   the premiums paid in the first ten years of the
                   policy. The agent can easily illustrate the return
                   of premium in this way and can, if desired,
                   increase the death benefit each year by an
                   amount equal to the sum of premiums paid to
                   date.

Change of Lifestyle

Case Study 7

AGE	YEAR	ANNUAL PREMIUM	4.0% BASIS (guaranteed)		8.0% BASIS (illustrative)		12.36% BASIS (current)	
			CASH VALUE	DEATH BENEFIT	CASH VALUE	DEATH BENEFIT	CASH VALUE	DEATH BENEFIT
36	1	2,000	904	100,000	980	100,000	995	100,000
37	2	2,000	2,556	100,000	2,767	100,000	2,860	100,000
38	3	2,000	4,257	100,000	4,688	100,000	4,944	100,000
39	4	2,000	6,010	100,000	6,752	100,000	7,277	100,000
40	5	2,000	7,812	100,000	8,970	100,000	9,887	100,000
41	6	2,000	9,664	100,000	11,357	100,000	12,813	100,000
42	7	2,000	11,567	100,000	13,927	100,000	16,094	100,000
43	8	2,000	13,524	100,000	16,694	100,000	19,775	100,000
44	9	2,000	15,534	100,000	19,672	100,000	23,905	100,000
45	10	2,000	17,598	100,000	22,877	100,000	28,539	100,000
➡ YEAR 11: $20,000 PARTIAL WITHDRAWAL								
46	11	0			2,642	100,000	9,103	100,000
47	12	0			2,368	100,000	9,722	100,000
48	13	0			2,027	100,000	10,380	100,000
49	14	0			1,609	100,000	11,078	100,000
50	15	0			1,103	100,000	11,818	100,000
51	16	2,000			2,478	100,000	14,665	100,000
52	17	2,000			3,920	100,000	17,837	100,000
53	18	2,000			5,431	100,000	21,377	100,000
54	19	2,000			7,010	100,000	25,329	100,000
55	20	2,000			8,654	100,000	29,747	100,000
60	25	2,000			18,025	100,000	61,548	100,000
65	30	2,000			29,275	100,000	119,406	144,406
70	35	2,000			42,638	100,000	221,113	246,113
75	40	2,000			60,972	100,000	398,908	438,810

Partnership/Corporate Buy-Sell   Case Study 8
Part A

Facts: Tom, age 30, and Ernie, age 35, form a partnership and need life insurance to fund a buy-sell agreement. The value of the partnership is determined to be $200,000.

Plan: They each purchase a $100,000 Universal Life policy on the other's life. They pay a minimum premium only until the business starts to develop a positive cash flow. Thus, they make an initial premium payment of $1,000 per year into each contract.

Comment: It is interesting to note a $1,000 level premium at ages 30 and 35 is sufficient to provide $100,000, or more, of death benefit protection to life expectancy (age 73) at the current interest rate, 12.36% and assume average rate of 8%. However, 4% interest only keeps the age 30 going to age 73 on the guaranteed side. The age 35 illustration requires additional cash to maintain the contract past age 64 on the 4% guaranteed side.

Partnership/Corporate Buy-Sell Part A

Case Study 8

A G E	Y E A R	ANNUAL PREMIUM	4.0% BASIS (guaranteed)		8.0% BASIS (illustrative)		12.36% BASIS (current)	
			CASH VALUE	DEATH BENEFIT	CASH VALUE	DEATH BENEFIT	CASH VALUE	DEATH BENEFIT
30	1	1,000	7	100,000	62	100,000	74	100,000
34	5	1,000	3,058	100,000	3,546	100,000	3,776	100,000
39	10	1,000	7,375	100,000	9,522	100,000	11,434	100,000
44	15	1,000	12,034	100,000	17,981	100,000	24,853	100,000
49	20	1,000	16,778	100,000	29,933	100,000	48,630	100,000
54	25	1,000	21,118	100,000	46,956	100,000	91,503	116,503
59	30	1,000	24,241	100,000	71,919	100,000	168,077	193,077
64	35	1,000	24,576	100,000	108,639	133,639	303,974	334,371
69	40	1,000	18,780	100,000	160,932	185,932	542,362	596,599
73	44	1,000	4,793	100,000	218,427	243,427	854,214	939,636

A G E	Y E A R	ANNUAL PREMIUM	4.0% BASIS (guaranteed)		8.0% BASIS (illustrative)		12.36% BASIS (current)	
			CASH VALUE	DEATH BENEFIT	CASH VALUE	DEATH BENEFIT	CASH VALUE	DEATH BENEFIT
35	1	1,000	0	100,000	39	100,000	51	100,000
39	5	1,000	2,745	100,000	3,294	100,000	3,505	100,000
44	10	1,000	6,281	100,000	8,692	100,000	10,441	100,000
49	15	1,000	9,550	100,000	15,978	100,000	22,241	100,000
54	20	1,000	11,871	100,000	25,733	100,000	42,699	100,000
59	25	1,000	12,073	100,000	39,034	100,000	79,589	104,589
64	30	1,000	7,841	100,000	57,613	100,000	145,663	170,663
69	35	1,000			85,042	110,042	262,055	288,261
73	39	1,000			115,214	140,214	415,037	456,541

Partnership/Corporate Buy-Sell   Case Study 8
Part B

Facts: Five years later Tom, age 35, and Ernie, age 40, incorporate the business and transfer ownership of the policies to the newly incorporated business.

Plan: Tom and Ernie increase the pure death benefit of the Universal Life contract to $250,000 each and agree to increase their premium to $2,000 per year for each contract.

Comment: At the guaranteed rate, the $2,000 premium in the 36th year for Tom and 26th year for Ernie is not sufficient to carry $250,000 to age 74. However, at the current rate of 12.36%, there is more than sufficient cash to carry the death benefit protection to age 74.

At the current rate of 12.36%, the cash value at age 74 is $1,420,890 and death benefit protection is $1,562,980 on Tom's policy. The cash value at age 74 on Ernie's policy is $606,401 and the death benefit is $667,042.

At current rates the key-man insurance will provide additional indemnification to the corporation.

Partnership/Corporate Buy-Sell Part B

Case Study 8

AGE	YEAR	ANNUAL PREMIUM	4.0% BASIS (guaranteed) CASH VALUE	4.0% BASIS (guaranteed) DEATH BENEFIT	8.0% BASIS (illustrative) CASH VALUE	8.0% BASIS (illustrative) DEATH BENEFIT	12.36% BASIS (current) CASH VALUE	12.36% BASIS (current) DEATH BENEFIT
30	1	1,000	7	100,000	62	100,000	74	100,000
34	5	1,000	3,058	100,000	3,546	100,000	3,776	100,000
35	6	2,000	4,290	250,000	5,100	250,000	5,534	250,000
39	10	2,000	10,007	250,000	13,127	250,000	15,556	250,000
44	15	2,000	17,011	250,000	26,465	250,000	35,943	250,000
49	20	2,000	22,905	250,000	44,483	250,000	71,097	250,000
54	25	2,000	25,787	250,000	68,636	250,000	132,928	250,000
59	30	2,000	22,366	250,000	101,625	250,000	245,748	270,748
64	35	2,000	6,075	250,000	147,804	250,000	448,660	493,526
69	40	2,000			216,950	250,000	804,162	884,579
73	44	2,000			298,789	328,668	1,269,250	1,396,180

AGE	YEAR	ANNUAL PREMIUM	4.0% BASIS (guaranteed) CASH VALUE	4.0% BASIS (guaranteed) DEATH BENEFIT	8.0% BASIS (illustrative) CASH VALUE	8.0% BASIS (illustrative) DEATH BENEFIT	12.36% BASIS (current) CASH VALUE	12.36% BASIS (current) DEATH BENEFIT
35	1	1,000	0	100,000	39	100,000	51	100,000
39	5	1,000	2,745	100,000	3,294	100,000	3,505	100,000
40	6	2,000	3,707	250,000	4,653	250,000	5,050	250,000
44	10	2,000	7,802	250,000	11,576	250,000	13,764	250,000
49	15	2,000	11,335	250,000	22,115	250,000	30,489	250,000
54	20	2,000	10,986	250,000	34,617	250,000	57,651	250,000
59	25	2,000	2,890	250,000	48,914	250,000	103,690	250,000
64	30	2,000			63,477	250,000	185,884	250,000
69	35	2,000			74,490	250,000	339,151	373,067
73	39	2,000			77,565	250,000	540,685	594,753

Deferred Compensation   Case Study 9

Facts: Five years later Tom, age 40, and Ernie, age 45,
                  decide to establish a deferred compensation
                  plan in their corporation. The deferred compen-
                  sation plan provides $50,000 per year for 10
                  years to their families if death occurs prior to
                  age 65, and post-retirement compensation of
                  $50,000 per year starting at age 65, lasting for
                  10 years.

Plan: Two additional Universal Life contracts for
                  $250,000 each are established on Tom and
                  Ernie. The owner and beneficiary of the con-
                  tracts is the corporation. $12,500 per year is
                  paid into each contract for a total premium of
                  $25,000.

Comments (1):   Assuming the corporation's tax bracket is
                  approximately 50%, $250,000 cash from the
                  Universal Life contract at death prior to age 65
                  would allow a $500,000 payment of funds
                  ($50,000 per year x 10 years). Any balance of
                  funds over $250,000 received from the contract
                  would be key-man insurance. For example, at
                  age 59, Tom's death would bring in anywhere
                  from $326,568 guaranteed to $903,299 (at
                  12.36% interest).
                      At age 65, the guaranteed death benefit in
                  Tom's contract, is $533,118 and at current
                  interest rates, $2,090,400. A substantial profit to
                  the corporation would develop, since the tax-
                  free money paid to the corporation at Tom's
                  death at age 59 or age 65 is substantially greater

296

than the amount needed to fund the deferred compensation benefits of $250,000.

Comments (2): At age 65 Tom and Ernie make a partial withdrawal of $50,000 per year for 10 years. The balance of the funds are left in the policy to provide key-man insurance to the corporation at their deaths.

The premium payments stop at age 65 and there are no loans taken, merely a cash withdrawal of funds each year. We note, in Ernie's case, there is sufficient cash at the current 12.36% interest rate but less than sufficient cash at the guaranteed 4% interest rate. The plan should be reviewed each year from inception to determine its adequacy. If we assume a 50% corporate tax bracket, the pay-out could still be accomplished with cash available on the guaranteed side, since the total cash needed after tax to pay out $500,000 is $250,000.

Deferred Compensation   Case Study 9

AGE	YEAR	ANNUAL PREMIUM	4.0% BASIS (guaranteed)		8.0% BASIS (illustrative)		12.36% BASIS (current)	
			CASH VALUE	DEATH BENEFIT	CASH VALUE	DEATH BENEFIT	CASH VALUE	DEATH BENEFIT
40	1	12,500	10,081	250,000	10,687	250,000	11,107	250,000
44	5	12,500	58,080	250,000	66,769	250,000	75,550	250,000
49	10	12,500	129,458	250,000	166,472	250,000	213,359	250,000
54	15	12,500	217,714	250,000	314,884	346,373	461,758	507,934
59	20	12,500	326,568	359,225	531,770	584,947	903,299	993,629
64	25	12,500	456,105	501,715	846,049	930,654	1,684,030	1,852,440
65	26	12,500	484,652	533,118	923,860	1,016,250	1,900,370	2,090,400
➡ YEARS 27 THROUGH 36: $50,000 PARTIAL WITHDRAWAL								
66	27	0	450,485	495,533	941,328	1,035,460	2,073,510	2,280,860
67	28	0	414,936	456,430	959,877	1,055,860	2,266,890	2,493,580
68	29	0	377,967	415,764	979,564	1,077,520	2,482,770	2,731,040
69	30	0	339,544	373,499	1,000,460	1,100,500	2,723,680	2,996,050
70	31	0	299,640	329,604	1,022,630	1,124,890	2,992,460	3,291,700
71	32	0	258,232	284,055	1,046,210	1,150,830	3,292,370	3,621,610
72	33	0	215,074	240,074	1,071,300	1,178,430	3,627,000	3,989,700
73	34	0	170,071	195,071	1,097,980	1,207,780	4,000,180	4,400,200
74	35	0	123,142	148,142	1,126,290	1,238,920	4,415,970	4,857,560
75	36	0	74,099	100,000	1,156,210	1,271,830	4,878,560	5,366,420
76	37	0	75,014	100,014	1,241,360	1,365,500	5,448,130	5,992,950
77	38	0	75,833	100,833	1,331,930	1,465,120	6,080,050	6,688,050
78	39	0	76,498	101,498	1,428,060	1,570,870	6,780,080	7,458,090
79	40	0	76,982	101,982	1,529,930	1,682,930	7,554,440	8,309,880

Deferred Compensation

Case Study 9

		ANNUAL PREMIUM	CASH VALUE	DEATH BENEFIT	CASH VALUE	DEATH BENEFIT	CASH VALUE	DEATH BENEFIT
45	1	12,500	9,636	250,000	10,432	250,000	10,846	250,000
49	5	12,500	55,420	250,000	64,907	250,000	73,518	250,000
54	10	12,500	122,997	250,000	161,642	250,000	207,736	250,000
59	15	12,500	206,933	250,000	306,832	337,516	450,880	495,968
64	20	12,500	312,158	343,374	518,384	570,223	881,027	969,130
65	21	12,500	335,418	368,960	570,792	627,871	1,000,250	1,100,270
	➡ YEARS 22 THROUGH 31: $50,000 PARTIAL WITHDRAWAL							
66	22	0	295,814	325,396	560,984	617,083	1,064,800	1,171,280
67	23	0	254,685	280,153	550,266	605,292	1,136,810	1,250,490
68	24	0	211,817	236,817	538,563	592,419	1,217,110	1,338,830
69	25	0	167,134	192,134	525,803	578,383	1,306,640	1,437,300
70	26	0	120,555	145,555	511,913	563,105	1,406,420	1,547,060
71	27	0	71,789	100,000	496,836	546,519	1,517,680	1,669,450
72	28	0	17,866	100,000	480,495	528,545	1,641,740	1,805,910
73	29	0			462,795	509,074	1,780,000	1,958,000
74	30	0			443,615	487,976	1,933,950	2,127,340
75	31	0			422,817	465,099	2,105,090	2,315,600
76	32	0			453,932	499,326	2,350,810	2,585,890
79	35	0			559,372	615,309	3,259,490	3,585,440
84	40	0			778,388	856,226	5,514,900	6,066,380

Pension Life Insurance   Case Study 10
Part A

Facts:

Jack, age 45, and his wife Mary, age 40, own a small corporation. They decide to install a 20% money purchase pension plan. They each draw $36,000 salary and a 20% contribution is $7,200 per year each. They decide to use 40% of the contribution to purchase Universal Life.

Plan:

$2,880 of each pension account is used to purchase Universal Life with an initial pure death benefit of $100,000. The balance of each account in the money purchase plan is currently invested in a money market fund.

Comment:

The premium of $2,880 is sufficient to keep both the guaranteed account and current interest account with sufficient cash to carry life insurance to life expectancy of age 74. The cash value of the plan could be used as part of the monthly income if retirement did take place.

Pension Life Insurance
Part A

Case Study 10

A G E	Y E A R	ANNUAL PREMIUM	4.0% BASIS (guaranteed) CASH VALUE	4.0% BASIS (guaranteed) DEATH BENEFIT	8.0% BASIS (illustrative) CASH VALUE	8.0% BASIS (illustrative) DEATH BENEFIT	12.36% BASIS (current) CASH VALUE	12.36% BASIS (current) DEATH BENEFIT
45	1	2,880	1,469	100,000	1,682	100,000	1,729	100,000
49	5	2,880	10,628	100,000	12,896	100,000	14,383	100,000
54	10	2,880	23,207	100,000	32,136	100,000	40,723	100,000
59	15	2,880	37,134	100,000	60,184	100,000	88,496	113,496
64	20	2,880	52,752	100,000	101,994	126,994	173,903	198,903
69	25	2,880	71,257	100,000	162,009	187,009	324,599	357,059
74	30	2,880	93,393	118,393	248,003	273,003	586,584	645,243

A G E	Y E A R	ANNUAL PREMIUM	4.0% BASIS (guaranteed) CASH VALUE	4.0% BASIS (guaranteed) DEATH BENEFIT	8.0% BASIS (illustrative) CASH VALUE	8.0% BASIS (illustrative) DEATH BENEFIT	12.36% BASIS (current) CASH VALUE	12.36% BASIS (current) DEATH BENEFIT
40	1	2,880	1,651	100,000	1,821	100,000	1,871	100,000
44	5	2,880	11,777	100,000	13,921	100,000	15,510	100,000
49	10	2,880	26,296	100,000	35,076	100,000	44,262	100,000
54	15	2,880	43,251	100,000	66,143	100,000	96,156	121,156
59	20	2,880	63,508	100,000	112,155	137,155	188,975	213,975
64	25	2,880	88,412	113,412	179,051	204,051	354,053	389,458
69	30	2,880	117,091	142,091	276,659	304,325	646,293	710,923
74	35	2,880	149,183	174,183	417,511	459,262	1,160,160	1,276,180

301

Pension Life Insurance Increased Part B

Case Study 10

Facts: Five years later Jack, age 50, and Mary, age 45, receive a salary increase of $14,000 per year and increase their contribution to the pension to 20% of the total $50,000 salary, or $10,000 per year each.

Plan: Each account in the pension plan is now receiving $10,000 per year. 40% of $10,000 or $4,000 is paid into the Universal Life contract. Jack and Mary also increase the pure death benefit of their contract to $150,000.

Comment: Again, the current contributions to the Universal Life contract are sufficient to keep full death protection for all indicated interest rates.

Pension Life Insurance Increased   Case Study 10
Part B

AGE	YEAR	ANNUAL PREMIUM	4.0% BASIS (guaranteed) CASH VALUE	4.0% BASIS (guaranteed) DEATH BENEFIT	8.0% BASIS (illustrative) CASH VALUE	8.0% BASIS (illustrative) DEATH BENEFIT	12.36% BASIS (current) CASH VALUE	12.36% BASIS (current) DEATH BENEFIT
45	1	2,880	1,469	100,000	1,682	100,000	1,729	100,000
49	5	2,880	10,628	100,000	12,896	100,000	14,383	100,000
50	6	4,000	13,634	150,000	16,960	150,000	19,301	150,000
54	10	4,000	26,254	150,000	36,550	150,000	45,786	150,000
59	15	4,000	42,714	150,000	70,428	150,000	102,132	150,000
64	20	4,000	59,489	150,000	120,803	150,000	205,338	230,338
69	25	4,000	76,069	150,000	196,096	221,096	387,628	426,391
74	30	4,000	92,526	150,000	304,204	334,625	704,202	774,623

AGE	YEAR	ANNUAL PREMIUM	4.0% BASIS (guaranteed) CASH VALUE	4.0% BASIS (guaranteed) DEATH BENEFIT	8.0% BASIS (illustrative) CASH VALUE	8.0% BASIS (illustrative) DEATH BENEFIT	12.36% BASIS (current) CASH VALUE	12.36% BASIS (current) DEATH BENEFIT
40	1	2,880	1,651	100,000	1,821	100,000	1,871	100,000
44	5	2,880	11,777	100,000	13,921	100,000	15,510	100,000
45	6	4,000	15,248	150,000	18,434	150,000	20,937	150,000
49	10	4,000	30,308	150,000	40,357	150,000	50,284	150,000
54	15	4,000	51,494	150,000	78,895	150,000	112,863	150,000
59	20	4,000	75,926	150,000	136,383	161,383	226,197	251,197
64	25	4,000	105,168	150,000	221,104	246,104	427,633	470,396
69	30	4,000	142,346	167,346	344,580	379,038	784,109	862,519
74	35	4,000	185,656	210,656	522,429	574,672	1,410,940	1,552,040

Pension Life Insurance "Paid-Up"   Case Study 10
Part C

Facts:

At age 65, Jack decides not to retire but to continue working. Jack and Mary both reduce their pure death benefit to the minimum allowed in the contract. Further premium payments are discontinued.

Plan:

These particular Universal Life policies are reduced to a total death benefit of $100,000, or the value of cash value plus 10%, whichever is greater.

Comment:

By reducing the death benefit to the minimum at Jack's 65th birthday, maximum cash can be accumulated for a possible future retirement date. At this point it would make more sense for the cash value to be rolled over, income tax free, to a higher paying single premium whole life policy.

Pension Life Insurance "Paid-Up" Part C   Case Study 10

AGE	YEAR	ANNUAL PREMIUM	4.0% BASIS (guaranteed) CASH VALUE	4.0% BASIS (guaranteed) DEATH BENEFIT	8.0% BASIS (illustrative) CASH VALUE	8.0% BASIS (illustrative) DEATH BENEFIT	12.36% BASIS (current) CASH VALUE	12.36% BASIS (current) DEATH BENEFIT
45	1	2,880	1,469	100,000	1,682	100,000	1,729	100,000
49	5	2,880	10,628	100,000	12,896	100,000	14,383	100,000
50	6	4,000	13,634	150,000	16,960	150,000	19,301	150,000
54	10	4,000	26,254	150,000	36,550	150,000	45,786	150,000
59	15	4,000	42,714	150,000	70,428	150,000	102,132	150,000
64	20	4,000	59,489	150,000	120,803	150,000	205,338	230,338
65	21	4,000	62,841	150,000	133,769	158,769	234,102	259,102
66	22	0	64,063	100,000	143,775	168,775	262,257	288,483
67	23	0	65,258	100,000	154,509	179,509	293,727	323,100
68	24	0	66,420	100,000	166,025	191,025	328,883	361,771
69	25	0	67,545	100,000	178,384	203,384	368,139	404,953
74	30	0	72,593	100,000	255,453	280,999	644,283	708,711

AGE	YEAR	ANNUAL PREMIUM	4.0% BASIS (guaranteed) CASH VALUE	4.0% BASIS (guaranteed) DEATH BENEFIT	8.0% BASIS (illustrative) CASH VALUE	8.0% BASIS (illustrative) DEATH BENEFIT	12.36% BASIS (current) CASH VALUE	12.36% BASIS (current) DEATH BENEFIT
40	1	2,880	1,651	100,000	1,821	100,000	1,871	100,000
44	5	2,880	11,777	100,000	13,921	100,000	15,510	100,000
45	6	4,000	15,248	150,000	18,434	150,000	20,937	150,000
49	10	4,000	30,308	150,000	40,357	150,000	50,284	150,000
54	15	4,000	51,494	150,000	78,895	150,000	112,863	150,000
59	20	4,000	75,926	150,000	136,383	161,383	226,197	251,197
60	21	4,000	81,309	150,000	150,881	175,881	257,840	283,624
61	22	4,000	86,897	150,000	166,509	191,509	293,324	322,656
62	23	4,000	92,716	150,000	183,355	208,355	333,098	366,408
63	24	4,000	98,794	150,000	201,517	226,517	377,675	415,442
64	25	4,000	105,168	150,000	221,104	246,104	427,633	470,396
65	26	4,000	111,881	150,000	242,233	267,233	483,625	531,988
69	30	0	126,592	151,592	326,951	359,647	764,558	841,014
74	35	0	145,980	170,980	473,996	521,396	1,350,470	1,485,520

Stock Redemption
Part A

Case Study 11

Facts: Bill, age 50 has inherited a million dollar plus
              company. His attorney has calculated that his
              estate will have liquidity needs of $1,000,000
              and has suggested the corporation purchase a
              Universal Life contract to redeem stock from
              Bill's estate.

Plan: A Universal Life contract with an initial pure
              death benefit of $1,000,000 is purchased. An ini-
              tial lump sum premium of $100,000 is made the
              first year and $10,000 each subsequent year.

Comment: At the current interest rate, the corporation will
              have over $1,000,000 in the Universal Life con-
              tract to redeem Bill's stock if he wants to sell
              his stock during his lifetime.

Stock Redemption
Part A

Case Study 11

AGE	YEAR	ANNUAL PREMIUM	4.0% BASIS (guaranteed)		8.0% BASIS (illustrative)		12.36% BASIS (current)	
			CASH VALUE	DEATH BENEFIT	CASH VALUE	DEATH BENEFIT	CASH VALUE	DEATH BENEFIT
50	1	100,000	85,197	1,000,000	90,996	1,000,000	94,772	1,000,000
51	2	10,000	89,645	1,000,000	102,159	1,000,000	110,632	1,000,000
52	3	10,000	93,526	1,000,000	113,803	1,000,000	128,073	1,000,000
53	4	10,000	96,747	1,000,000	125,934	1,000,000	147,273	1,000,000
54	5	10,000	99,204	1,000,000	138,531	1,000,000	168,408	1,000,000
59	10	10,000	95,063	1,000,000	208,417	1,000,000	312,498	1,000,000
64	15	10,000	43,111	1,000,000	287,255	1,000,000	559,660	1,000,000
65	16	10,000	23,160	1,000,000	303,636	1,000,000	629,331	1,000,000
66	17	10,000			319,923	1,000,000	708,508	1,000,000
69	20	10,000			367,711	1,000,000	1,021,220	1,123,350
74	25	10,000			449,221	1,000,000	1,852,650	2,037,920
79	30	10,000			522,783	1,000,000	3,269,240	3,596,170

Stock Redemption   Case Study 11
Increase Insurance
Part B

Facts: At Bill's age 55, his attorney recommends an
              additional $500,000 life insurance for the corpo-
              rate stock redemption plan.

Plan: Bill increases his Universal Life contract from
              $1,000,000 to $1,500,000. (A medical exam for
              increase was required.) He also increases his
              premium from $10,000 per year to $25,000 per
              year.

Comment: By increasing the premium to $25,000 per year
              in the sixth year under the current 12.36% inter-
              est assumption, the pure death benefit increases
              at age 74 to $2,839,790 and the cash value
              increases to $2,581,630. Additional cash premi-
              ums would need to have been paid at the guar-
              anteed interest rates of 4% to keep the pure
              death benefit in force to life expectancy.

Stock Redemption
Increase Insurance
Part B

Case Study 11

AGE	YEAR	ANNUAL PREMIUM	4.0% BASIS (guaranteed) CASH VALUE	4.0% BASIS (guaranteed) DEATH BENEFIT	8.0% BASIS (illustrative) CASH VALUE	8.0% BASIS (illustrative) DEATH BENEFIT	12.36% BASIS (current) CASH VALUE	12.36% BASIS (current) DEATH BENEFIT
50	1	100,000	85,197	1,000,000	90,996	1,000,000	94,772	1,000,000
51	2	10,000	89,645	1,000,000	102,159	1,000,000	110,632	1,000,000
52	3	10,000	93,526	1,000,000	113,803	1,000,000	128,073	1,000,000
53	4	10,000	96,747	1,000,000	125,934	1,000,000	147,273	1,000,000
54	5	10,000	99,204	1,000,000	138,531	1,000,000	168,408	1,000,000
55	6	25,000	107,970	1,500,000	161,233	1,500,000	201,826	1,500,000
56	7	25,000	116,023	1,500,000	185,442	1,500,000	239,219	1,500,000
57	8	25,000	122,649	1,500,000	210,706	1,500,000	280,535	1,500,000
58	9	25,000	127,604	1,500,000	237,029	1,500,000	326,251	1,500,000
59	10	25,000	130,622	1,500,000	264,377	1,500,000	376,885	1,500,000
64	15	25,000	103,746	1,500,000	414,861	1,500,000	729,999	1,500,000
65	16	25,000	86,464	1,500,000	447,828	1,500,000	828,669	1,500,000
66	17	25,000	63,527	1,500,000	481,538	1,500,000	940,420	1,500,000
67	18	25,000	33,892	1,500,000	516,023	1,500,000	1,067,730	1,500,000
68	19	25,000			551,418	1,500,000	1,213,710	1,500,000
69	20	25,000			587,966	1,500,000	1,382,210	1,520,430
74	25	25,000			806,113	1,500,000	2,581,630	2,839,790
79	30	25,000			1,123,770	1,500,000	4,626,530	5,089,190

Stock Redemption
Partial Withdrawal
Part C

Case Study 11

Facts: At Bill's age 71 (the 20th year), the corporation withdraws its total investment of premiums of $400,000. This reduces the corporation's net investment in the contract to $0.

Plan: The corporation requests a withdrawal of $400,000 in cash from the contract to reduce its net cost to $0.

Comment: By withdrawing $400,000 in the 20th year the death benefit under the illustrative 8.0% interest assumption the pure death benefit decreased from $1,000,000 to $600,000.

Stock Redemption
Partial Withdrawal
Part C

Case Study 11

A G E	Y E A R	ANNUAL PREMIUM	4.0% BASIS (guaranteed)		8.0% BASIS (illustrative)		12.36% BASIS (current)	
			CASH VALUE	DEATH BENEFIT	CASH VALUE	DEATH BENEFIT	CASH VALUE	DEATH BENEFIT
50	1	100,000	85,197	1,000,000	90,996	1,000,000	94,772	1,000,000
54	5	10,000	99,204	1,000,000	138,531	1,000,000	168,408	1,000,000
55	6	25,000	115,162	1,000,000	166,418	1,000,000	207,135	1,000,000
59	10	25,000	175,994	1,000,000	298,011	1,000,000	414,240	1,000,000
64	15	25,000	237,742	1,000,000	522,161	1,000,000	862,080	1,000,000
69	20	25,000	263,225	1,000,000	859,567	1,000,000	1,682,690	1,850,960
➡ YEAR 21: $400,000 PARTIAL WITHDRAWAL								
70	21	25,000			517,031	600,000	1,461,040	1,607,150
71	22	25,000			580,603	638,663	1,660,200	1,826,220
74	25	25,000			800,360	880,396	2,407,310	2,648,040
79	30	25,000			1,278,640	1,406,510	4,324,890	4,757,380

Key-Person Permanent Life Insurance Part A

Case Study 12

Facts:	Bill's company hires a bright Ph.D. from Harvard to run its research department. The company's future depends on this man's talent. Bill's chief financial officer recommends a $500,000 key-man policy be purchased on the Ph.D's life.
Plan:	A $500,000 key-man policy is purchased on the Ph.D. and a premium of $10,000 is paid each year. Since the Ph.D. is only 35 years old, a death benefit of $500,000 *plus the cash value* is provided. It is felt the increased death benefit will be needed to balance inflation.
Comment:	By keeping the death benefit at $500,000 plus the cash value, an automatic inflation provision has been built into the contract. At age 65 the guaranteed death benefit has gone to $794,452, but on the current interest side the death benefit has risen to $2,826,770. This illustration shows again the tremendous flexibility and versatility of Universal Life.

Key-Person Permanent
Life Insurance
Part A

Case Study 12

A G E	Y E A R	ANNUAL PREMIUM	4.0% BASIS (guaranteed) CASH VALUE	DEATH BENEFIT	8.0% BASIS (illustrative) CASH VALUE	DEATH BENEFIT	12.36% BASIS (current) CASH VALUE	DEATH BENEFIT
35	1	10,000	7,023	507,023	7,594	507,594	7,899	507,899
40	6	10,000	51,453	551,453	61,618	561,618	71,316	571,316
45	11	10,000	101,363	601,363	138,373	638,373	181,972	681,972
50	16	10,000	155,390	655,390	246,103	746,103	374,553	874,553
55	21	10,000	210,274	710,274	396,396	896,396	710,511	1,210,510
60	26	10,000	260,171	760,171	604,936	1,104,940	1,298,380	1,798,380
65	31	10,000	294,452	794,452	889,821	1,389,820	2,326,770	2,826,770
70	36	10,000	294,541	794,541	1,272,270	1,772,270	4,126,480	4,626,480
74	40	10,000	253,213	753,213	1,674,130	2,174,130	6,501,760	7,151,940

Key-Person Split-Dollar Part B

Case Study 12

Facts: The Ph.D. is doing a splendid job and the corporation decides to provide an additional fringe benefit in the form of a split-dollar policy.

Plan: A second Universal Life $250,000 split-dollar policy is purchased for the Ph.D. who is now age 40. The corporation decides to pay a $10,000 premium per year for five years and then discontinue further payments.

Comments: The P.S. 58 costs to the Ph.D. will be based on the lower of the P.S. 58 costs published in the IRS regulations or the cost of term insurance offered by the insurer.

Because the Universal Life policy can quickly build a cash value in excess of the premiums paid, it may not be a viable product for a split-dollar plan. Under Revenue Ruling 66-110, 1966-1 C.B. 12, if the employee benefits from the policyholder dividends on a split-dollar contract, the dividends are taxable to him as an extra economic benefit. In this case, the fifth year cash value at the intermediate interest rate of 8% is $51,705 compared to total premiums paid of only $50,000. This means the policyholder will be required to include as income $1,705 in addition to the P.S. 58 costs on a net $250,000 of pure death benefit.

This has not been a problem with traditional whole life policies because the interest return in the form of cash values and dividends has been low enough that it takes many years for the total value to exceed the premium paid.

Key-Person Split-Dollar
Part B

Case Study 12

A G E	Y E A R	ANNUAL PREMIUM	4.0% BASIS (guaranteed)		8.0% BASIS (illustrative)		12.36% BASIS (current)	
			CASH VALUE	DEATH BENEFIT	CASH VALUE	DEATH BENEFIT	CASH VALUE	DEATH BENEFIT
40	1	10,000	7,678	257,678	8,201	258,201	8,520	258,520
41	2	10,000	16,472	266,472	17,942	267,924	18,978	268,978
42	3	10,000	25,533	275,533	28,380	278,380	30,682	280,682
43	4	10,000	34,865	284,865	39,622	289,622	43,782	293,782
44	5	10,000	44,472	294,472	51,705	301,705	58,440	308,440
49	10	0	46,934	250,000	70,696	250,000	99,006	250,000
54	15	0	45,933	250,000	96,706	250,000	171,268	250,000
59	20	0	38,085	250,000	133,171	250,000	303,325	333,658
64	25	0	16,585	250,000	186,064	250,000	537,850	591,634
65	26	0	9,582	250,000	199,567	250,000	602,814	663,095
66	27	0	1,305	250,000	214,368	250,000	675,454	743,000
69	30	0			267,190	293,908	948,599	1,043,460
74	35	0			384,055	422,460	1,660,990	1,827,090

315

Key-Person Term Insurance   Case Study 13

Facts:
The Ph.D. recommends the company hire Susan, a female scientist, age 52, to put together a program that will take about 15 years of pure research. A key-person policy is purchased to indemnify the corporation if she dies before the 15 year program is completed.

Plan:
Since Susan is 52 and the key-person policy only covers 15 years, a term to age 66 contract is purchased. The corporation asks that a level target premium be calculated by the insurance company to provide it with the lowest cost possible using an 8% interest assumption, on a $350,000 death benefit. It is mutually decided that a fair interest assumption over 15 years would be the 8%.

Comment:
The computer is asked to calculate a target premium (level premium) for $350,000 on a female, age 52, for 15 years at a target interest assumption of 8%. The actuarial determination is that a premium of $3,792.00 be paid each year for 15 years. If the actual interest earned is more than 8%, a cash value will remain at age 66. If exactly 8% is earned as a current rate, than the cash value at 66 will be $0. If less than 8% is earned, the additional premiums must be paid or the policy will lapse before age 66.

Key-Person Term Insurance   Case Study 13

A G E	Y E A R	ANNUAL PREMIUM	4.0% BASIS (guaranteed) CASH VALUE	4.0% BASIS (guaranteed) DEATH BENEFIT	8.0% BASIS (illustrative) CASH VALUE	8.0% BASIS (illustrative) DEATH BENEFIT	12.36% BASIS (current) CASH VALUE	12.36% BASIS (current) DEATH BENEFIT
52	1	3,792	0	350,000	521	350,000	521	350,000
53	2	3,792			1,951	350,000	1,951	350,000
54	3	3,792			3,319	350,000	3,319	350,000
55	4	3,792			4,580	350,000	4,580	350,000
56	5	3,792			5,707	350,000	5,708	350,000
57	6	3,792			6,661	350,000	6,662	350,000
58	7	3,792			7,403	350,000	7,403	350,000
59	8	3,792			7,892	350,000	7,892	350,000
60	9	3,792			8,088	350,000	8,088	350,000
61	10	3,792			7,910	350,000	7,911	350,000
62	11	3,792			7,290	350,000	7,291	350,000
63	12	3,792			6,183	350,000	6,184	350,000
64	13	3,792			4,580	350,000	4,581	350,000
65	14	3,792			2,499	350,000	2,500	350,000
66	15	3,792			13	350,000	15	350,000

CHAPTER 12

Marketing Universal Life

Now that TEFRA has established the ground rules for Universal Life and companies are rapidly introducing their Universal Life products, it is important to discuss marketing techniques. First, we will discuss the use of Universal Life in qualified plans. Next, Universal Life and deferred compensation. In a third marketing area, we will examine the advantages Universal Life has over whole life minimum deposit approaches. We believe that, in practice, minimum deposit is overly complicated, often inadequately administered and, under the Economic Recovery Tax Act of 1981, a potential tax trap for the unwary.

Qualified Plans

The advantage of Universal Life in the qualified plan setting is the flexibility of the policy. The amount of premium can be varied, and the pure death benefit of the contract can be adjusted without the issuance of a new policy. In cases where the pure death benefit is significantly increased, underwriting requirements apply; but the same policy can include amounts of insurance subject to different mortality costs if the insured is no longer eligible for standard insurance. Suppose a defined contribution plan is established which provides that 30% of the contributions made for the benefit of a participant be used for the purchase of Universal Life. If the contribution is increased for a participant the premium automatically increases, without the issuance of a new policy. In a typical situation, Option B can be elected so the participant will receive the benefit of the cash value increases in his total death benefit. Also, if the participant desires to increase the pure death benefit of his Universal Life policy, he can easily and inexpensively do so within the same contract.

In a defined benefit plan, the flexibility is equally important. Issuance of multiple policies can be avoided. It is important that the insurance in a defined benefit plan be defined so the annual premium paid is less than 50% of the yearly contributions made in behalf of the participant (or less than 25% if Universal Life is determined to be term insurance, an issue discussed later in this chapter).

In this case, the death benefit can be the sum of the insurance plus the side fund attributable to the contributions made on behalf of a participant. The actual amount of pure death benefit elected does not matter as long as the premium is less than 50% of the contribution. Option B again may be the most sensible approach. Thus, the total death benefit will automatically keep up with inflation.

If the death benefit of an insurance contract is fixed at 100 times the monthly retirement benefit to which a participant will be entitled, the death benefit paid from a qualified plan can only equal the insurance proceeds and cannot consist of any portion of the side fund. It would be inappropriate to elect Option B in this case because, in all likelihood, the total death benefit of the contract would exceed the 100 times benefit. In any event, when the death benefit is expressed as a multiple of the normal retirement benefit, Universal Life prevents the issuance of multiple policies.

Universal Life companies find the issue of large policies for qualified plans to be profitable. However, many Universal Life companies will not issue Universal Life contracts for less than $25,000 of face coverage. Qualified plans may require small policies, and the Universal Life company which deals most effectively with the need for $5,000 to $10,000 issues may also be one that will sell the profitable larger policies. Easy issue of small policies may be developed as a loss leader by some Universal Life companies in an effort to corner the qualified plan market. Also, small policies may be handled as a rider on the policy of a participant. This makes sense only in the defined benefit plan area where there can be a commingling of funds including the payment of insurance costs.

QUALIFIED PLAN ADMINISTRATION

To our knowledge, no Universal Life company has aggressively sought to handle the administration of qualified plans which contain Universal Life. Presently, administration has been handled by the professionals outside the home offices, typically independent accountants and actuaries. As larger insurance companies enter the Universal Life market, we expect to see services and products provided as a package. Those who first undertake the combination may have a loss leader on their hands, but the competition is clearly moving in that direction. Certainly, Universal Life requires more administrative work. Among the matters to be dealt with are: 1) the annual statement of account on each policy; 2) the lack of a judicial and regulatory framework and the questions this encourages; and 3) for existing qualified plans, the need to either convert traditional policies to Universal Life or administer both types of policies in a single plan.

TOP HEAVY PLANS

TEFRA will promulgate a host of new requirements beginning in 1984 for plans of small businesses in which benefits and contributions are primarily for the benefit of owners and officers. These so-called top-heavy plans are prohibited from making distributions to key-employers of newly contributed money prior to their attainment of age 59½. Also, there are now significant limitations on borrowing from a qualified plan.

These lock-in features will cause many key-employees to develop new approaches in their attempt to garner current benefits from their qualified plans.

One of the most logical, current benefits to receive is life insurance protection. The only cost to the purchaser of life insurance within a qualified plan is the P.S. 58 costs. Universal Life companies will develop term insurance rates within the contract that can be used in lieu of the P.S. 58 rates. Also, if a company has term insurance available at rates lower than the term can contained within the Universal Life contract, this lower term rate can and will be used instead of the P.S. 58 rate.

IS A UNIVERSAL LIFE POLICY TERM OR WHOLE LIFE INSURANCE?

Many Universal Life companies have taken the position that as long as there is lifetime protection within the contract, the Universal Life policy should be considered whole life insurance and subject to the 50% limitation for purchase in qualified plans. Other companies, to be on the safe side, are treating Universal Life as term insurance.

What if a policy is designed to run out of lifetime protection and become simply a term product? IRS guidance is needed on the parameters required for the Universal Life policies to be considered as whole life insurance within a qualified plan. As a practical test, we propose that if yearly premium payments, based upon current interest assumptions and guaranteed mortality charges, would support the death benefits within a contract to age 75 or older, the policy should be determined to be a whole life policy.

ESTATE PLANNING CONCERNS

Perhaps more important than any topic considered thus far is the dramatic change made by TEFRA in the estate exclusion of qualified plan assets. Whereas there used to be a potentially unlimited exclusion now, under IRC Section 2039(g), the exclusion is limited to $100,000 unless the beneficiary is the surviving spouse. If the beneficiary is the surviving spouse, the unlimited marital deduction applies.

Many people have purchased large amounts of life insurance within qualified plans so their beneficiaries will receive a death benefit which is both income and estate tax free. With the change in the law and in light of the limited tax exclusion, large amounts of life insurance within qualified plans will have to be reconsidered.

If it is important for the life insurance proceeds to be kept out of the client's estate, the plan participant should purchase the life insurance on his life from the plan for the cash value of the policy. This purchase is an exception to the prohibited transaction rules as provided by Prohibited Transaction Exemptions 77-8 and 77-9. The policy can then be transferred to an irrevocable trust which will cause the life insurance proceeds to be excluded from the participant's estate if he lives for more than three years after making the transfer. Usually with whole life insurance, the policy cannot be minimum deposited unless four out of seven years premium have been paid as provided by IRC

323

Section 264. This means that if the policy is transferred out of the qualified plan before the eighth year, a new qualification period may begin, and four out of the next seven years premium will have to be paid. For reasons discussed below, Universal Life can provide all the benefits of a minimum deposit policy without any of the complications.

It has also been part of the design of the irrevocable, or so-called Super Trust, that money can be appointed back to the grantor of the trust in certain situations. In a minimum deposit case, this enables the grantor's net outlay of cash to be zero. It works this way. The grantor pays the interest to the trust required for borrowings from the policy to pay premiums and receives an interest deduction for the amount paid. Then, in an unrelated transaction and perhaps after the passage of two years or so, the trustee, at the direction of the grantor's spouse, appoints back to the grantor approximately one-half of the interest paid. The trustee gets the appoint-back money by borrowing from the life insurance contract. If the grantor has been in a 50% tax bracket, his net cost is one-half the interest paid. He recovers this cost upon the appointment back by the trustee of money borrowed from the policy.

However, Private Letter Ruling 8213074 puts this technique in question. This ruling states that the annual gift tax exclusion will not apply if the trustee has the ability to appoint property from the trust thus jeopardizing the interest of the Crummey beneficiaries. This is a private rather than a general revenue ruling. Careful drafting may be able to get around the problem, such as giving the Crummey beneficiaries a right of first refusal on the appointment of any principal from the trust or providing a 30-day period to withdraw contributions before the appointment of any principal is permitted. However, at a minimum, this PLR creates one more obstacle to the effective use of minimum deposit within an irrevocable trust utilizing a life insurance product initially purchased within a qualified plan.

Where does all this leave Universal Life? If there is a possibility that life insurance purchased within a qualified plan will be transferred out, the life insurance purchase should be Universal Life. Universal Life does not have to meet any of the requirements of minimum deposit since the policyholder can simply stop the payment of premiums and allow the cash value to carry the policy for as long as possible. Even if a Universal Life policy is transferred to an irrevocable trust, the irrevocable trust will not have to provide the appoint-back provisions because the grantor will only have to pay in whatever is needed in additional premiums, if anything.

Summary

Universal Life fits qualified plans well because of its flexibility and adaptability to situations in which it may be transferred to nonqualified plans. As this book went to press, we learned that a major mutual company has developed Universal Life for exclusive use in the qualified plan market. Some questions still remain concerning administration and the term or whole life issue. Nevertheless, Universal Life is likely to be the dominant qualified plan product of the 1980's.

Deferred Compensation

This section assumes that the reader has a general knowledge of deferred compensation and salary continuation plans. Our intent is to comment on the advantages of using Universal Life to fund the program rather than discuss the mechanics of the program.

Under an employee directed deferred compensation program, the employee agrees to a salary reduction in return for a promise on the part of a company to provide him or her with income at retirement plus a pre-retirement death benefit. A typical arrangement provides a pre-retirement death benefit of $20,000 per year for ten years, and a post-retirement death benefit of $20,000 per year for ten years in exchange for a current salary reduction, for example $300 per month, on the part of the employee. This $300 per month reduces the employee's income and is used by the corporation to purchase a life insurance policy to fund both the pre- and post-retirement death benefits.

The advantage of using a Universal Life contract in this situation is that high current interest rates available under the Universal Life policy limit the number of years needed to fund the arrangement and provide the designated benefits. It might be necessary with a traditional whole life policy to fund the contract up to age 65. With a Universal Life contract, if interest rates remain high, fewer premiums will have to be paid to guarantee the benefits.

In the case of an employer installed deferred compensation plan (also called a "salary continuation plan"), it is normal for the corporation to provide the pre- and post-retirement death benefits to the employee in exchange for his promise not to compete at retirement. The cost of providing these benefits often causes corporations to hesitate in establishing these programs. Heretofore, such programs were provided through life insurance policies requiring a fixed premium. The Universal Life policy offers relief in that 1) substantially fewer premiums may be required as discussed above, and 2) premiums can be omitted in slow business years and additional premiums paid in good years. In addition, if premiums are not paid under a traditional whole life policy, there is an interest charge for any loans taken against the policies to pay premiums. This is an additional cost to the corporation. There is no interest for monies withdrawn if the special withdrawal privilege of Universal Life is used.

We have provided a simple example of deferred compensation in Chapter 11, "Marketing Ideas and Case Studies." Other benefits of Universal Life are:

1) Flexibility of death benefits. Over the duration of a pro-

gram, the amount of pre- and post-retirement death benefits may need to be altered. Universal Life provides a per-
fect vehicle for this since the amounts of insurance can be
increased or decreased as the need arises. Increases will
usually require some evidence of insurability. One contract can be adjusted to provide the benefits desired.

2) Flexible premiums. Universal Life insurance allows the
amount of contribution to be adjusted each year according to a) the company's ability to pay premiums in good
and bad years, and b) the need to pay sufficient premiums
to keep the funding at the level prescribed in the agreement. For example, if high interest rates are earned, premiums may be reduced so the cash value of the contract
remains sufficient to fund the benefits. On the other hand,
if low interest rates prevail, additional premiums can be
paid to maintain the cash value at a fully funded level.

3) Fewer premiums. Universal Life insurance offers the
opportunity for a corporation to pay one premium or a
series of larger premiums which pay for all the benefits.
The decision makers of many corporations do not like
continuing obligations. In good years they may prefer to
contribute the money necessary to fund the entire
arrangement. Accelerated premium payments should be
checked to be certain they do not run afoul of the
TEFRA guidelines.

Also, by taking advantage of the premium flexibility, it
is possible to fund the deferred compensation agreement
during the employees most productive working years
when he is generating the greatest profits for the
company.

4) Large single premiums at age 65. Many corporations
today are faced with tight financial situations and a limited cash flow. They would like to provide pre- and post-
retirement death benefits for the employees, but would

rather fund the program in later years when their profits are higher. The corporation can pay the minimum premium during the early years of the contract, and pay the larger premium to fund the post-retirement death benefits in later years.

5) Usage of Option B. Universal Life insurance can be easily structured so the death benefit equals the specified level insurance amount plus the cash value. The corporation can pay sufficient premiums which funds the pre-retirement death benefit, and at the employee's death prior to retirement, returns the cash value to the corporation.

In essence, the corporation can provide the death benefits and get the premiums back. This approach can be applied to the post-retirement death benefits as well. If Option B is used and sufficient premiums are paid, the corporation may make withdrawals each year from the contract to pay post-retirement benefits to the employee. At the employee's eventual death, the premiums will be returned to the corporation.

6) No interest charges. Many traditional whole life programs establish a minimum deposit arrangement whereby the corporation pays four out of the first seven premiums to fund the deferred compensation plan.

Future cash value increases would be used to pay the premium with the company paying the interest. One advantage of the Universal Life insurance policy is that if only two or three premiums are paid, there are no interest charges incurred. Many corporations are not 50% taxpayers and cannot take maximum advantage of an interest deduction. A Universal Life contract works well in this situation. The policy continues as long as the interest on the cash value covers the monthly costs. Another application of this approach is that, at age 65 when the employee retires, withdrawals can be made from the Universal Life contract to fund promised retirement benefits. Under the contract's withdrawal provision, there is no interest charged.

7) No excess cash accumulation. Some corporations are faced with the problem of excess accumulations of cash which could be subject to a penalty tax in an IRS audit. If excess cash is available, the Universal Life contract carried to fund the deferred compensation program can be utilized. For example, if a corporation had an excess accumulation of $100,000 for the current tax year, it could, subject to the guideline premiums test, pay a single premium into the Universal Life contract, thereby removing the cash from an unallocated corporate account.

Summary

In summary, the creative features of the Universal Life policy make it an outstanding funding vehicle in the deferred compensation area.

Minimum Deposit

Many agents have found that they can market substantial amounts of whole life by using a process called minimum deposit. Some buyers, however, are unwilling to commit substantial assets to cash values. Minimum deposit solves the problem by providing a vehicle for marketing whole life via a series of loans. When these loans are made, the cash value of the policy is substantially reduced. As the reader probably knows, the basic form of minimum deposit involves paying four out of the first seven years' premiums to tax qualify the policy. Future cash value increases and dividends on participating policies can be used to pay the premiums as they come due. A loan is taken against the policy for the amount of premium paid, and the insurance company charges interest. The rate on most new whole life policies is 8%. (Interest rates will rise substantially when the new varia-ble loan interest rate provision is adopted by the industry.)

After having tax qualified the policy, the client can then deduct the interest for income tax purposes. As an observation, it can be said that most minimum deposit business is sold to generate a higher commission than is paid on term insurance. For a high tax bracket taxpayer, minimum deposit may be less expensive than term insurance in the long run. In some cases, minimum deposit does not benefit the client. In the next part of this chapter, we will review the weaknesses of minimum deposit and show the advantages of Universal Life in place of the mini-mum deposit sale.

Disadvantages of Minimum Deposit

Agents don't understand it. Most policyholders are not suffi-ciently sophisticated to understand the minimum deposit con-cept. Dissatisfaction with minimum deposit arises whenever increasing loans accrue against the policy and interest notices are received along with premium notices. A large number of people borrow on the policy for a period of four or five years, then decide to surrender it and buy something they can under-stand. Few people know what is actually happening after the fourth premium is paid and the loans and interest become due. This can lead to a confrontation between the policyholder and the agent. It is questionable how much minimum deposit busi-ness will actually remain in force until the policyholder's death since there are many changes in a client's situations that could lead him to surrender the policy.

Policyholders do not always qualify the interest. In some instances the agent doesn't tell the policyholder that he has to pay the first four out of seven years. Often the client decides to sacrifice the deductibility of the interest and pay the minimum premium due in each of the first seven years. The interest charges in later years, particularly after age 70, become substantial. If they are not tax deductible, the policyholder cannot look only at his after-tax cost, but has to pay the full interest. Then, the policy no longer is viable as a minimum deposit policy and usually costs much more than a term policy.

Not every client is a 50% taxpayer. Most minimum deposit illustrations show a 50% taxpayer. In the near future a taxpayer will have to earn over $150,000 per year to be in this bracket. Most taxpayers will be paying in at a lower rate. As the tax bracket goes down, the viability of minimum deposit goes down.

Loans become substantial. It is common practice to elect a special term dividend option to provide added death benefits equal to the amount of the policy loan. At the younger ages, the cost of this option is small because both the loan and the cost of insurance are small. As the insured ages and reaches say, age 70, both the loan and the term dividend option cost increase greatly. The combination can become so expensive that the minimum deposit concept is no longer viable.

There is a tax trap at surrender. A number of agents do not explain to their clients that minimum deposit has a built-in tax trap in later years. The IRS considers the cost basis of the contract to be the premiums paid minus the dividends. Here is an example. Consider a $100,000 policy with a cash value of $70,000, all of which is loaned out under the minimum deposit plan. After many years, the cost basis can be very small. To make the point, let us assume the total premiums paid less dividends reaches $0. If the policy is surrendered at an advanced age and the cash value is $75,000, the amount taxable as ordinary income is $75,000. If the policyowner is a 50% taxpayer, a current income tax of $37,500 is due with no money from the contract to pay it. This can be a substantial problem!

There are new tax traps starting in 1985. The Economic Recovery Tax Act of 1981 has a provision called the Interest

Exclusion. Effective January 1, 1985, a new 15% exclusion for "net savings interest" will be allowed with respect to the first $3,000 of such interest earned by an unmarried taxpayer ($6,000 in the case of a married couple filing jointly). Applying the 15% gives a maximum deduction of $450 for a single person and $900 for a married couple. However, in calculating the exclusion for net savings interest, interest income must be reduced by interest payments made with respect to consumer loans. This includes credit card loans, or other installment credit, *including interest paid on insurance loans.*[1] (No reduction is required for the interest paid on a home mortgage or a business-connected borrowing.)

The trap is apparent. The buyer of the minimum deposit policy paying interest to an insurance company after January 1, 1985, will have a reduction in his net aftertax benefit. As one example, a married couple with $6,000 of interest earned and $6,000 of interest paid under a minimum deposit plan will lose the entire 15% exclusion of $900. If they are in the 50% tax bracket, the cost is $450 more tax.

Many customers prefer to build a strong cash position. With inflation compounded by recession and unemployment worries, the attitude of the public is changing. The attractiveness of debt, even nonrepayable life insurance loans, decreases historically in times such as these. Minimum deposit is, we think, less acceptable now than it has been in recent years.

There are no cash values at retirement. Many people continue to view their insurance program as a means of generating cash for retirement. Many clients have been disappointed by the low purchasing power that has accumulated in their life insurance cash values. Recognizing the problem of inflation does not diminish their desire for security in retirement. The need for

---

[1] Emphasis added.

loan-free interest sensitive insurance products suggests the decline of minimum deposit in today's marketplace.

Advantages of Universal Life over Minimum Deposit

If four or fewer premiums are paid, the Universal Life insurance will continue. The cash values will grow as long as there is sufficient money in the contract. No loan interest has to be paid. Withdrawals can be made on a regular basis without interest. Universal Life does not always pay as high a commission as whole life, but it pays a substantial commission and, at the same time, usually has a meaningful cash value in the first policy year. With traditional whole life products the cash value, if any, is small for the first two years.

People understand Universal Life. A descriptive buyer's guide is often used at the time of sale to explain Universal Life. The annual statement of account is sent to the policyholder which summarizes the premiums paid each month, the expenses charged, the interest paid, the cost of insurance, the withdrawals, and the cash values available.

There is no need to tax qualify the policy. By using Option B, which provides a death benefit of the specified level amount of insurance plus the cash values, any withdrawals that are made will not reduce the insurance benefit below the specified amount. This is not the same in the typical minimum deposit program. In addition, it is comforting to know that the Universal Life policy does not require the taxpayer to be a 50% taxpayer until he dies to obtain the maximum tax advantages from his contract.

There is a positive difference in the tax trap. Whereas the minimum deposit contract usually provides no cash to pay the taxes due, Universal Life, with a substantial cash value in the contract, provides cash to pay the ordinary income tax. The policyholder may elect to take the proceeds from his Universal Life policy in installments over a period of years, thus spreading the tax burden. The 1985 tax trap, represented by the Interest Exclusion Allowance, does not apply to Universal Life because there are no interest payments involved.

Debt avoidance creates an incentive. The fact that many consumers are avoiding debt and want retirement cash values at 65 are important reasons for people to buy Universal Life. In fact, the policy design encourages people to put additional money into the policy. Since the interest accumulates on a tax sheltered basis, money grows faster inside the Universal Life contract than it would grow in numerous other investments. People don't have to go into debt to get a tax benefit. Instead, they pay premiums into their policy as they find funds available and, as a result, accumulate substantial cash values. It is exciting to think that once again agents can go to their clients and suggest that they contribute not only the normal target premiums needed to make the policy work, but additional amounts that will accumulate on a tax sheltered basis.

Summary

Minimum deposit may have advantages for certain high income taxpayers who feel they will always be in a 50% tax bracket. These people are willing to put up with the extra administration, paper work, and complications to try to secure potential tax benefits from their life insurance policies.

Such policyholders are a small minority. To put it facetiously, there is a limited market for loans and loan interest. A typical policyholder is much more interested in building a sound, substantial cash value life insurance program which takes advantage of tax sheltered interest and in a well-funded life insurance program at retirement from which money can be withdrawn as needed.

CHAPTER 13

The Replacement Issue

A financial planning seminar was held in Milwaukee, Wisconsin in early November, 1982. The agenda for the seminar differed from the usual topics of recent years. The speakers discussed:

- The explosion of change within the life insurance industry;
- Second and third generation Universal Life; and
- Replacement—who will do it? Will it be done?

Two of the speakers compared the life insurance industry with the automotive industry. Both said that, unlike General Motors and others, the life insurance industry was making its move *before* it was too late. Both expected life insurance sales to rise dramatically in the future. With this as background, the Chief Executive Officer of a large brokerage operation said, "Go out and replace your term insurance that was sold more than three years ago and all your whole life insurance. If you don't, someone else will."

He backed up his belief in this statement by producing a flyer he recently mailed to thousands of agents which stated, in part:

WHO WILL REPLACE
YOUR CLIENT'S OBSOLETE
WHOLE LIFE AND TERM:

THE BANKER
STOCK BROKER
SAVINGS AND LOAN
DEPARTMENT STORE BOOTH
OR YOU?

Any reader of recent insurance articles and advertising can catalog a surge of material motivated by this belief. The mid-1980s may well become an era of replacement hysteria. In this chapter we will discuss the replacement issue. Our emphasis is on permanent insurance, traditional whole life compared to Universal Life, the latter sold with planned premiums above the minimum levels as was discussed in Chapter 5, "Creating the Proposal." The financial interests of the three parties involved—consumer, company and agent—are reviewed.

Replacement Pros and Cons for the Consumer

Replacement of whole life is done in the interest of the consumer because the Universal Life product is a better deal. True or false.

TRUE. The interest rates projected for Universal Life are higher, the mortality costs are generally better, the loading costs are often lower (in part because commissions are often lower), and the policyholder has more flexibility with the product.

Also, FALSE. The policyholder has already paid the front-end costs of the policy he or she has, a new policy may not be underwritten at standard rates, and the insurer of the old policy may be developing a new policy that will be offered in exchange, with reduced loading, for the old policy. (See our discussion in Chapter 9, "How Others Expect to Compete" and the "Insurance Company Questions" in Chapter 10, "Questions and Answers.")

True or false. To again stress the key policy factor, as interest rates decline, the old policy may eventually pay dividends comparable to the return on the Universal Life contract. If this happens soon enough, the new policy costs will not be recovered and the policyholder will lose.

Many people will admit that there are some whole life products in force that ought to be replaced by a good Universal Life product (or a good traditional policy for that matter) without the agent or policyholder blinking an eye. On the other hand, a heavily commissioned new policy of any kind will likely have such a stiff loading (or surrender) charge that replacement of a good whole life product with such a new policy would benefit only the agent.

What about replacement of a good whole life product by a good Universal Life product? A thorough analysis is in order. The agent must run his computer proposal, projecting a fair intermediate interest rate, and compare the Universal Life plan with the whole life policy. Research is needed to ascertain what future benefits the insurer of the whole life policy expects to make available on the old insurance. Dividend scales are frequently increased, annually in some companies; the possibility of an update or favorable exchange to a new traditional policy exists. Some idea of the effect of such events on the value of the old policy, however rough, is useful.

This may sound like a lot of trouble, and it is. But for the agent to do less could well be a disservice to the client, eventually discrediting the agent. Making the analysis will surely enhance the agent's standing.

How Companies Handle Internal Replacement

There is great uncertainty in the industry dealing with the question of how to handle internal replacement. Balancing the equitable needs of policyholders with the financial integrity of the company is the clear objective. The uncertainty arises from the inherent losses to the company when investment earnings on the company's current assets must be used to pay the higher interest necessary to sell a competitive Universal Life policy.

If the higher interest rate continues long enough, the company's solvency may be jeopardized. The policyholders, whom the company sought to benefit by accepting internal replacement, will then wind up with a problem rather than a benefit. Those who are still around when the crunch comes may have both their cash values and prospective death benefits impaired. At the least, the company may be forced to reduce future interest credits to a level well below other companies, thereby risking a spiral of disintermediation or sharp reduction in continuing premium income as policyholders exercise their rights under the policy.

One mutual company offered a full commission on the exchange of its whole life policies for the Universal Life product offered by its stock subsidiary. As you can imagine, some of its agents had a field day; a great deal of money was paid in "easy" commissions. A cash drain out of the mutual ensued. The situation worsened to the point where the company substantially modified its commission rules and reduced the incentive to the agents by giving them only two weeks notice of the change.

Those agents who had approached the replacement issue in a deliberate and thoughtful manner were understandably bitter. The agents who had worked at replacing everything in sight were resentful because their windfall was cut off. This was a lesson learned the hard way.

Other companies have offered full or partial commissions on internal replacement of old policies. A typical set of rules might follow this simplified example.
IF . . .

The planned premium for the first policy year of the Universal Life policy is increased to twice the annualized premium of the old policy (or policies),

AND . . .

The policyholder's death benefit on the Universal Life policy (excluding supplemental benefits) is increased by a specified amount or percentage, often 100%,

THEN . . .

The Company pays Universal Life commissions of the full first-year commission on the increase,

AND . . .

Full or partial first-year commission on the premium continued from the old business,

BUT . . .

Little or no commission on the transferred cash value paid into the Universal Life policy as a lump sum.

This approach should work better than that previously described. But, how well such rules will resolve the replacement issue from the company's point of view remains to be seen.

There are more unanswered questions.

- Will the doubling of premiums be more apparent than real, with the premiums in renewal years falling short of expectations?
- Will the smaller policies that cannot be upgraded be replaced externally?
- Will the company be able to determine that an internal replacement has taken place when the rules are not met?

Consider the problems in defining the rules which allow for

policy loans to be taken out for a variety of purposes other than internal replacement. Loans are also more difficult to identify in current computer records than surrenders. Over the years, the latter have been monitored more closely to measure the quality of an agent's life insurance business. Such questions will be answered by the experience of those who are dealing as best they can with the replacement issue.

Loading and Other Considerations

The replacement issue is further compounded by the variety of possible loading practices. Loading may be set to cover: 1) commissions and other field compensation paid according to the company's rules; 2) the expense of underwriting and issuing the new policy, at least to the extent that this expense is covered in a newly issued Universal Life policy which does not involve an exchange; and 3) the expense of terminating the old business. If the loading charges on the new Universal Life policy are set high enough, the company may be able to profit, temporarily, from internal replacements. Gains from company taxes under TEFRA may also be available. Any "profit" from loading or tax is likely to be used up by the crediting of higher interest rates on the Universal Life policy values than would have been credited on the traditional business.

The company tax situation is complex. We mention it here because it introduces another uncertainty. The reader who wishes to have a better understanding of the current home office tax issues will find useful background material in actuarial literature. In a nutshell, it is possible that the exchange of traditional policies will result in taxable gains to the company which are not current operating gains. Thus, a tax may be payable with no current income available to pay it.

Another part of the replacement issue is intensely practical. Universal Life companies realize that, if they do not offer reasonable compensation to their agents who wish to replace internally, such agents may replace that business with another insurer. Under these circumstances, it is vitally important to structure a commission program that is beneficial to the agent, is compatible with the company's long term objectives and is, at the same time, beneficial to the policyholder who seeks to increase his death benefits and/or otherwise improve his insurance program. The fear of some companies is that, if they encourage their agents to replace existing whole life policies, one of two things may happen, both negative: 1) the consumer will shop around for the best Universal Life product available and place his business with another company; or 2) so much business will be transferred to the higher interest rate Universal Life product that a severe financial strain will result.

What about the companies which sell traditional permanent insurance but do not offer Universal Life? The companies that are doing nothing (there are fewer and fewer of these with each passing month) are in for a continued cash drain. These companies have taken the position that it is better to fight (Universal Life) than to switch (to higher interest return products). They often have a portfolio of investments which consist of long-term intermediate interest (7%-9%) bonds and mortgages written during the 1960s and early 1970s.

A continuing decline in interest rates, which appears to have begun in the fall of 1982, will help. However, it may not help enough. For many of these companies, the replacement issue has become an issue of survival. Loans and surrenders have reached a new high. The sale of traditional high premium policies continues to drop. Lower interest rates ease the replacement pressure, but lower rates also reduce the interest earnings that have helped the companies cover the inflated expenses of doing business. Unless these companies can design a currently competitive product and replace their lost business at a reasonable cost, their viability will be seriously impaired.

The Outlook

To return to the policyholder's dilemma, the difficulty of evaluating a replacement proposal is compounded greatly during these times. The possibility of a higher load may substantially reduce the benefit of an exchange. Even with conscientious analysis by the agent, the difficulty of knowing what action the company may take to improve existing policies is extreme. As one example from the summer of 1982 shows, several companies, close to offering substantially updated programs, backed off when TEFRA was passed by Congress. The tax rules affecting companies and policyholders continue to be under extensive review by both Congress and the Treasury Department. When the basis upon which major financial decisions must be made is subject to unpredictable shifts, the ability to evaluate any offer made to the policyholder is severely impaired.

Universal Life has added another dimension to the replacement issue. In addition to the complex problems discussed above, new competitors are emerging. Shearson-American Express (stock brokers), Sears Roebuck & Co. (retail sales), and the Kroger Company (food) are all in the life insurance business. Others will enter. These large firms are attracted to mass marketing. If an agent does not offer an opportunity to his clients to replace whole life, one of these newcomers most likely will. The replacement issue has become an issue of survival for some companies and for many agents. The handling of this issue by the industry, its critics and its regulators will be a key focus of the middle 1980s.

Index

Becker, Ted, 31
Belth, Joseph M., 25
Bond(s), 16, 20, 46, 57, 189, 195, 224, 258
Borrow, 14, 16, 41, 44, 47, 56, 167–8, 172, 183–7, 191, 222, 236, 249, 261, 263, 269, 271
Brown, Rice E., 22
Business Insurance, 54, 118, 274
Butkiewicz, Ron, 12
Buyer's Guide (Life Insurance), 21, 25, 255
Buy-sell, 110, 274–5, 292–5

C

California Department, 28, 193
Carpenter, David R., 229
CARRIAGE RETURN, 132
Carter, President Jimmy, 23
Cases
  Cohen v. Commissioner, 180
  Commissioner v. Meyer, 173
  Commissioner v. Treganowan, 169
  A. Ralph Evans v. Commissioner, 178, 212
  Falkoff v. Commissioner, 185
  Goldstone v. United States, 173
  Griffith v. United States, 181
  Estate of W. T. Hales, 40 B.T.A. 1245(1939), 180
  Helvering v. Horst, 185
  Helvering v. LeGierse, 189, 173–4
  Keller v. Commissioner, 173
  Kess v. United States, 173
  Robert W. & Mary F. Minnis, T.C. 1049(1979), 184–6
  Mosley v. Commissioner, 171–72
  Old Colony Trust v. Commissioner, 172
  Primuth v. Commissioner, 185
  Republic Nat'l Life Ins. v. United States, 201
  S.E.C. v. Variable Life Ins. Co., 169
Challenger, 229
Chapin, Walter, 29
Charge(s), 192–4, 202, 232, 250–1, 265–6
Chartered Life Underwriter, 250
Children, 35–6, 41, 58, 72–3, 101–3, 273, 278

M

N

Q

R

S